RUSSIAN REFUGE

Susan Wiley Hardwick

RUSSIAN REFUGE

Religion, Migration, and Settlement
on the North American Pacific Rim

THE UNIVERSITY OF CHICAGO PRESS
CHICAGO & LONDON

Susan Wiley Hardwick is professor of geography at
California State University, Chico.

The University of Chicago Press, Chicago 60637
The University of Chicago Press, Ltd., London
© 1993 by The University of Chicago
All rights reserved. Published 1993
Printed in the United States of America
02 01 00 99 98 97 96 95 94 93   1 2 3 4 5
ISBN: 0-226-31610-6 (cloth)
       0-226-31611-4 (paper)

Library of Congress Cataloging-in-Publication Data

Hardwick, Susan Wiley.
    Russian refuge : religion, migration, and settlement on the North
American Pacific rim / Susan Wiley Hardwick.
        p.   cm.
    Includes bibliographical references and index.
    1. Russian Americans—Northwest, Pacific.   2. Refugees, Religious—
Northwest, Pacific.   3. Russians—British Columbia.   4. Refugees,
Religious—British Columbia.   5. Russian Americans—Alaska.
    6. Refugees, Religious—Alaska.   7. Northwest, Pacific—Emigration
and immigration.   8. British Columbia—Emigration and immigration.
    9. Alaska—Emigration and immigration.   I. Title.
F855.2.R9H37   1993
979.5'0049171—dc20   93-10519
                                                                CIP

To Don,

who made it all seem possible

CONTENTS

LIST OF ILLUSTRATIONS

LIST OF TABLES

PREFACE

THE INSPIRATION FOR THIS book began in 1978 in a graduate seminar taught by Professor Dennis Dingemans at the University of California, Davis. At the same time that I was conducting research on ethnic neighborhoods in nearby Sacramento for Dr. Dingeman's required seminar paper, one of my own students, David Karakazoff, asked why *his* ethnic group was not included in my lectures and class discussions on the ethnic geography of California. This research on Russian immigrants thus originated in both a student's request for attention and a required research assignment in a graduate seminar. Little did I know the subject would entice me into fifteen years of intensive work on an immigrant group almost entirely overlooked by other scholars. The seminar paper eventually grew into a dissertation that compared the residential and commercial patterns of all major ethnic groups in Sacramento to the Russian-American experience.

One year after my dissertation was completed, in 1987, Soviet president Mikhail Gorbachev made the startling announcement that victims of religious persecution had permission to leave the USSR for the first time in seventy years. These persecuted groups were subsequently admitted to the United States and Canada as refugees. By the end of 1990 over one hundred thousand had settled in the United States alone. In 1991 and 1992 fifty thousand more arrived per year. The vast majority of these newcomers were Jews, Baptists, and Pentecostals.

Equally surprising was the major destination choice for non-Jewish Russian immigrants. Instead of choosing well-known "melting pot" cities on the California coast such as Los Angeles and San Francisco, these migrants settled in the Central Valley city of Sacramento, in the heart of the historic Russian neighborhood I had studied for my dissertation several years earlier. By early 1993 there were over eight thousand new refugees from the former Soviet Union living in California's capital city.

This book is the result of many years of work with Russian immigrants in California, Oregon, Washington, British Columbia, and Alaska. Russians were also interviewed in the Soviet Union during the spring and summer of 1991. Fieldwork on site in the cities and small towns of what is now, once again, known as *Russia* provided a context for understanding the migration experience more completely. As families interviewed in their homeland migrated to the American and Canadian West, the interview process continued. Long-term interviews extending through time and space made comparisons between groups possible.

A great many people provided both professional and personal support in the research and writing of this book. The Russian immigrants themselves, most of all, gave countless hours of time and energy to the project. I particularly appreciated the help and constant support of Mikhail Lokteff and Slava and Nadya Bolyshkanov in Sacramento. Their advice and encouragement were invaluable as the project evolved. General ideas about managing the large scope of the project and developing a structure for the work were provided by Dr. Dennis Dingemans of the University of California, Davis; David Hooson, University of California, Berkeley; Ronald Wixman, University of Oregon; James Gibson, York University; and James Allen, California State University, Northridge. I also appreciated the long-term guidance of Dr. Dale Heckman, Siberian expert for the California Postsecondary Education Commission, who offered encouragement from dissertation draft to final book manuscript.

Thanks are also extended to specialists on each of the religious groups for reading preliminary drafts of the manuscript and/or for offering advice on my discussion of particular Russian religious groups. Of special note are Ethel Dunn and A. J. Conovaloff for their generous help with the Molokans; Dr. Richard Morris, Pat Chitty, and Oleg Bychkov for information on Old Believers; professors Basil Dmytryshyn and Clem Padick for their knowledge of early Orthodox Russians in Washington, Oregon, and California; Michael Chursenoff and Nell Coger for their help with the Doukhobors in Canada; Professor Paul Steeves and Bruce Robinson for assistance with the story of Russian Baptists; and Dr. Kent Hill for his helpful advice on conducting research on Russian Pentecostals. The support of all these willing and enthusiastic advisors is greatly appreciated.

The published work of others too numerous to list here, useful in providing background for the fieldwork and interviews on more recent

Russian settlement in the study area, is listed in the bibliography. I am especially indebted to the work of anthropologist Ethel Dunn on Molokans and Doukhobors and the excellent publications of Canadian geographer Dr. James Gibson on Russian settlement in frontier America. Their work, along with other archival and published sources cited in the book, was consulted at the Bancroft Library, University of California, Berkeley; the Hoover Library at Stanford University; the Library of Congress; the Oregon Historical Society in Portland; the libraries of the University of British Columbia and the University of Washington; and Rasmuson Library at the University of Alaska, Fairbanks. I am particularly grateful to have had the opportunity to conduct extensive archival research in the Slavic Collections of the University of Illinois due to the generous support of the Russian and East European Center there.

In addition to this support, travel expenses and fieldwork costs for the research were provided by generous grants from the Association of American Geographers and the California State University, Chico Foundation. This support, along with the encouragement of the faculty of the California State University, Chico Department of Geography and Planning, who supported my full year's sabbatical from all teaching responsibilities, made the final writing of this book possible.

I also wish to thank the talented cartographers who worked hard to bring my data to life visually. Jennifer Helzer and Charles Nelson worked hard throughout the final year of the project to produce high-quality, and often extremely complicated maps to accompany my narrative. Jennifer's overall support provided an almost daily dose of encouragement. The work of research assistants Pamela Posey and Ann Teubert is also warmly appreciated.

The encouragement and guidance of the University of Chicago Press editor Penelope Kaiserlian have been invaluable as the final stages of the project evolved. Her abiding interest in the topic, editorial advice, and supportive behind-the-scenes efforts made the final publication of this book possible. Her belief in me is warmly appreciated. The careful scrutiny of copy editor Joann Hoy made the book not only more readable but more accurate. I appreciate her efforts to improve *Russian Refuge* in its final stages of development. Any errors in content, however, are my own responsibility.

Finally, I wish to extend my deepest gratitude to my husband, mentor, and friend, Dr. Donald Holtgrieve. Without his guidance and constant support, *Russian Refuge* would never have become a reality.

ONE
Introduction

——————————————— Nadezhda ———————————————

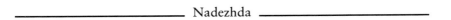

It happened over thirty years ago, but she can remember it as if it had all happened yesterday. Nadezhda Bolyshkanov was a young child then, living in the Uzbekistan city of Tashkent. Her father had been arrested and imprisoned by Communist authorities for his religious beliefs. Nadezhda and her older brother and sister had been taken away from their parents for reeducation in state-mandated values. Every morning when she woke up, she felt afraid and alone. Sometimes she still does.

Now Nadezhda is a young mother herself, living on the other side of the world in Sacramento, California. She and her husband and their four children left Tashkent two years ago to begin their lives over again in a new country. Baby Victor was born soon after they arrived in the United States.

Nadezhda has religious freedom now. She also has a much improved economic situation, but sometimes new problems seem almost as overwhelming as the old. The challenges of learning a new language, finding employment, making decisions about almost everything in a land of choice, and adjusting to the stresses of living in a multicultural neighborhood face Nadezhda and her family every day.

Despite these challenges, life in Sacramento is the best life she and her family have ever known and, she says, more than she could ever have imagined before she left Russia. Nadezhda's mother, the daughter of a church choir director, was born in a small Siberian village near Novosibirsk. When she was eight years old, her family was taken into the taiga and left to die. Their crime was that they believed in God. Exercising

1

their will to survive to its limit, they found their way to Kazakhstan. At first, the Russians found valuable and supportive friends among their Muslim neighbors there. In Kornilovka, Nadezhda's mother met her future husband when he was on military leave. After their marriage in 1940, he went to war in Eastern Europe and returned home more than five years later to a son and a wife he hardly knew. But he felt grateful to be alive after his wartime experiences, and, soon after arriving home, he became a believer in his wife's religion.

Nadezhda's parents lived in Tashkent with their three sons and seven daughters for most of their married life. They were active members of one of the three large Russian Baptist churches there and worked hard to keep their children loyal to their faith.

When Nadezhda was eighteen, she met her future husband at church, and they soon began to plan for their life together. As the number of children in Nadezhda and Slava's family increased, so did their hopes for the future. When ethnic conflict intensified in the former Soviet Union's Middle Eastern republics during the early years of glasnost, Nadezhda's family decided to move to a small town near Moscow with a more homogeneous Russian population. But economic conditions, political uncertainty, and the sudden change in Soviet emigration policy encouraged Nadezhda and her family to make the difficult decision to leave their homeland forever. "We did it for our children. If we had been alone there, we would have stayed no matter how bad it might have been" (Nadezhda Bolyshkanov interview, West Sacramento, 9 September 1990).

After a year and a half of planning, filling out paperwork, attending countless government interviews, and making final arrangements, their decision to settle in California happened almost by accident. After arriving in New York exhausted from the long trip, "an American official asked us where we were going. For some reason, I just shouted 'San Francisco.' I do not know why I said that because our sponsors lived in New England. It must have been the will of God."

Nadezhda's family was greeted at the San Francisco Airport by an old friend from Tashkent. He told them about the Russian neighborhood and Russian churches in nearby Sacramento and offered them a place to stay. They have lived in California's capital city ever since. In 1991 and 1992 Nadezhda's parents and sisters and their families came to Sacramento from Russia to begin their new lives in a new and sometimes lonely place.

This story of one young woman's experiences is typical of the stories of tens of thousands of other Russian immigrants currently living in the United States and Canada. Nadezhda and her family, like other immigrant families searching for a safer and more economically and politically stable place to raise their children, migrated long distances to begin a new life. They arrived in North America hoping to preserve the best part of their old lives as they learned to adapt to a new life in a new place. Many have chosen to settle in the states of California, Oregon, Washington, and Alaska and in the Canadian province of British Columbia.

For over two centuries, this Pacific region has served as an important migration destination for Russians. Of particular interest are the location patterns of six Russian religious groups that cluster in distinct enclaves held together by religious affiliation. These groups include Orthodox, Old Believer, Doukhobor, Molokan, Baptist, and Pentecostal Russians.

Although there is an enormous literature about the processes of ethnic acculturation and assimilation in American life, little has been written about the cultural and social adjustments of non-Jewish Russian groups.[1] Because of the abundance of literature on Russian Jewish émigrés in North America, and because they are, culturally and ethnically, Russian Jews rather than Jewish Russians, this study focuses only on the experiences of non-Jewish ethnic Russians.

Within the vastness and diversity of western North America, numerous ethnic and religious groups have met and mingled over time. The impact of religion and ethnicity on migration, culture change, landscape evolution, and adaptation to life in North America presents a complex and interrelated set of problems for cultural geographers and other social scientists. While some ethnic and religious groups have been studied intensively in an effort to understand the North American immigrant experience, other groups have been mentioned less often or not at all. Non-Jewish Russian immigrants and their descendants, for example, have been almost entirely overlooked in the literature. In the early 1990s, as thousands of postglasnost Russian refugees settle in the United States and Canada, it is important to begin to document their adaptation to their new environment. The Russian story is similar to the stories of tens of thousands of other immigrants in North America, but their fascinating story also has unique elements.

Russian migration, settlement, landscape, and adaptation to life on the North American Pacific Rim form the central themes of this book. Research questions focus specifically on the importance of the role of religion in migration and settlement decision making by immigrant groups. Important associated questions include an analysis of factors leading to religious conversion in the former USSR and the reasons for the subsequent migration of Russian immigrants into the study area. This book also investigates and documents the historic and contemporary cultural landscape of Russian religious groups in the study area. These patterns and related social processes provide a structure for the study of hundreds of thousands of people from Russia and other parts of the former USSR who have resettled in this large and diverse region.

Since the earliest arrival of newcomers in the study area, Russians have remained an important group. In some ways, they have been typical of other immigrants who left their homeland for political and religious reasons in search of a new life. Many came to find economic opportunities in a new and more prosperous land. Many viewed the United States and Canada as places of economic opportunity and vast, untapped natural resources where they could readily amass great wealth.

Among the diverse immigrant groups who made up the earliest wave of immigration into the western United States and Canada, Russians blended fairly easily into the American mainstream. Their ethnic and racial identity and cultural background, in general, fit comfortably into the majority American belief system. Their skin color, ethnic background, religious preferences, and European heritage provided opportunities to blend easily into what would eventually come to be known as the "melting pot."

Yet, in some ways, Russians have not been typical of other Euramerican immigrant groups in North America, and their spatial patterns of settlement reflect this difference. Russian residential enclaves have been relatively slow to disperse through time, not only in urban areas but in isolated rural areas as well. Distinct Russian neighborhoods in many North American cities continue to persist through several generations into the 1990s. Many are located on the edge of the city in well-bounded, isolated enclaves. Rural Russian nodes in the study area usually lie far away from populated urban centers, isolated by distance and other socioeconomic barriers.

Several factors have contributed historically to this Russian tendency to cluster in distinct settlement nodes. Until the late 1980s, the Soviet Union was viewed as the supreme enemy of the American people. Russian immigrants arriving in former decades, therefore, had to bear the burden of this negative perception. Many were viewed as hostile Communists, enemies of the American government, or spies. In some measure, it was the reaction against this perception that encouraged many Russians to remain in more safe and secure ethnic enclaves. For almost a century, Russians remained the people Americans "loved to hate."

Even in this post–Cold War political climate, Americans often possess confused, residual negative perceptions about anything *Russian*.

Russians also carry the stigma of belonging to a strange and relatively unknown variant of mainstream Christianity. Eastern Orthodox dogma and ritual often seem uncomfortably "pagan" to more fundamentalist Christians. The perception lingers that Russians come from a country that is not truly European. Seen as originating in a land practicing the worst form of "Oriental despotism," the Russian heritage was viewed as lacking a connection with "more desirable" European roots (Wittfogel 1957). These ethnic and religious factors have all contributed to the Russian sense of being cut off from American mainstream life and have slowed assimilation and residential dispersal in urban and rural North America.

Russians have also been slow to assimilate into American life because of the cultural baggage they brought with them. Most Russian Christians left home because of their religious beliefs. Long persecuted by government and Orthodox church authorities, deprived of economic opportunities, completely cut off from admission into colleges and universities, most people who are the subject of this study migrated to the United States and Canada under great duress. Experiences in their homeland left many with scars that have not healed, even in the more open environment of the United States and Canada. Their need to remain unobtrusive and geographically isolated has sometimes created "invisible" ethnic landscapes of anonymity, where only trained eyes can tell they are in a Russian neighborhood.

Another unique aspect of Russian settlement in the study area deserves mention. Unlike other European immigrant groups in the United States and Canada, Russians first settled on the West Coast rather than on the East Coast. This historically significant factor, along with the other locational and sociocultural issues discussed above, make an analysis of Russian settlement and cultural change on the Pacific Rim of North America a significant topic of study.

Perhaps the most important reason to study the Russian experience in North America has arisen in recent years. Since 1988, a sudden and somewhat startling influx of new Russian immigrants into the region has begun to change the ethnic character of the American and Canadian West, as *glasnost* (openness), *perestroika* (restructuring), and other policies affecting emigration from the former Soviet Union have made it possible for thousands of new refugees to resettle in the United States and Canada. Over 140,000 have migrated to the United States since 1987, and more than 100,000 more were expected before the close of

1992. Emigration policies in the republics of the former Soviet Union are currently less restrictive than at any time since the early part of this century. In the chaos of political and economic restructuring, it is uncertain how long this open-door policy will continue. But whatever the future holds, changes in Russia are increasingly being reflected in the North American cultural and religious landscape, as new immigrants settle in distinctive nodes in many parts of the region.

There are, then, four major components of this analysis of Russian migration to the Pacific Rim of North America: migration decision making, settlement patterns, the cultural landscape, and adjustment to a new life and land. Each theme is discussed in the chapters that follow.

The Study Area

For the purpose of this study, the North American Pacific Rim is defined as that area included within the borders of the American states of Alaska, Washington, Oregon, and California, and the Canadian province of British Columbia (map 1). Extending along more than forty degrees of latitude, from the remote villages of the Aleutian chain to the semitropical coast of southern California, this elongated Pacific region forms an extremely large and diverse area for investigation. Despite its immense size, however, the region extending from northern Alaska to Mexico possesses a great many unifying characteristics.

The physical environment of the Pacific Rim region provides a backdrop for this study of ethnic settlement. Patterns of landforms, weather and climate, water resources, and vegetation may be viewed as parts of a well-developed system of north-south mountains and interior valleys. In both elevation and relief, this is a land of extremes. California's coast ranges and higher interior Sierra Nevada merge into the Pacific Northwest's Cascade Range, forming an almost unbroken barrier to east-west movement. A moderate maritime climate dominates coastlines along the entire region, with precipitation decreasing and temperatures increasing significantly from north to south. Interior valleys lie in drier rain-shadow locations and are often irrigated for agricultural development.

The physical geography of the study area is significant for this study for several reasons. First, due to limitations in transportation technology, the earliest Russian settlement in Alaska and coastal California necessarily was limited to bays and coastal promontories. Later settlement by immigrant groups who formed agricultural colonies focused on fertile, well-drained valleys, most often just east of the coastal mountains. Recent arrivals have preferred more urban places. These Pacific Rim cities

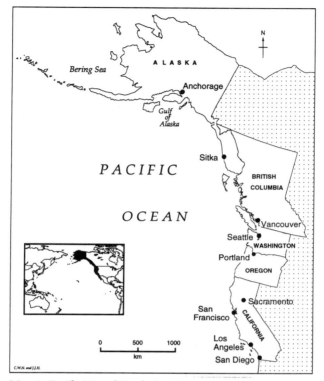

Map 1. Pacific Rim of North America

lie in a north-south linear pattern linked to transportation routes and coastal access.

A unifying set of cultural and economic characteristics also links the study area. The entire region was once populated by large numbers of native people who were all but eradicated by the arrival of Euramerican settlers. Historic European settlement favored rivers and transportation corridors throughout. Today, the region resonates with ethnic diversity. There is a strong current of Hispanic culture in the south and native American culture in the north. Ethnic pluralism, coupled with a perception of isolation from the rest of the continent, has created a sense of freedom and openness in much of the region, which carries over into political decision making and economic development. It is most often the individual that matters here, rather than the group. Individual freedom at any cost is respected and encouraged along this most *western* edge of the Canadian and American West.

In recent decades the Pacific Rim has emerged as a vitally important economic and political region and is rapidly becoming one of the most important economic zones on earth. As cultural and economic connections between Japan and North America have grown stronger, the potential for similar trade and transportation networks among other nations has become evident. Although trade agreements with the former Soviet Union have thus far been slow to develop, Russia hopes to triple its Pacific trade in the next ten years. Local officials in Vladivostock are now developing a tourist industry in this formerly closed Pacific coast city. Soviet president Gorbachev made a commitment in 1990 to join the Pacific Economic Cooperation Conference, a private group that aims to encourage development in the region. The new Russian government under Boris Yeltsin seems to be following this same path of support for increased Pacific Rim contacts. Linkages between the United States and the Russian Far East were made more convenient when the first regular airline connection between the San Francisco Bay area and Vladivostock began operations in early 1991, signaling a new era of exchange between the two nations. Speaking prophetically almost 150 years ago, the Russian scholar Aleksandr Herzen called the Pacific Rim "the Mediterranean of the Future" (Trofimenko 1989, 239).

The Pacific Rim of North America was selected for this study of the Russian experience for three main reasons.

1. The earliest Russian settlement in North America began here, and the region tells a continuous cohesive story of the Russian experience.

2. Russian religious groups vary dramatically in California, Oregon, Washington, Alaska, and British Columbia. A distinct spatial pattern of Russians exists there that is based on ethnic and religious affiliations.

3. Glasnost- and postglasnost-era immigration from the former Soviet Union has increased the number of Russians in the study area by tens of thousands in the early 1990s. Selected places along the Pacific Rim have become preferred resettlement sites for a majority of recent Russian immigrants.

Humanistic Geography as an Approach to This Topic

Although numerous geographic studies have been published on migration, ethnic settlement, and the cultural landscape, there are very few intensive, long-term studies using a humanistic approach.[2] An emphasis on the importance of analyzing human perceptions, impressions, and emotional feelings about *place* first began to find a voice in the geographic literature in the 1970s. This approach evolved as a reaction against the sterility of purely quantitative applications to spatial analysis. "The determinism, economism, and abstraction of the early quantitative publications seemed to abolish human intentionality, culture, and man himself" (Ley 1981, 250). A return to this more sensitive concern for human issues and a rejection of the "scientific pretentiousness" of highly quantified work is the foundation upon which this study of Russians in North America is built.

Establishing reliable and replicable methodologies for work in humanistic geography has not been easy. Some authors have advocated the use of oral histories and in-depth interviewing (Buttimer and Hagerstrand 1980), while others have questioned the dependability and predictability of these methodologies. There can be no doubt that exploring and analyzing the world in some systematic fashion through the face-to-face questioning of people in their own environment is a challenging approach to data gathering. Yet only by deciphering the meaning of the minds, hearts, and words of the people themselves can a full understanding of the ethnic experience be captured. Their sense of place, interpretation of space, and perceptions of past and present realities form the basis for understanding their spatial patterns. These social constructs overlay other geographic patterns and lead the way to a deeper understanding of the settlement process.

Much concern has been raised about methodologies employed in humanistic studies because they lack a solid grounding in theory. The positivist view insists on imposing order on data through the innovation of theories and preconceived structures. Predictability and replication of research guide the data-gathering process and final analysis. The analysis of humans and their decisions as expressed on the landscape, however, cannot be approached in the same way as the more theoretical approach used in the analysis of other geographic data. The human geographer has no need of his or her own theories because he or she is concerned with the theories expressed in the actions of those being investigated (Guelke 1974, 193). It is essential that the voices of the people under investigation be heard and that their voices provide a living text for geographic analysis. According to anthropologist Clifford Geertz, "The point for now is only that ethnography is *thick description* . . . Doing ethnography is like trying to read (in the sense of 'construct a reading of') a manuscript—foreign, faded, full of ellipses, incoherences, suspicious recommendations, and tendentious commentaries, but written not in conventionalized graphs of sound but in transient examples of shaped behavior" (1973, 9–10).

Methodologies developed for this study of Russians in North America center on the importance of gaining information about the ethnic experience from the participants themselves. Intensive "geoethnographic" interviews and field observations of Russian immigrant life and landscape, therefore, are used to complement archival and census data throughout.

In recent years, as new methodologies in ethnic geography have grown out of computer technologies, other long-respected geographic methods have often been overshadowed. In an attempt to make the study of human geography as objective as possible, statistical analysis and computer applications often distance researchers from their subject of research and from their study areas. Field inquiry and personal interviews with the people themselves have largely been replaced with computer models and mathematical formulae.

It is a central argument of this book that a complete investigation of the ethnic experience must grow out of a variety of methods. Census and archival data are used most effectively when corroborated and verified by intensive ethnographic interviews and extensive field observation. This type of comprehensive data gathering for broad-based regional studies on migration and settlement has been especially challenging for geographers who depend on fieldwork as a primary methodology. Collecting information from ethnographic interviews and on-site observation over a large area is both expensive and time consuming. With increasingly detailed census data available in the 1990s, it is easy to see why many researchers have depended almost entirely on computer models and statistical predictions in their attempt to understand the ethnic experience.[3] But much complementary work remains to be accomplished through the use of *geoethnographic* field methods.

The study of migration has remained particularly distant from humanistic methodologies. Migration is broadly defined as movement for the purposes of a permanent or semipermanent change of residence. Moves may be as short as across town or across the hall of an apartment building or as long as those that cross international borders from one continent to another. Migration often affects cultural and economic conditions of the receiving area as well as of the source area. Because the process involves *movement*, one of the fundamental themes of geography, geographers have been interested for several decades in the examination of migration as a spatial process. Lee's effort to explain the volume, streams, and characteristics of migrants expanded Ravenstein's pioneering work on the subject (Lee 1966; Ravenstein 1889). Later work by geographers and other scholars has evaluated the reasons for moving, by using rational and, more recently, behavioral models. Wolpert was the first geographer to focus on individual decision making in migration behavior rather than on statistical group data (Wolpert 1964, 1965). His focus on individual *place utility* of one's current residence and the migrants' perception of migration destinations opened up a wide range of migration topics. In later studies, Wolpert analyzed migrants' ability to handle stress. His work examined the decision to move based on stress-coping mechanisms and available alternatives (Wolpert 1965). Other geographers interested in applying a behavioral approach to the study of migration include Golledge (1980) and Roseman (1971, 1977).

A number of popular assumptions about migration as a spatial and social process need further testing. Migrants are usually a select group, and their characteristics may not represent the demographic profile of typical people from their homeland. The majority of today's migrants are often viewed as economic migrants, in search of an improved standard of living for themselves and their families. Yet according to the work of Hugo and others, cultural and ethnic connections and family ties also influence the decision to migrate and intensify migration streams (Hugo 1981). Russians, like many other immigrant groups in North America, have migrated here individually, in families, and in groups. Chain migration is flowing at its fullest in the early 1990s, as families and church members join earlier pioneer migrants. Most Russians follow well-defined paths to their new home and are greeted there by family and friends. The importance of religious networks in migration decision making is especially fascinating for geographic analysis and is addressed in detail in this study.

Religion is, in fact, the primary variable affecting Russian migration decision making and settlement patterns. An understanding of the role of religious beliefs in migration and settlement and their connections to the larger culture system operating in Russian immigrant communities is central to this study.

Past work by religious geographers has been limited primarily to an analysis of the distribution of religious groups and their imprint on the cultural landscape.[4] These studies offer fascinating reading and established in the field of geography a strong belief in studying religious geography. Few studies, however, have linked religion to other sociocultural variables. Thus far, the relationships between religion and the economic and political structure of its cultural context have not been adequately explored. As synthesizers of information, as experts in seeing the "big picture," as scholars interested in exploring the relationships between various aspects of culture, geographers now need to begin to move into a broader interpretation of religious influences on space and place (Levine 1986).

Methods

This analysis of the Russian experience in North America via a *humanistic perspective* discards preconceived notions of theory and prediction. Rather, conclusions depend on the experiences and decision making of the Russian immigrants themselves. An understanding of social and historical processes and their resulting spatial patterns based on individual and group decisions, then, form the heart of this analysis.

Fieldwork and intensive face-to-face interviewing with Russian immigrants is not easy. Most fear outsiders and remain guarded throughout preliminary discussions. Experiences in their homeland cause many to be withdrawn and unwilling to give information about their past lives. Fear of persecution by authorities lingers decades after resettlement in North America. Most view outsiders as intruders and are unwilling, at first, to divulge details about past and present experiences, living in fear of repercussions. Those who are willing to talk are usually uncomfortable with tape-recorded interviews or even with detailed note taking by the interviewer. Two attempts to distribute and collect written questionnaires to community groups and individuals for this study were completely unsuccessful. "It was OK to talk to people in Soviet Union, but we never, *ever* put anything in writing" (Samuel L. interview, Davis, California, November 1990).

Long-term data gathering through numerous follow-up interviews was necessary for the completion of this book. Fifteen years of contact with the Russian communities in Sacramento and San Francisco (and "survival" Russian-language skills) laid a foundation for the trust needed to begin formal work on the project. Attendance at numerous community and family functions, such as weddings, funerals, christenings, anniversary dinners, and club meetings, in Russian enclaves from Alaska to San Diego increased communication and trust. Two hundred and sixty-six in-depth interviews with Russians in both western North America and the former Soviet Union were ultimately gathered for this analysis.

After almost two years of preliminary work on site in the study area, a scheme for interviewing individuals was designed. All generations were included in the interview process, with a balance of male and female respondents. Although community and church leaders were interviewed in depth, an emphasis on understanding the experiences and perceptions of "real people" in each neighborhood dominated the interview process. Women and children were interviewed as often as men. Individuals were interviewed in all Russian settlement nodes in the study area, from Alaska to San Diego. Family members of recent immigrants who planned to emigrate to North America as soon as their paperwork was completed were interviewed in the Soviet Union in the spring and summer of 1991; follow-up interviews were conducted in California upon their arrival there. The interview process thus captured the full range of emotions and decisions involved in the entire migration experience—from Russian homeland to new North American environment.

Most of the data analyzed and cited in the following chapters took many months, and in some cases several years, to collect. Once trust was established, however, the interviewees became willing participants in the study. As discussed in chapter 6, close human connections were vitally important to Russians in their homeland because of the often abusive political and economic system that dominated their lives. The research for this book was entirely dependent on establishing this close level of trust necessary for honest communication about experiences.

Over fifteen years, my role as outsider and inquirer became the role of friend, interpreter, information source, arbitrator, and peacemaker. My function became everything except neutral observer. Instead, I became a de facto family member. Only then could an accurate and complete account of this group's experiences be compiled. What the immigrants told me, I now offer to you, using the Pacific Rim of North America as a regional setting and religion, migration, and settlement as overall geographic themes in this chronicle of the Russian immigrant experience.

TWO

Origins

TODAY'S WORLD IS A world in flux. Every day thousands of people move away from their homes and resettle in new places. Some move by choice, seeking climatic or economic amenities. Others are forced to move by deteriorating conditions at home. During the past one hundred years, tens of thousands of people have emigrated from Russia and the Soviet Union in response to deteriorating economic, political, and social conditions there. During 1991 and 1992, more than one hundred thousand have arrived in the United States, rapidly filling our government's quota for people from the former Soviet Union in the first few months of each year. Many are religious and political refugees, forced to leave their homes in haste, never to return again. Most come to North America with hopes of finding a life of freedom and acceptance for themselves and their children. Others have settled in western Europe, Australia, New Zealand, and Latin America. This chapter identifies and discusses the origins of ethnic Russians in North America. It begins with a brief overview of the geography of the former Soviet Union and then describes the origin, diffusion, and location patterns of the six religious groups discussed in later chapters.

The Russian and Soviet Homeland

The country the Russian émigrés left behind is a vast and diverse land (map 2). The former Soviet Union (now known as the Commonwealth of Independent States and Baltic nations) was the largest country on earth, extending through eleven time zones and covering an area more than two and a half times the size of the United States. Most of this land

14

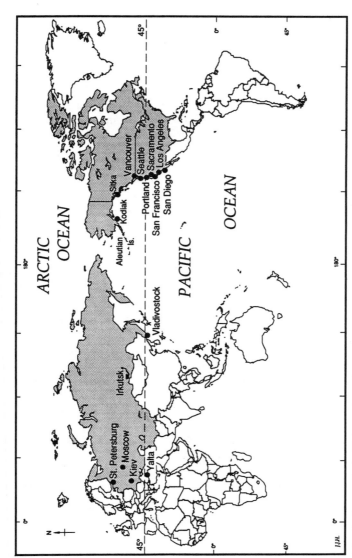

Map 2. Former Soviet Union and North America

is located north of the forty-fifth parallel, the line that extends from central Maine to northern Oregon and lies exactly halfway between the North Pole and the equator. Yalta, one of the nation's southernmost resort cities, is at the same latitude as Portland, Oregon, while Kiev, the capital city of Ukraine, is as far north as the Aleutian Islands.

Because of its northern location, the former USSR long experienced severe challenges in supporting its population. Food production is difficult in a land where permafrost lies under one-half of the soil. Nearly one-third of the country is too cold or too dry for agricultural production. In contrast, the rich chernozem soils of Ukraine are the most fertile soils on earth. The natural systems of the former Soviet Union thus have provided both opportunities and limitations for its diverse population.

Although this book investigates the migration experiences of ethnic Russians, the Commonwealth of Independent States and Baltic nations include over one hundred different ethnic groups located within their international boundaries. Russia, largest of the former Soviet Union's fifteen autonomous republics, contains more than half of the population and covers more than 75 percent of the total land area of the commonwealth.

This homeland of ethnic Russians is a combination of vast meadowlands, mountains, cultivated farms, forests, and steppe. The steppe has been a frontier zone during several thousand turbulent years of human history. Numerous invasions and subsequent disruptions in individual lives have shaped and reshaped this huge area. Today, Russians live in all fifteen of the former republics, as political and demographic change dispersed this large group to all parts of the nation (map 3). Their political power in outlying republics, along with a growing (or at least more visible) sense of nationalism and ethnic pride in the 1990s, has resulted in ethnic conflict in many of the non-Russian republics during the glasnost era and since the formation of the commonwealth. In the 1980s and early 1990s, all republics pushed for independence from the Soviet system in one way or other. The Baltic and Ukrainian provinces have been particularly insistent on maintaining their internal autonomy, resisting Soviet rule in the streets and in local government decision making. Finally, in late 1991, the world witnessed the breakup of the largest country on earth and the reformation of the tenuously united Commonwealth of Independent States.

Religious Origins

Ethnic conflict, immense size, and varying natural resources are not the only factors that created physical and human diversity in Russia and the

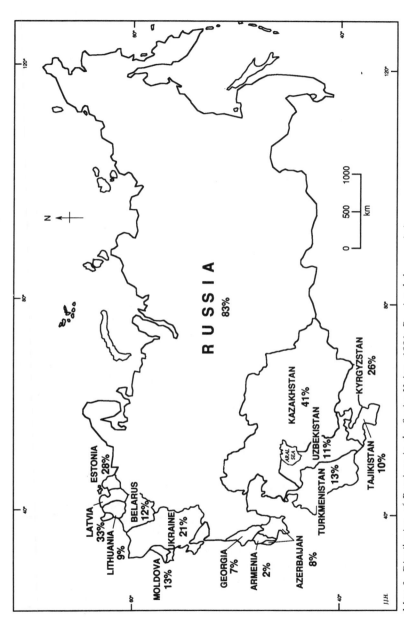

Map 3. Distribution of Russians in the Soviet Union, 1991. Reprinted, by permission, From DeBlij and Muller 1992, 147.

Soviet Union. Religious affiliations add yet another layer of complexity to the spatial and social patterns of this vast land. Perceived by Prince Vladimir of Kievan Rus in 988 A.D. as the best chance for unification of his diverse state, his decision to import an official religion for his people added further fragmentation to an already divisive nation. Differences of opinion about theology and beliefs over the years resulted in the development of numerous incompatible religious sects, evolving in direct opposition to the Orthodox church.

Until the Great Schism of 1666, however, the beliefs and dogmas of Vladimir's choice of Eastern Orthodoxy were a powerful force in unifying and shaping the culture of emerging Russia. And despite increasing differences of opinion about religion, in terms of total numbers of believers the Russian Orthodox church has remained the most important single ecclesiastical body in Russia and the USSR for over a thousand years.

The history of the Russian Christian church began in ancient Kiev, now the capital of Ukraine. This node of early Russian culture developed on a fertile plain alongside a large, navigable river on a busy trade route linking Europe and Asia. The commercial linkages of Vladimir's Rus with the Byzantine Empire centered at Constantinople made conversion to Eastern Christianity a strong probability. Credit for this decision, however, is often given to the conversion of Vladimir's grandmother Grand Princess Olga of Kiev to Christianity in 957 (Pushkarev 1989, 1). Legends abound concerning Vladimir's choice of Eastern Christianity. According to numerous historical accounts, Vladimir sent out government emissaries to observe three major world religions, including Eastern and Western Christianity, Islam, and Judaism. He selected Eastern Christianity primarily because of the reports on its charismatic mysticism and the beauty and splendor of the magnificent cathedral of St. Sophia in Constantinople. In 988, Vladimir forced the entire population of Kievan Rus into the Dnieper River for Russia's first mass baptism.

Along with religious teachings, Vladimir's choice of Eastern Orthodoxy ultimately led to the implementation of the Cyrillic alphabet. Brothers Cyril and Methodius, missionaries to the Slavs, first developed the Slavonic alphabet and translated the Holy Scriptures into Old Church Slavonic. Ties with Byzantium remained strong during the first centuries of Christianity, and when Rome and Byzantium split in 1054, Russian Christians remained loyal to the East.

Christian literature, art, architecture, and music were brought to Kievan Rus from the Greeks. Ties with western Europe were also strong during the first centuries of Christianity in Rus. Vladimir's son Yaroslav built an Orthodox cathedral dedicated to Hagia Sophia, the Divine Wisdom, in his capital city and married his daughters to the ruling princes of Europe (fig. 1; Meyendorf 1962, 103). However, the close ties between Europe and Rus were interrupted by the Mongol invasion.

The domination of the much hated Golden Horde in the thirteenth century severely retarded Russia's cultural development. For over 350 years, the Mongol yoke intensified the separation between East and West. During the period of rule of the various khans, Russian people were enslaved, and lands were held only as feudal dependencies. However, churches were allowed to remain open and free from taxation. Religious beliefs, prayer, and protection inside church buildings thus became the only solace in a difficult life. Numerous hermitages and monasteries were built in the forests during this period to provide a few places where life was safe and quiet. The long period of enslavement brought a deepening of religious faith. Russia's isolation and the shared persecution of its people during the era of Mongol rule strongly contributed to the identity of the Russian nation. As monasteries increased in number during the period of the Mongol yoke, they also grew in wealth and ownership of land. Because the church did not divide its landholdings into inherited parcels, the amount of land under the control of the Orthodox church increased substantially.

Another development during this period was the deepening relationship between church and state in a mutual effort opposed to the Mongol invaders. After the period of Mongol domination, the way was cleared for the creation of a large Orthodox Christian state, unique thus far in Russian history (Parsons 1987, 2). This close integration of church and state in Russia was to continue until the Bolshevik revolution in 1917.

After Kiev was destroyed by the Mongols in 1240, thousands of Russians migrated to the north into the safety of distant forests. Under the reign of Metropolitan Peter (1308–26), Moscow became the new center of Eastern Orthodoxy, maintaining the vitality of Christianity in the far north (Bourdeaux 1966, 22). Moscow quickly grew from an obscure village into the religious capital of all the Russias (Meyendorf 1962, 105). After Constantinople was conquered by the Turks in 1453, Moscow's role in church leadership became even more vital. The rapidly expanding city ultimately became known as the third Rome. According to a letter to Czar Basil III from the monk Philotheus, "The first Rome collapsed owing to its heresies, the second Rome fell a victim to the Turks, but a new and third Rome has sprung up in the north, illuminating the whole universe like the sun" (Bourdeaux 1966, 24).

The growth of the church and the comparative political stability of Russia during the decline of Byzantium resulted in the church's being recognized as autocephalous. This meant that the Russian Orthodox church was now viewed as an equal partner with Byzantium in the feder-

Figure 1. St. Sophia's Cathedral in Kiev, Ukraine, is the "mother church" of Russian Orthodoxy. Photo by author.

ation of national Greek Orthodox churches (Timasheff 1942, 2). In 1589, Moscow named its own Russian patriarch.[1]

The Russian state had almost no problems with non-Christians or religious nonconformists until the sixteenth century. That century witnessed violent disagreements about the direction of the church in Russia. Some felt church and state should remain closely allied and envisioned Moscow, the third Rome, as the center of their great nation. Others preached that the church should remain independent from Moscow, remain loyal to Constantinople, and emphasize monasticism, simplicity, and poverty. The church ultimately accepted the idea proposed by the first group. Moscow was made the seat of power for both church and state, and the church retained all its vast properties and wealth.

From the sixteenth through the early twentieth century, the relationship between church and state vacillated between complete unity and complete disunity, depending on the decisions of the governing czar. Despite this instability, the Russian church developed its own literature, art, and culture. Russian culture came to be more and more associated with the Orthodox church and its teachings.[2] This close connection with culture and politics, along with the continued support of monasteries, theological seminaries, and religious education for the young, strengthened the church's membership over the centuries. It is estimated that, by 1914, the Russian Orthodox church had approximately one hundred million believers in Russia (Meyendorf 1962, 117).

Membership in the official Russian church would have grown larger if a series of internal schisms had not occurred in the mid-seventeenth century. These events significantly reduced the number of believers in the Russian Orthodox church. The first major schism occurred when the idea of Moscow as the third Rome suffered under the rule of Patriarch Nikon (1652–58), who tried to establish the dominance of the spiritual over the state. Nikon also hoped to reform the Russian church in an effort to bring it more into line with other Eastern Christian rites and rituals. Accomplishing his first objective rather easily, he moved forcefully into his second objective. However, millions of faithful Orthodox believers, taking the concept of the third Rome seriously, rebelled against him. This event was to have long-term effects on church unity and would eventually result in the emigration of large numbers of disillusioned believers.

The Emergence of Russian Sects

To comprehend the profound significance of the events of the Great Schism (Raskol) of the mid-seventeenth century, one must appreciate the fanatical devotion of Russian Christians to everything traditional (Bourdeaux 1966, 28). In 1666, a major schism developed between those who claimed to be followers of the original Orthodox faith and those who allied themselves with Patriarch Nikon's proposed changes in church doctrine. One of the major factors causing church reform during this era was the correction of poorly translated church books. Translations and printing were done only in monasteries at this time; inaccuracies resulting from careless work had become common in church books and therefore found their way into church doctrine.

In 1551, the Council of the Stoglav met to discuss issues of ritual and dogma; its decisions were published as revisions to church materials. It was at this time that many incorrect translations were changed, with requirements that church members were to use only the "corrected" versions (Morris 1981, 34).

This council's decisions became divisive only after the introduction of the printing press in 1552. Newly published books were then disseminated widely. The result was a confusion of translations and "truths." The schism that resulted from this confusion and from the decisions of Patriarch Nikon was to have major religious and social ramifications, which would extend into the present day.

OLD BELIEVERS

Old Believers (Starovery) consider themselves the only true Orthodox Christians. Despite changes suggested by the ruling patriarchate, this dissenting sectarian group insisted on remaining faithful to the original teachings of the church. Because they refused to follow the reforms of Patriarch Nikon and Czar Alexis, the Old Believers were eventually driven out of their Russian homeland by excommunication, threats, and violence. Tens of thousands migrated east into remote Siberian villages. Others moved west, resettling in Romania and Poland, hoping to maintain their faith in a more tolerant place. Their fundamental religious beliefs and seventeenth-century culture traveled with the Old Believers wherever they went, as duplicate settlement nodes were established far from the original culture hearth of Russian Orthodoxy.[3]

The irreparable schism began when Nikon, appointed as patriarch in 1652, decided to bring the Russian church back to some of its original Byzantine rituals. Czar Alexis agreed to the plan, probably because he wanted to show support for a unified Eastern church during a difficult time of Turkish oppression in Constantinople. Unfortunately, Nikon had no idea how much resistance he would encounter, especially from rural Orthodox believers who did not understand his motives. Most offensive to the Old Believers were his suggestions regarding the number of fingers used to cross oneself (three instead of two), the spelling of the name of Jesus, the number of hallelujahs sung at certain times in the liturgy, and changes in several other church rituals.[4] It shquld be added here that Nikon's rather caustic personality and autocratic tendencies apparently made his suggestions even less palatable to the masses of believers.

In contrast, the founder of the Old Ritualist (Staroobriadtsy) or Old Believer movement was Archpriest Avvakum, a charismatic leader with a deep spiritual sense that appealed to his mostly illiterate followers. Avvakum's autobiography remains a classic of the era and was the first book to be written in "modern" Russian rather than in Old Church Slavonic. As a traditional Orthodox priest, Avvakum strongly believed that everything *Russian* was sacred and perfect and needed no alteration. The Raskolniki accused the Nikonians of countless heresies, as Avvakum and his Old Believers refused to go along with the proposed reforms. But even Avvakum's close personal relationship with Czar Alexis did not protect him or his followers from exile and punishment. Nikon ultimately excommunicated his uncompromising adversaries.

In confusion and anger, thousands of Old Believers retreated to villages in the forests outside Moscow, awaiting the end of the world. After Peter the Great, son of Alexis, became czar, they were convinced he was the Antichrist predicted in the Bible. Peter's refusal to follow prescribed church ritual and his overall contempt for religion convinced the Old Believers that they had to find a way to escape him. Before the end of the seventeenth century, there were numerous reported cases of Old Believer mass suicides and immolations inside burning buildings. At least twenty thousand people perished in panic during this early stage of the schism (Bourdeaux 1966, 30).[5]

The religious resistance eventually divided into two opposing sects. One believes that the church cannot exist without a priesthood. It maintains that it is necessary to have a regular clergy, ordained by the holy Orthodox church and converted to Old Believer principles. This group became known as Popovtsy (priest-possessing).

The second type of Old Believer completely rejects everything about the Nikon-reformed Orthodox church, including ordained priests. These priestless believers (Bezpopovtsy) practice their religion without an ordained leader or church hierarchy. Literate laypersons conduct baptisms and other important ceremonies, and Bezpopovtsy confess their sins to each other. During the rule of Peter the Great, Bezpopovtsy were permitted to organize and observe their own rites and customs. They eventually settled in the far north in the vast Nizhni Novgorod area of Russia (Bolshakoff 1950, 69–70). By the end of the nineteenth century, Bezpopovtsy had settled along the shores of the White Sea, along the Polish-Russian border in the settlements of Vetka and Starodub, in Siberia, in the convent of Vygoretsk, and in villages near Vyg, their most important center. Tolerated by Peter the Great, the Vyg monastery and its dependencies, in particular, grew in strength and added vigor to the development of the Russian Arctic (Crummey 1970, xiv). Unfortunately, Nicholas I closed Vyg in 1855, and its colonies then fell into poverty and disrepair (Bolshakoff 1950, 72).

The Popovtsy, on the other hand, were located farther south. They had settled in small villages among the Cossacks of the Don, Volga, and Ural rivers. The Popovtsy had come more from the Russian bourgeoisie, as many had been well-to-do peasants and Cossacks. They remained relatively intact after the Soviet revolution and had an estimated three million followers in the late 1940s (Bolshakoff 1950, 81).

The Bezpopovtsy wandered farther every century, settling in the northern forests and ultimately migrating across the steppe and tundra of Siberia. After the Revolution ended in 1922, many moved across the Sino-Soviet border, settling in small villages in central China. A few isolated congregations remained in the Baltics and Poland. Bolshakoff estimated in 1950 that, although there were at least eight million Bezpopovtsy Old Believers in Russia in 1879, the Revolution coupled with geographic dispersal probably reduced the total numbers of the sect by many millions. Map 4 illustrates the wide dispersal of Old Believers in Russia. Further information on their dramatic migration to North America is presented in chapter 4.

DOUKHOBORS

Other sectarian groups emerged in opposition to the Orthodox church in the years following the Old Believer movement. Several other sects developed in Russia as a spin-off of the Great Schism, such as the Khlysty and the Skoptsy, but their teachings were too extreme for many who were initially attracted to their emphasis on inner spiritualism.[6] Throughout the eighteenth century, both rational and mystical anti-Orthodox doctrines continued to spread secretly throughout Russia (Bolshakoff 1950, 97). The movement eventually spawned the formation of yet another new sect, the Doukhobors (spirit wrestlers).

Details about the emergence of this sect are unavailable. Doukhobors were inspired by dissident members of other, more extreme sectarian groups. The Doukhobors became a recognized group at least as early as the middle of the eighteenth century when Silvan Kolesnikov began preaching in the Ukrainian village of Nikol'skoe (Avakumovic 1979,

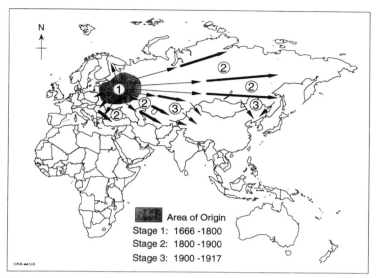

Map 4. Origin and diffusion of Old Believers, 1666–1917

30). The name "spirit wrestlers" was first used by the archbishop of Ekaterinoslav as an insult, implying that they were fighting *against* the Holy Ghost. The group adopted it and changed its meaning to reflect their fight to work *with* the indwelling spirit (Woodcock and Avakumovic 1968, 19).

Doukhobors reject the idea of baptism and all other sacraments and religious ceremonies, have no official priesthood, and reject the Bible as their official source of doctrine. Instead, Doukhobors believe that every person has the answer within themselves, that God is present in every person. This focus on the importance of the inner spirit lies at the heart of Doukhobor teachings. Basic elements of existence are represented by three symbolic items—a loaf of bread, a cellar of salt, and a jug of water. These three symbols are present on every Doukhobor table during worship services.[7]

Ukraine was the origin and nodal center of Doukhobor settlement until the early eighteenth century. Many Doukhobors then migrated or were exiled to the distant edges of the Russian Empire. They moved to Finland, Arkhangelsk, to the Solovetski Islands of the White Sea, near the Sea of Azov, to islands off the coast of Estonia, and to Siberia (Woodcock and Avakumovic 1968, 31). During the reign of Alexander I (1801–25), the Doukhobors were deported in 1802 by the Russian government to Milky Waters (Molochnye Vody) in Taurida, northeast of the Sea of

Azov, in an effort to keep them away from other Orthodox believers. Settlers were to be given forty acres of free land, an interest-free loan of one hundred rubles, and a promise of five years of no taxes. The fertile soil and favorable climate of this region were familiar agricultural amenities to the former residents of Ukraine. Their successes were noted by other Doukhobors from the Tambov and Voronezh provinces, who joined them at Milky Waters after 1804. Small groups of other Doukhobors continued to settle in the fertile region, including groups from the Caucasus and Finland. In 1827, 3,985 Doukhobors had settled in nine villages along the river and lake of Milky Waters (Woodcock and Avakumovic 1968, 38).

The czar's amnesty also encouraged non-Doukhobors to join the faith. Because the benefits of becoming a member of this sect outweighed the deterrents, many newcomers joined the fertile settlements at Milky Waters. Numerous army leaders, exiled criminals, prisoners, army deserters, Tartars, gypsies, and other non-Doukhobors somehow convinced Russian authorities they were members of the sect and needed to rejoin their "forgiven" brethren (Popoff 1964, 9–10).

The blended groups of new residents soon organized an agricultural commune where everyone received everything according to need. The Doukhobors shared common herds, granaries, and gardens and were hospitable to visitors. They tried to live by their main principle of mutual love, although Mennonites and other new German residents of the area complained about their aloofness and extreme social distance. Because of their isolation from other groups, the Doukhobors developed their own socioeconomic system.

Despite these economic successes, there was a great deal of inconsistency in the day-to-day lives of Doukhobors. On the one hand, individuals made decisions based on their own consciences and worked on a purely volunteer basis. On the other hand, they lived within a highly centralized theocracy, characterized by extreme dependence on the decisions of a strong leader. Such authority was always subject to criticism and opposition from dissident individuals and factions (Jamieson 1955, 44–45).

Notwithstanding these inner conflicts in the Doukhobors' society, their economic success threatened the Russian government, since the former frontier region soon became settled by Orthodox farmers as well. The success of the sectarian group soon became an embarrassment to Czar Alexander's administration, which searched for ways to deport them to a more isolated place. The migration of Russian settlers into the Transcaucasus dates from 1830 when the first government order was issued to resettle sectarians and schismatics in the region (Ismail-Zade 1976,

27). These were primarily members of the Doukhobor and Molokan sects. Between 1840 and 1844, large groups of Doukhobors were transported to the Caucasus Mountains, where they established farms in treeless valleys at about the six-thousand-foot level (Bockemuehl 1968, 8). By 1845, more than four thousand had left the fertile Crimea for a new life in the province of Tiflis. Nine settlements were established here along with four more villages in the province of Elizabetpol. Using survival skills learned in their earlier migrations, the Doukhobors once again organized a successful communal economic system. According to summaries of total population cited by Soviet scholar A. I. Klibanov, data published by V. A. Sukhorev in 1944 listed at least twenty thousand Doukhobors in communities in the Caucasus. This agrees with G. V. Verigin's report written previous to emigration, in 1896 (Klibanov 1982, 112).

Much of the financial success of Doukhobors in the Caucasus may be attributed to their willingness to transport supplies for the Russian army during the Crimean War. Although their religion did not permit them to serve in the military, their efforts to transport supplies and to house soldiers during the war won them favor from government authorities and significantly boosted their financial status (Avrich 1962, 265).[8]

Doukhobor settlement was not limited to the rugged Caucasus Mountains. It has been well documented that this sectarian group also settled in many other parts of Russia, even in Siberia. Ethel Dunn established that, by 1898, there were already over twenty thousand Doukhobors and other sectarian groups as far east as the distant Amur region. Some of them had come as exiles, but probably many more had come for the promise of religious liberty (Dunn 1971, 349).

Doukhobors of the Transcaucasus eventually became involved in a power struggle regarding religious leadership. One group, led by Peter Verigin, came into contact with Count Leo Tolstoy, the celebrated Russian religious thinker and writer. The two had many beliefs in common, especially the rejection of private property and taxation. Both also held strict pacifist attitudes. In addition, the Doukhobor's extreme reverence for the land, which had sustained the group from its inception, paralleled Tolstoy's own devotion to Mother Earth. Due to the similarity of their religious and social viewpoints, Tolstoy ultimately helped over seven thousand Doukhobors resettle in Canada.

Thousands of other, more conservative Doukhobors remained in Russia after the Canadian migration. They lived in relative peace with the Russian government although they continued to resist missionary efforts of the official Orthodox church. Soviet sources have collected data on villages still located along the Russian-Turkish-Armenian border in southern Georgia. The residents of these villages resisted Communist demands to collectivize their production and refused to send their children to public schools. In 1939, when collectivization of agricultural land was relatively complete in the USSR, one-third of all land in Doukhobor villages was still privately owned (Kolarz 1961, 355). A second node of Soviet Doukhobor settlement was in the Salsk district in the Rostov province. Many who lived in this area ultimately suffered persecution by government authorities because of their religion. In an interesting and rare reverse-migration process, several hundred Canadian Doukhobors who had returned to the USSR after the Revolution were also a part of the imprisonment and overall anti-Doukhobor attacks in this part of the Soviet Union.

During the glasnost era, the increasingly open Soviet government offered free rural land to Doukhobors for resettlement and communal farming. Finally acknowledging their successes in agricultural production, authorities are also encouraging the descendants of Doukhobors who emigrated to Canada almost one hundred years ago to return to these proposed sectarian agricultural settlements (Paul Steeves interview, Urbana, Illinois, 12 July 1991).

MOLOKANS

The distribution of Doukhobors and Molokans in European Russia in the early twentieth century shown in map 5 illustrates the close spatial relationship between these two sectarian groups. Their spiritual connections are also strong, although significant differences do exist between the two Russian Protestant groups.

The rapid diffusion of Molokan beliefs is remarkable. Of all the movements within pre-twentieth-century Russian sectarianism, Molokanism has had the largest number of followers (Klibanov 1965, 181). Despite the migration of at least thirty-five hundred Molokans to California at the turn of the century, Kolarz estimated that there were at least 1.2 million Molokans still living in Russia at the time of the Revolution (1961, 349). Most were living in the Transcaucasus, with clusters in the cities of Baku and Tiflis and in dozens of small villages in Azerbaijan. As recently as the 1950s, a group of Molokans in Moldova attempted to establish a center for the sect in conjunction with the 150th anniversary of its founding (Dunn 1971, 365).

Molokans were a rationalist sect that rejected priests and all established formalism of the official Orthodox church. They were originally a part of the Doukhobor group but split off from them in 1823 because of certain disagreements on doctrine (Conybeare 1962, 304). The con-

Map 5. Doukhobors and Molokans in European Russia, 1800–1910. Reprinted, by permission, from Klibanov 1982, 149.

tempt of the Doukhobors for the teachings of the Bible alarmed many of the average Russian peasants as they sought a more acceptable anti-Orthodox belief system (Bolshakoff 1950, 106). This desire attracted them to Molokanism.

Molokans trace their specific origin to a laborer named Semen Matveevich Uklein, a son-in-law of a Doukhobor leader. Organizing a group of seventy followers, Uklein led a march into the city of Tambov, preaching his belief in Mosaic dietary law and the fundamentalist teachings of the Bible (Bolshakoff 1950, 105–6). The word *Molokan* was originally derived from the Russian word for milk, *moloko,* because Molokans rejected Orthodox fasts and therefore, unlike Orthodox believers, drank milk during Lent.[9] It is interesting to note here that Molokans reject all fasts but observe Mosaic dietary law. They may have learned this from Simeon Dalmativ, a minister of the covert group, the Judaizers, who influenced Semen Uklein. A complete discussion of Judaizers is beyond the scope of this book, but their story offers a fascinating story of religious origin and diffusion (Bolshakoff 1950, 107–8.) Another Russian Christian sectarian group connected with Jewish teachings was the Subbotniki (Sabbatarians), who observed Jewish holy days, refused to eat pork, and conducted their religious services in Hebrew. After the Molokans emigrated to southern California, a close relationship existed between the Molokans and a small group of Subbotniks in Los Angeles (Dunn 1983–92, sec. 6). Subbotniks, however, were a minor religious group in western North America and so are not discussed in detail in this analysis.[10]

Molokans call themselves True Spiritual Christians. They believe in the teachings of the Bible but, like the Doukhobors, reject all sacraments. As was common in other Russian religious groups, events and personalities divided the Molokan faith. Three groups evolved, the Postoiannye, the Pryguny, and the Maksimisty. The Pryguny are especially significant to this study because they formed the largest group of early émigrés to southern California. This subgroup is also known as the Jumpers because they express themselves physically during worship much like Pentecostals. Sacred dancing and prophesying are important in their worship service.

The newest subgroup, Pryguny-Maksimisty, named in honor of a religious leader of some of the Molokans, Maksim Rudometkin, often moved away from the other groups to form their own communities. They have also revised Molokan writings (much to the chagrin of more traditional Postoiannye and Pryguny) to include the teachings of Rudometkin. According to Ethel Dunn, the three groups have different attitudes about their larger society and their place in it (1971, 367). The Maksimisty are today the most urbanized and the most conservative. Because of their extreme mysticism, Maksimisty are suspicious of outsiders who do not believe as they do. Divisions between these three groups of Molokans are expanded upon in chapter 4 since they are reflected in the settlement patterns and church memberships in Molokan communities in Oregon and California.

After the movement's origin in the fertile chernozem plains of Ukraine, it rapidly diffused to Stavropol, the Crimea, other villages in the Tambov region, Voronezh, Samara, Saratov, and Astrakhan Guberniias, as well as the Transcaucasus, Central Asia, and the farthest eastern borders of Russia (Bonch-Bruevich 1959, 295). In the 1840s, the government decided to send the Molokans as far away from their center of power as possible. They resettled in the Caucasus Mountains, forming a buffer between Christian Armenians and Muslim Turks in the region. The Molokans adjusted extremely well to life in this remote region of Russia, making a significant contribution to the development of the Transcaucasus. By the 1880s, Doukhobors and Molokans probably made up half of the population of the Amur region (Priamur'e 1909, 110). According to Litvintsev's 1887 article about Russian sectarians, "It would not be an exaggeration to call the city of Blagoveshchensk a Molokan city, as many do" (550).

But the settlement patterns of Russian Molokans during the nineteenth and early twentieth centuries were not limited to rural villages. In contrast to Doukhobor attachment to the land, Molokans often worked in commerce and trade. Many of them owned factories and small businesses, often becoming successful entrepreneurs and rising to positions of respect and authority in small communities. Others remained on prosperous individual farmsteads. Mechanization of all kinds of agricultural work in Molokan villages was common even in the 1890s (Klibanov 1982, 191).

The economic prosperity of Molokan believers as compared to Orthodox and Doukhobors was due almost entirely to religious differences. Orthodox Russians were tied to tradition and remained committed to the importance of serfdom; Doukhobors shared land communally and so were also less capitalistic and enterprising than the Molokan farmers. Soviet historian Klibanov argues that it was the development of this capitalist agriculture that set Molokans apart from the other sectarian groups (1982, 198–99). While their economic success may have provided more opportunities for religious influence and increased chances for the conversion of local people, it also contributed to dissension and class differentiation within Molokan communities in the early twentieth century. Doukhobor and Molokan land use and economic development in Russia at this time no doubt set the stage for their differing adjustment to life in North America.

Although there are thousands of Molokans still living in certain parts of the Commonwealth of Independent States, especially in villages in Azerbaijan, the number of Molokan believers has dwindled considerably, primarily because of the conversion of many thousands to the evangelical Christian and Baptist faiths in the twentieth century. A sixty-six-year-old Russian woman from the village of Peski, O. S. Roguleva, recalled that, in the years before the Revolution, Molokans converted to Baptism twenty or thirty at a time (Tul'tseva 1977, 26). Sometimes whole villages would convert at one time.

The Baptist faith is today the largest Protestant groups in the Soviet Union. Baptists and other evangelical Christians such as Pentecostals, Lutherans, Methodists, Seventh-day Adventists, and Mennonites are all significant denominations in the former Soviet Union (table 1). Large

Table 1
Religions in the Soviet Union

Religion	Believers
Orthodox	50–70 million
Muslim	35–43 million
Eastern Rite Catholic	>3 million
Georgian Orthodox	3 million
Roman Catholic	>2 million
Armenian Apostolic	2 million
Baptist	½–2 million
Old Believer	>1 million
Lutheran	600,000
Buddhist	500,000
Jew	500,000
Pentecostal	100,000
Seventh-day Adventist	40,000
Mennonite	40,000
Methodist	3,000
Jehovah's Witness	N/A

Source: Steeves 1989, 126.

numbers of only two of these groups, Russian Baptists and Pentecostals, now live on the North American Pacific Rim. The discussion of the origin and diffusion of Russian evangelicals in this chapter is therefore limited to these two groups.

BAPTISTS

The growth of fundamentalist Protestant beliefs in Russia and the Soviet Union during the past century has exceeded that of all other sectarian groups. Baptists were the earliest of the evangelical groups to organize in Russia and still remain the largest in total numbers of believers. Today, Baptists in the Commonwealth of Independent States are more numerous than those in any other nation except the United States (Pollock 1964, 91).

Baptist beliefs were brought into Ukraine from Germany as early as the 1830s. Evangelical ministers encouraged Mennonites in Ukraine to practice baptism by immersion, experience conscious conversion, and hold revival meetings. Durasoff marks the official beginning of the evangelical movement in Russia with the invitation of Russian spiritual leader Abraham Unger to German Baptist minister Johann Oncken to come to his country in 1869 (1969, 33–34). Other scholars emphasize the baptism of Molokan leader Nikita Voronin in a small stream near Tiflis in

1867 as an important event in starting the evangelical movement among ethnic Russians (Sawatsky 1981, 29; Steeves 1976, 3; Blane 1964, 6–7). The complete story of Voronin's secret baptism is told in detail in Steeves's seminal work on the subject of Russian Baptists. According to Steeves, Voronin's growing dissatisfaction with his fellow Molokans' resistance to water baptism led to his personal contact with a German Baptist in Tiflis who baptized him (Steeves 1976, 3). Despite the specifics of its beginnings, the evangelical movement had grown to about 100,000 Baptists and 250,000 total evangelical Christians by the end of the Russian Revolution in 1922 (Sawatsky 1981, 29). By 1929, there were more than 300,000 Baptists in the Soviet Union (Steeves 1976, iii).

Economic and political factors also contributed to the growth of early Protestant groups. The extraordinary social ferment that began in Russia during the Crimean War culminated in the emancipation of the serfs in 1861. This political reform, along with numerous other social reforms, added a major impetus to religious change. Openness to new ideas, the availability of Scriptures translated into vernacular Russian, and improved literacy rates among the peasants of Russia encouraged the growth of Bible-based, fundamentalist Christian groups. This era also witnessed public exposure of the corrupt Orthodox church hierarchy. Evidence of this corruption was cited by the governor of the Perm province: "The Orthodox clergymen exercise no moral influence over the people, they are prejudiced, dull, and too strictly scholastic in their attitudes. In private life the motives of the clergy are mercenary and selfish, of which the masses are well aware" (Miliukov 1943, 126).

Evangelical Baptists originated almost simultaneously in three parts of Russia at this time of change. Evangelical Christians were variously known as Baptists in the Caucasus, Stundists in Ukraine, and Pashkovites in St. Petersburg (Durasoff 1969, 36). The Ukrainian stream had gained particular strength because thousands of Russians were influenced by German Protestants who settled there during the time of Catherine the Great (1762–96). Russian agriculturalists participated in German *Stunde* (Bible hours) in the early 1800s. Most of the Stundists, as they came to be known, believed in baptism by immersion and in the conversion experience. This early exposure to Baptist ideas laid a foundation for receptivity to the ideas of German Baptist missionaries who came later. Large numbers of Molokans also resided in Ukraine and, as discussed earlier, were often open to conversion to the related Baptist belief system. By 1877, the number of Russians believing in the new faith had grown to over 250,000 in ten provinces between the Austrian border and the Volga River (Durasoff 1969, 41). Early Baptist congregations in southern European Russia are shown in map 6.

Map 6. Early Baptist and evangelical Christians in European Russia. Adapted from Klibanov 1982, 226.

The first evangelicals in St. Petersburg had been converted by a British missionary who held revival meetings in the high-status salons of the nation's capital in 1874. One of the many aristocratic converts, Colonel V. A. Pashkov, became the Russian leader of this branch of the movement. His energy and commitment to active missionary activity caused the movement to become known locally as Pashkovism. (One of the two Baptist churches in suburban St. Petersburg is shown in figure 2.)

Between 1867 and 1874, then, three separate but similar Baptist movements spread through various parts of Russia. As did the Molokans, Doukhobors, and other Russian sectarian groups, all three questioned the authority of the Orthodox church. All resisted traditional ideas of a priesthood and refused to venerate icons and the Virgin Mary. All were deeply spiritual but in a more simple and direct way, rejecting the ritual and mysticism of Eastern Orthodoxy. All believed in conscious and often

Figure 2. A Sunday morning view from one of the Baptist churches in suburban St. Petersburg, May 1991. Photo by author.

cataclysmic conversion and trusted the Bible as the only authority on religious life. They also participated in active missionary work with their neighbors (Blane 1964, 17–18). But each of the three groups was also unique. Their social status, economic background, and place of origin differed, making collaboration increasingly difficult.

Communication among the widely scattered groups of Baptists intensified in the 1880s. In 1882, the first conference of Russian and German Baptists was held in the Taurida province, northeast of the Crimea (Steeves 1976, 22). The conference organized missionary activity and solidified the various groups of believers.

This growing movement was further unified by the arrests and imprisonment of believers following the first Baptist conference held in St. Petersburg in 1884. Here, peasants from the Ukraine and Caucasus groups first met with St. Petersburg aristocrats. A participant in this first conference recalled: "Especially at meal time was the evangelical brotherhood revealed, a peasant sat next to a count, and cultured ladies waited on their simple brothers. This remains for me the brightest memory of my life" (*Bratskii Vestnik*, June–July 1945, 30).

These meetings were interrupted by continued persecution by the Orthodox-dominated state. Leaders were arrested and later summoned before authorities and presented with an ultimatum that if they wished to live in Russia they would "no longer preach, hold meetings, pray with their own words, or have communion with Stundists and other spiritual groups" (*Bratskii Vestnik*, Jan.–Feb. 1947, 44). This persecution continued until the government edict of 1905 permitted evangelicals in Russia the freedom of assembly.

Following the passage of this important law, the All-Russian Evangelical Christian Union was formed in 1909. The union eventually established suborganizations in each of the Russian provinces so as to expand missionary work, publish information, and conduct religious education in every part of the country. This effort increased the number of Baptists and evangelical Christians substantially in the 1920s. As a result of these efforts, the evangelical church grew from 107,000 in 1905 to 350,000 by 1921 and to 500,000 by 1929 (Hill 1989, 115). This phenomenal period of growth was aided by numerous conversions in prisoner-of-war camps during World War I. At least two thousand new Russian evangelicals returned home from the camps after the war and diffused the faith into diverse regions of the country (Sawatsky 1981, 38).

Evangelical Christian missionaries from outside Russia and the Soviet Union focused most of their attention on ethnic Russians as targets for conversion. There were two major reasons for this. First, Baptist missionaries worked in Poland, Ukraine, and the Baltic nations in the 1920s and 1930s. They targeted Russians there because they were a minority group and had weak or nonexistent religious affiliations. Other residents were already members of other churches. Second, Russian Baptist missionaries from the United States had been active supporters of these missionary efforts, and they preferred to support the conversion of other Russians. In 1939, when the USSR signed a nonaggression pact with Hitler, these nations became part of the Soviet Union, bringing numerous new Russian evangelicals into the Soviet Union (Ronald Wixman interview, University of Oregon, 3 March 1991).

Mission funding and overall support from Baptists in the United States was essential in accelerating the rapid diffusion of the new faith. Whereas Molokans, Doukhobors, and other sectarian groups had been distinctly Russian movements, Baptist beliefs originated outside Russia. These groups continue to be strongly supported by North American evangelical Christians. As will be discussed in more detail in chapter 5, these linkages with the West have been a vitally important factor influencing glasnost-era decisions by Russian Protestant groups to emigrate to North America.

PENTECOSTALS

The world first became aware of Russian Pentecostals in 1963 when worldwide media coverage revealed the story of thirty-two Russian Pentecostals from Chernogorsk in Siberia who had rushed, without warning, into the American embassy in Moscow to seek asylum. They were representatives of over one hundred Pentecostals from their village who desperately wanted to emigrate (Hill 1989, 28–29). After Soviet authorities denied all accusations of religious persecution in the USSR, the Pentecostals were loaded onto a bus and then onto trains and returned to their village.

Replaying the same dramatic story (and never giving up hope of emigrating to the United States), another group of nineteen Pentecostal families sought refuge in the American embassy in Moscow in 1978. The Chmykhalov and Vaschenko families, or the Siberian Seven as they were popularly called in Western news reports, lived in the embassy basement for five years while the United States and Soviet government debated their case. Finally, in 1983, after years of media coverage and letter-writing campaigns by North American and European Christians, the Soviet government allowed the families to emigrate.

Like Russian Baptists, the origin and rapid spread of Pentecostalism was aided by the support of believers outside the country. In 1911, just a few years after the beginnings of Pentecostalism in the United States, American Pentecostal missionaries started a congregation in Vyborg, on the Finnish border. Drawing on the support of Baptists and at the same time relying on internal schisms in Baptist church congregations, the movement spread to St. Petersburg by 1914. Pentecostal beliefs reached as far as Novgorod and Moscow and even into the Caucasus in the next several years of missionary activity (Fletcher 1985, 28).

This origin in the northern part of the country was superseded by growth in the Odessa area in the early 1920s. The main branch of Pentecostalism in the Soviet Union was started in Odessa by a former Russian Baptist minister, Ivan Efimovich Voronaev. After serving with the Cossacks under the czar, Voronaev became a minister in central Siberia in the town of Irkutsk. Following a period of persecution of Protestants under the Orthodox-dominated state church, Voronaev emigrated to San Francisco via Harbin, Manchuria, in 1911. He founded a Russian Baptist church in San Francisco and planted the seeds for churches in Los Angeles and Seattle, then moved his family to New York City, where he served as minister of a Russian Baptist church in Manhattan (Synan 1984, 66). Influenced by his daughter who began attending a Pentecostal church on Forty-second Street and by his Pentecostal neighbors, Voronaev eventually attended a cottage prayer meeting, where, it is reported, he had his first Pentecostal experience of speaking in tongues. Soon after, in 1919, Voronaev founded the first Russian Pentecostal church in the United States in New York City (Durasoff 1969, 1972).

In 1920, with the support of the American Assembly of God, the entire Voronaev family returned to their homeland to preach their revised message. First traveling to Varna, Bulgaria, and organizing several churches there, the missionaries moved on to Odessa, which was to serve as the node of Pentecostal activity in Eastern Europe and the USSR for several decades. Within five years, over 350 congregations with a membership of approximately seventeen thousand had been established. Map 7 charts Voronaev's long and complex journey from central Siberia to Odessa by way of North America.

Although this rapidly growing Pentecostal movement in Russia and the Soviet Union has been strictly a twentieth-century phenomena, a foundation for the practice of emotional and expressive Christianity had been laid centuries earlier. As discussed earlier, in the middle of the seventeenth century, a sect known as the Khlysty (the flagellants) broke off from the official Orthodox church to create their own mystical belief system. Among their many unique ideas, Khlysty participated in strenuous worship services involving high-energy dancing, singing, and praising God (Fletcher 1985, 13–14). Rejecting all traditional church sacraments, the Khlysty focused on two sacraments of their own. The first was a reverence for suffering. To them, suffering provided the believer with purification and was a positive and necessary part of worship. The second, and perhaps even more pertinent as a foundation for later Pentecostal successes, was their belief in the importance of the gift of the Holy Spirit. The presence of the Spirit during worship services was established by numerous expressive and emotional experiences exhibited by believers. Dancing during worship often resulted in exhaustion followed by the experience of glossolalia, or speaking in tongues. Although a wide variety of types of Khlysty evolved over the years, some with rather bizarre behavioral requirements, the practice of expressive worship continued to remain important into the twentieth century. Soviet leaders, in fact, often mistook early Pentecostals for this earlier sectarian group (Fletcher 1985, 18).

Another foundation for the rapid acceptance of Pentecostal beliefs in the Soviet Union was laid in the nineteenth and early twentieth centuries by a branch of the Molokans known as the Pryguny. As discussed earlier,

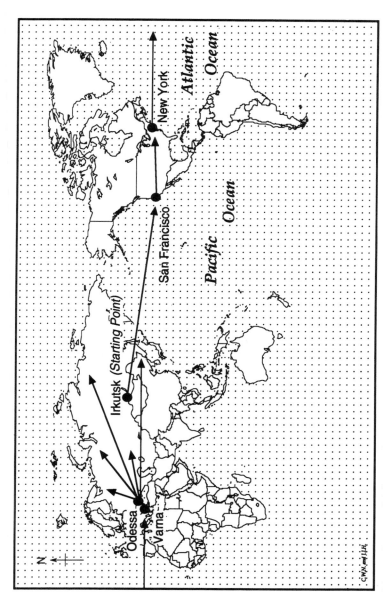

Map 7. Origin and diffusion of Russian Pentecostals, 1911–25.

these Molokans practiced a form of worship that often involved jumping and shouting as an expression of the presence of the Holy Spirit. Of particular importance was the large number of Molokan Pryguny in the Odessa region at the time Pentecostal missionary Voronaev arrived. Molokan Pryguny, Khlysty, and numerous other sectarian groups undoubtedly laid a receptive foundation for the acceptance of Pentecostal teachings in the Soviet Union in the 1920s. Baptists also provided a large group of potential converts and a church home for early Pentecostal missionaries (map 6).

Pentecostal and Baptist believers are today found in most parts of the former Soviet Union. It is estimated that there are at least one hundred thousand Pentecostals remaining there (Steeves 1989, 126). In an effort to avoid persecution, Pentecostal communities often moved from place to place en masse. According to Alexeyeva (1987, 215), there are communities in the westernmost regions of Russia; in the Far East (Nakhodka and Vladivostock); along the path of their movements from west to east in the Rovno, Zhitomir, and Kaluga regions; in Ukraine, Stavropol, and Krasnodar regions; and in Azerbaijan, Georgia, Siberia, and central Asia. Constant persecution, the negative attitudes of Soviet society, and the unique belief system of Pentecostals have resulted in a strong solidarity among the various congregations. Most consider themselves members of one large family, call each other brothers and sisters, and generally form a cohesive body. Pentecostals also migrated to new places because of their continued apocalyptic search for a legendary country where the forces of evil do not rule (Kolarz 1961, 334). In this regard, they were much like the Old Believers, who moved in large groups to escape the evils of the Antichrist. As described in chapter 5, these beliefs and traits encouraged glasnost-era emigration out of the USSR, tightly structured chain migration patterns, and the formation of a cohesive sense of community among Russian Pentecostals in the United States and Canada in the early 1990s.

Why did this charismatic, *non-Russian* style of religious expression spread so rapidly throughout the USSR and have such a strong influence on its people? An analysis of a complex mix of economic, social, political, and even psychological factors is necessary to explain the rapid diffusion of this religious phenomenon. First, since the movement traditionally affected the poor, Pentecostalism is even more attractive as a proletarian and grass-roots movement than is the Baptist faith. The traditional Russian Christian religion, Eastern Orthodoxy, long associated with restrictive state policies forced on the masses of people from the *top*, made Pentecostalism, a grass-roots movement from the *bottom*, a more attractive alternative. A certain mystique has drawn young people in particular to evangelical services. There is something romantic and revolutionary about the movement, since it has been banned for decades and it takes some courage to belong to it. In addition, religious services often take place in secretive settings, which appeals to young people. Mountains, forests, and half-dark rooms are common sanctuaries for worship. It has been said that the evangelical religions serve the same function for today's younger generation that underground political meetings did for their parents and grandparents in earlier revolutionary movements (Nichol 1966, 193–98).

Another reason for the rapid diffusion of evangelical Protestantism in Russia, the Soviet Union, and most recently the Commonwealth of Independent States relates to its easily comprehensible, rationally oriented worldview. The basic tenets of the faith can be mastered in a relatively short time by a person of average intelligence. The approach is dogmatic and deterministic, qualities that offer the movement the ability to satisfy its followers. It allows members to feel they are part of an inevitable process whose success is preordained. This deterministic element encourages a fatalistic acceptance of life's spiritual and material problems.

It is also of interest to speculate on the role of the physical environment in the development of this Russian fatalistic attitude. Many scholars regard religious behavior as essentially a response of humans to features in their natural environment. Day-to-day life in a harsh, politically repressed environment may lead to a sense of inadequacy and a tendency to seek a substitute for environmental security. In terms of evangelical beliefs, the image of God as a loving, personal friend may offer security in an often difficult environmental setting.

Four major factors, therefore, have influenced the rapid diffusion of Pentecostalism in Russia and the Soviet Union. First, it was a grass-roots movement arising within the masses of Russian peasants rather than an authoritarian, state-dominated religion forced on people from the top. Second, evangelical beliefs are direct, rational, and easy to understand. This makes them easier to teach and learn. Third, charismatic Christianity is viewed by many who are disillusioned with socialism as romantic and revolutionary. With its secretiveness, emotionalism, and personal commitment, the religion offers a satisfying replacement for communism. Finally, the harsh physical environment and repressed political environment may have offered fertile ground for a religion based on the concept of a loving, personal, and constantly supportive God.

Interrelationships between Religious Groups

Figure 3 illustrates the close connections between various Russian religious groups. One depended on the evolution and spread of the other.

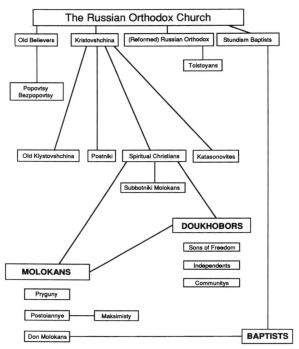

Figure 3. Evolution of religious groups in Russia. Adapted from E. Dunn's translation of Klibanov 1982, 20–21.

As has been shown, the Old Believer movement developed as a response to Eastern Orthodoxy, Doukhoborism grew out of the same schism, Molokanism evolved as a protest against Doukhoborism, Baptists often were converted from Molokan believers, and, finally, Baptists provided the most fertile ground for conversion to Pentecostalism. In fact, the relationships come full circle. The successes of the various sectarian groups might not have been as dramatic had the setting not been prepared for them by the deep spirituality of earlier Orthodox seekers (Kolarz 1961, 283). After the Russian Revolution, the paths of their spread and strength changed dramatically.

Religion and the Soviet State

At the end of the Revolution in 1922, Protestant groups were tolerated by the new government primarily because they were viewed as anti-Orthodox. In addition, evangelical Christians had been persecuted during czarist times and so were not viewed as supporters of the old regime.

Both Russian and foreign Baptists originally misjudged the true nature of the Communist government, thinking it a new form of democracy during the first years after the Revolution (Kolarz 1961, 287). Anti-religious measures of the new Communist government (confiscation of church property, closing of churches) did not affect most Protestant believers.

Eastern Orthodox believers were, on the other hand, severely perse-cuted because of their long-term close association with the hated czarist government. Church property and land formerly belonging to Russian Orthodox groups was turned over to sectarians in an effort to divide and conquer.

But the Law on Religious Associations severely curtailed the continued growth of all religious groups in the USSR. From the beginning of the Soviet regime, atheism was strongly supported by the government. Before 1929, however, religious persecution mainly focused on the Russian Or-thodox and Muslim faiths (Alexeyeva 1987, 201). After the passage of the 1929 law, both Protestant and Orthodox church buildings were converted to use by the new League of the Militant Godless or made into dance halls or social clubs. Religious education of children under the age of eighteen became illegal, and church libraries were closed. As a direct result of this law, the 1930s witnessed not only a radical reduc-tion in visible growth of the Baptist and Pentecostal movement in the USSR, but also a decrease in the number of Orthodox churches and of their members. Thousands of believers were sent to Siberian prisons. There, unexpectedly, missionary work spread quickly. Numerous stories of dramatic prison conversions to evangelical Christianity continue to come from people who lived through this era. Their dramatic stories became well known to readers outside the Soviet Union through the sympathetic presence of the Baptist prisoner Alyosha in Solzhenitsyn's powerful novel *One Day in the Life of Ivan Denisovich* (1963). Twelve to twenty million people were sent to forced labor camps during these years, many in the most remote parts of the country (Fletcher 1985, 48). This geographic dispersal spread religious teachings to remote areas. Whole communities were exiled to Siberia as persecution intensified dur-ing the Stalin years, thus diffusing evangelical Christianity far and wide.

The onset of Russia's involvement in World War II in 1940 brought a total reversal of religious policy—increased support of all religious groups by the Soviet government. Stalin's wartime policies sought unifi-cation of the Soviet Union, since he viewed religion as a potentially useful, unifying factor. In the early years of the war, the Soviet govern-ment shifted abruptly from religious persecution to an attitude of cooper-ation. This new relationship was governed by the state-appointed Council for Russian Orthodox Church Affairs and the Council for the Affairs of Religious Cults created in 1943. The most recent Council for Religious Affairs, founded in 1965, combined these two bodies. In 1944, a government-supported All-Union Council of Evangelical Christians and Baptists (AUCECB) was organized to oversee the officially approved activities of these Protestant groups. This organization had its own internal problems from the beginning because the state forced two opposing groups, the Baptists and the evangelical Christians, to merge into one governing body. A year after it was founded, Pentecostals were invited to join, and, in 1963, Mennonites were admitted. One year after the Pentecostals became part of the AUCECB, the majority of them resigned over differences in church doctrine, especially as it related to Pentecostal speaking in tongues.

The Soviet-approved organizations met with mixed reactions among church members. Some undoubtedly felt a sense of relief after the years of persecution in the 1930s. Others mistrusted the government and refused to register their churches with the council. Still other congregations registered the church initially but gave false information about its actual membership list to the authorities (Nikolai Ivannik interview, West Sacramento, 29 November 1990). As a result, evangelical believers found themselves faced with many divisive decisions about associating with particular churches. Many went underground during this period, returning to the secret religious life they had known in the 1930s.

Tolerance of the church in the USSR after World War II depended on decisions by the current Soviet leadership. The last five years of Stalin's rule saw a renewed effort to thwart church membership. Contact with foreigners was almost completely cut off, making outside support of evangelical groups difficult. Convicted unregistered believers received long prison terms. After Stalin's death in 1953, conditions improved somewhat, although church membership was still tightly controlled by the state council. Even so, membership in evangelical churches increased substantially in the 1950s, although both registered and unregistered believers continued to face persecution at many levels. The unregistered faced prison terms, labor camp sentences, fines, and stays in psychiatric hospitals, while the registered faced job discrimination and were banned from admission into institutions of higher education. Despite these difficulties, *Bratskii Vestnik* estimated the number of evangelical Christian/ Baptist believers in the Soviet Union in the early 1950s as at least three million (March–April 1954, 91).

During the Khrushchev years (1959–64), over half of the evangelical churches in the USSR were closed along with thousands of Orthodox churches (Hill 1989, 127). Although Khrushchev was viewed by many within the system as a liberal because he denounced Stalin, he continued to approve often violent policies that persecuted religious believers in the Soviet Union. Faced with dealing with religious groups who refused to go away, he tightened up state policies to discourage their further growth. In 1959, the government-sponsored periodical *Science and Religion* began publication in a continuing effort to speak out against religious beliefs.

In the early 1960s, churches found themselves in the challenging position of trying to abide by the 1929 laws as well as by the restrictions placed on them by their own AUCECB. Many of the leaders of this group had suffered long prison terms because of their religious beliefs. It can be assumed that their decision to work with the government for official church approval during this era was based on their perception that this would protect their membership from similar fates. Much to the shock and anger of many members of the AUCECB, however, the council completely acquiesced to Khrushchev's demands and even established its own set of state-supported restrictive guidelines (Hill 1989, 130). A deep schism in evangelical church unity resulted from the policies of the AUCECB during this period of tight state supervision over church records. During the decades of heightened Soviet persecution of the church in the 1950s and 1960s, the council's representatives even told the World Council of Churches and other international Christian groups that freedom of religion was guaranteed in the Soviet Union. Church leaders also falsely told thousands of foreign visitors to Moscow that religious freedom was no longer an issue in the Soviet Union (Sawatsky 1981, 205).

In 1965, after the refusal of church groups to recognize the AUCECB, an independent Baptist church body was organized in the USSR. The newly formed Council of Churches of the Evangelical Christian–Baptists (CCECB) established an energetic system of missionary activity, especially among Orthodox believers in eastern Siberia and the Soviet Far East (Alexeyeva 1987, 206).

The period immediately after Khrushchev and preceding Gorbachev's policies of glasnost, perestroika, and associated religious openness continued the Soviet antireligious policies. Both registered and unregistered members of evangelical groups continued to be harassed by the state. Through the first half of the 1980s, unregistered Christians were often arrested and imprisoned (Y. Yakovlev interview, Seattle, November 1991). Deep schisms remained in the church hierarchy, although the AUCECB had approximately 350,000 members in 1980 (Hill 1989, 143). Its rival group, the CCECB, was down to about one hundred thousand members in the same year (Sawatsky 1981, 211, 442, 468). Congregations of Baptists, Pentecostals, Mennonites, Seventh-day Adventists, and others registered on their own, ignoring the official church hierarchy altogether (Hill 1989, 143). Growing animosity among those who registered independently, those who registered through the CCECB or the AUCECB, and those who were unregistered divided church membership into many factions by 1985. This fragmentation remains a divisive issue also among Russian immigrants in the United States and Canada working on behalf of fellow believers in the USSR.

Gorbachev and the Gospel

The years since 1988 have witnessed remarkable changes in religious freedom in the USSR. In November 1990, ending decades of state-sponsored atheism, the new Law on Freedom of Conscience and Religious Organizations was passed by the Soviet legislature. This official decision was the first change in policy since the restrictive 1929 Law on Religious Associations. The new law prohibited discrimination against believers in the USSR and allowed them to sponsor Sunday schools for their children and to conduct home prayer services. The law also ended Bolshevik control of all religious institutions and their policy of required education on atheism. It recognized all religions as equal under the law and barred the state from legally interfering in religious affairs. After the establishment of the new Commonwealth of Independent States in 1991, this Soviet law set the stage for complete religious freedom in the new republics.[11]

The new law on religion was the direct result of the policies of Soviet president Mikhail Gorbachev, who assumed the leadership of the USSR in 1985. His policies of glasnost and perestroika extended into the sphere of religious freedom. After decades of persecution, believers now have the freedom to worship openly. Although he is no longer in power, Gorbachev's vision for the restructuring process, including personal and economic transformation of the Soviet people, helped shape today's policies. According to Gorbachev, "Our main job is to lift the individual spiritually, respecting his inner world and giving him moral strength . . . an individual must know and feel that his contribution is needed, and his dignity is not being infringed upon, that he is being treated with trust and respect" (1988, 16).

The new law on religious freedom did not appear in a vacuum. Two years before it was passed, a well-publicized and internationally attended celebration of the Millennium of Christianity in the Soviet Union became an important event commemorating national unity. During the year before the historic event marking one thousand years of Christianity in Russia and the Soviet Union, despite a seventy-year history of persecuting believers, Soviet leaders began releasing religious prisoners. Following the celebration, the open publication of articles of support for religious groups in national journals and newspapers was permitted for the first time in decades.

The celebration of the Millennium of Christianity in Russia and the Soviet Union and the new law on religious freedom have encouraged thousands of Russians to be baptized in the Orthodox church. It has been suggested that this renewed interest in religion is a reflection of the nation's desire to return to the old way, the pre-Soviet way, rather than a search for real spiritual ideals. There is some concern among church leaders that the Orthodox faith is becoming a culture bearer rather than a God bearer, as the Russian people continue their search for a better way (Bourdeaux 1990, 105). This secularization of spiritual values is reflected in the large number of groups within the former Soviet Union who support a return to the monarchy and, with it, the traditional Russian way of life. The Monarchy party is currently a powerful political force in this movement. Their goal, in this controversial era of political restructuring, is to return the country to czarist rule. Many of the members of this party and other similar groups are now active, vocal members of the Orthodox church. Many have little or no background in Christian teachings and thus have little understanding of the spiritual aspects of the faith. Orthodox activists are working with these converts to assure their continued commitment to religion as a spiritual issue rather than a historical-cultural phenomenon (Bourdeaux 1990, 108).

Evangelical groups in the Soviet Union during the era of glasnost also witnessed a resurgence of membership and activities. These belief systems were originally imported from outside the country and so do not represent a return to the desire for traditional Russian culture as does Orthodoxy. Most of the financial support for Russian Baptist, Pentecostal, and other evangelical groups continues to come from the United States. Their members, rather than being attracted to traditional Russianness, are drawn to becoming Americanized. Their growing influence in the country adds fuel to the growing Russian obsession with all things American.

It is becoming clear, then, that Russians attracted to Eastern Orthodoxy and those attracted to evangelical Christianity form two different groups. Orthodoxy, with its mysterious mysticism, quiet beauty, and unquestioning acceptance of the person, without the believer doing much active work, is no doubt very appealing to someone who has had long-term hopes of changing the system. The frustration of living in a society where change comes slowly or not at all has encouraged many to return to the church of their cultural roots. Russian evangelicals, on the other hand, usually have lived out of the political and economic mainstream of Russian society and are more often in powerless socioeconomic positions. Patriotic Russians are rarely attracted to their membership.

This difference is one of several factors behind the decision of thousands of evangelical Christians to migrate to the United States and Canada. The Protestant connection with North American culture and the Orthodox connection with Russian culture may result in yet another schism in Russian society as the postglasnost era evolves.

THREE

Early North American Imprints

Rᴜssɪᴀɴs ᴡᴇʀᴇ ᴛʜᴇ first Europeans to discover the Northwest coast of North America and the islands of the North Pacific, although the area had been occupied by indigenous populations for thousands of years. Russian records, diaries, narrative accounts, and maps provide an early overview of the geography of this vast region and continue to offer fascinating glimpses into life in frontier America.

Until the postglasnost era, geographic connections between North America and Russia were never more direct than during the first era of Russian settlement in Alaska and California. In a somewhat ironic twist of history (but not of geography), Russian missionaries and fur traders penetrated lands east of the Urals, finally reaching the shores of the North American continent in the early 1700s. A myriad of information sources have been published about this frontier era of Russian expansion into America.[1] Until recently, however, most have dealt with the successes and ultimate failures of fur traders and the history of the Russian-American Company.[2] This chapter links the missionary activity of the Orthodox church with the settlement history of the region to illustrate the central role of religion in Russian frontier-era settlement.

The details of this story are not always positive. With the arrival of Russian missionaries and hunters, native people in the region suddenly found themselves besieged by an exceedingly foreign and often confusing culture and an aggressive and often brutal economic system.

Direct geographic linkages between Asia and North America are often overlooked. Map projections that divide the Pacific Ocean, commonly used in Russia and North America, diminish a clear awareness of the direct connection between the two continents. Less than one hundred miles separate the two continents. The narrow Bering Strait links the east coast of Russia to the west coast of North America; its islands extend in a long arc connecting mainland Alaska to the Commander Islands. They are the tops of volcanic mountains that appear on both continents. This direct connection provided North and South America with its first human occupants, as ancestors of "Americans" trekked across the land bridge between the two continents during previous ice ages when sea level was low enough to expose land.

During the frontier era of Russian expansion into the region, Alaska became the pivot of an empire that extended across three continents. In more recent years, twentieth-century air travel has increased the importance of this strategic location between North America and Eurasia.

Despite the physical proximity of North America and Asia, however, climatic and oceanic hazards in the region made human connections difficult during and after glacial eras. Since the Aleutians separate the cold waters of the Bering Sea from the warmer Japanese current, fog is an almost daily condition. Frequent high winds and heavy rainstorms also make travel difficult. Yet to Russians who had been living in cold continental Siberia, the Aleutians seemed almost tropical with their grassy ground cover and their comparatively mild climate induced by the Japanese current. Even more important to the Russians, these grasses supported a wide variety of fur-bearing animals. The fur from these mammals first encouraged Russian expansion.

Pre-Russian human settlement was sparse, with the most density on the eastern end of the island chain. Ethnographer Lydia Black categorizes the native people encountered by Russians on the Aleutians and the Alaskan mainland as two distinct groups of Aleuts; the Inupiaq and Yupik Eskimo on the northern and western coasts of Alaska; the Alutiiq on the Kodiak archipelago; the Chugach (Koniag), Eyak, Tlingit, Haida, and Tsimshian on the Northwest coast; and various Athabaskan-speaking groups in coastal settlements along the Cook Inlet and in interior regions (Black 1989, 48). These native people reacted to Russian occupation of the region in different ways, but all were affected by long-term impacts of cultural contact.

Russian occupation of Alaska from the early 1700s to the sale of the territory to the United States in 1867 was, in many ways, a typical example of colonial imperialism. Motivations for expansion into the North Pacific by imperial Russia, the extraction of resources, and the expansion of territory were very similar to those of the other colonizing nations of the time, such as Spain and England. Russian expansion into western North America was different in several aspects, however, from that of most other European colonists of the same period. Participants in the eastward expansion of Russian territory into North America were not colonists or pioneers in any sense. Their decision to leave their homeland was motivated entirely by profit. Most were employees of the Russian-American Company and made the long and treacherous journey to Alaska to hunt and barter furs, not to establish permanent residency there. Although these economic sojourners established settlements in the region, very few stayed on after the sale of Alaska to the United States. This makes the long-term impact of the Russian religion on the region all the more remarkable. According to Gibson,

Initially the fur trade was the *raison d'etre* of the Russian occupation of Siberia and Alaska. In the process the intruders altered the numbers and mores of the aborigines by introducing European diseases and spirits, Russian language, Orthodox faith, Slavic collectivism, capitalistic exploitation, and inequalitarian society. Although native cultures were changed less drastically and less bloodily than in New Spain, New France, or New England, the natives and their lands were unmistakably Russified. (1980, 127–28)

Russian Orthodox Diffusion East of the Urals

Russia's eastward expansion into Siberia began in the 1600s. After three centuries of Mongol rule and the challenges of living with the often brutal decisions of the first Russian czar, Ivan the Terrible, the people of Russia faced challenges of survival day by day. They felt trapped between two opposing religious movements as Catholic nations encroached upon their western and southern boundaries and Muslims moved in from the east. Russian culture increasingly became laden with economic, political, and religious pressures. At the same time, the people's identity as *Russian* and *Orthodox* solidified during these years of outside pressures. Ethnic Russians identified themselves as much by their religious beliefs as by their place of birth. Masses of people lived in extreme poverty after centuries of oppression during the Tartar yoke, which lasted from 1247 to 1480.

With the lands of old Kievan Rus and almost all of European Russia in ruin, it seemed the only hope for survival and freedom lay east of the Ural Mountains. Due to the proximity of Siberia to China and the Far East, however, the Mongols continued to view this remote region as a reasonable part of their empire. The first Russian penetration of western Siberia occurred in 1579 when a band of Cossacks led by Ermak Timofeivich overcame a Tartar kingdom on the Ob River. This opened up the increasingly Russianized frontier for penetration by fur trappers, hunters, and woodsmen from Russia's northwestern forests. These wilderness survivors, known as the *promyshlenniki,* were soon joined by merchants, traders, and missionaries as the rush to open up new and potentially wealthy lands continued.

In less than twenty years, western Siberia was linked from north to south by forts and associated small settlements. As Riasanovsky points out, the settlement of these lands forged ahead as a form of Slavic Manifest Destiny "in the name of Russia" drove expansion to the east (1977, 213–16). By 1639, a settlement at Okhotsk had been founded. Soon after the turn of the century, in 1711, Kamchatka was discovered. This set the stage for the establishment of direct connections with North America.

Recent sources on the subject of Russian expansion across Siberia emphasize the incredible speed of the conquest of this inhospitable region (Dmytryshyn, Crownhart-Vaughan, and Vaughan 1989, xxviii). Reasons given for this speed include government support from St. Petersburg, the use of superior weapons by the Russians, lack of resistance from native people, absence of competing European forces, and last, but by no means least, the motivation and resourcefulness of the Russians themselves.

Although often overlooked in the literature, Orthodox missionaries played a major role in the settlement process during this early period of Russian expansion eastward. Native people were baptized by the thousands and given Russian names. Many of these newly Russified natives were rewarded for their conversion by being released from paying taxes to the Cossack rulers and by promises of employment by the hunters and traders. This conversion of native people, Russian/native marriages, baptizing of children, and promises of religiously determined economic gain laid a foundation for religious conversion policies established in Siberia and the Far East that would be used later in North America.

Early North American Contacts

Throughout the reign of Peter the Great (1682–1725), a long-term interest in empire building, territorial expansion, and scientific excursions was sustained. Peter gave orders on his deathbed to a Danish officer in the Russian navy, Vitus Bering, to lead an expedition across the North Pacific. Bering's expedition was inspired by the earlier findings of two young cartographers, Ivan Evreinov and Fedor Luzhun, who were ordered by Peter to map everything east of Kamchatka (Dmytryshyn, Crownhart-Vaughan, and Vaughan 1988, xxxiii, xxxiv). Evreinov and Luzhun were prevented from reaching North America by antiquated ships and storms at sea, but their successful visit to the Kurile Islands and Kamchatka whetted Peter's appetite for eastward expansion. The specified purpose of Bering's expedition was summarized in Peter's official statement, the "Instructions from the Emperor to Captain Bering to Find Out Whether Asia and America Are Connected" (Makarova 1975, 33). It is obvious from the text of these instructions that Peter had more than scientific curiosity in mind when he sent Bering to the North Pacific. His less-than-subtle goal was to establish trade dominance in resources taken from the islands and waters of the "Eastern Sea" and to claim new territory for Russia. Bering thereafter embarked on a five-thousand-mile trip across Siberia to Okhotsk, where he was instructed to build a ship for the upcoming expedition.

After years of preparation, Bering's first voyage led to the discovery in 1728 that Asia and America were separate continents. He also discovered the straits that still bear his name. His second expedition in 1741 resulted in disaster after his ship became lost in the foggy North Pacific. Before this tragedy, however, Bering saw and mapped the St. Elias Mountains. After this first Russian view of Alaska, Bering's ship was wrecked in the Bering Sea. His crew carried him ashore where he later died. Survivors spent the year of 1741 hunting furs, thereafter setting in motion an economic system that was to dominate Russian America throughout the frontier era as pelts of seals, foxes, and sea otters were taken en masse to Petropavlosk.

At the same time, the second ship in Bering's expedition continued its search for American land. Its captain, Aleksei Chirikov, sighted the northwest coast of North America between 48 and 49 degrees north latitude (Golovin 1979, 5). Chirikov and his crew spent several days exploring the coast of Alaska and the Aleutian Islands, although they could not land. Both Chirikov and Bering's reports of large numbers of fur-bearing animals in the region further awakened the entrepreneurial spirit among Russian merchants in Siberia.

Chirikov's discovery and Bering's calamity on a fur-rich island launched a burst of activity much like the California Gold Rush. By the 1760s, Russian trappers were hunting in the region, and merchants were making plans for settlement. Between 1743 and 1799, private companies explored the Commander, Kurile, Aleutian, and Pribilof islands and the coast of Alaska (Tripp 1980, 9). The Bering and Chirikov expeditions had opened up a huge unsettled region that led to almost a century of Russian domination.[3]

Russian Settlement in North America: Stage 1

The first phase of Russian occupation of Alaska extended from 1743 to 1799. Gibson (1976, 3–9) and Federova (1973) described the earliest phase of Russian expansion in America as a period when a steady stream of Russian trappers and government officials established permanent bases in the region. They characterized this period as "distinguished by the establishment of permanent Russian settlements which were usually sited atop promontories at the mouths of rivers or at the heads of bays along the mainland or insular coasts" (Gibson 1976, 5).

Three factors influenced settlement decision making that favored coastlines during this time period—the hostility of native Americans in the interior, proximity of fur-bearing marine animals, and access to maritime transportation to distant markets. The first permanent settlement to be established was the town of Three Saints Harbor on the southwestern coast of Kodiak Island in 1784. This town remained the primary settlement of Russian America until 1791 when lumber supplies ran low and the decision was made to establish another settlement on the island, St. Paul's Harbor. Russian settlements were subsequently established during this stage of settlement at Fort St. George (1787) and St. Nicholas Redoubt (1791), both on the Kenai Peninsula; St. Constantin Redoubt (1793) on Nuchek (Hinchinbrook) Island on Chuvash Inlet; and Slavorossiya on Yakutat Bay in 1795 (Gibson 1976, 6–7). It is significant that all settlements were named for Eastern Orthodox saints, a practice continued by recent Russian migrants to the Kenai Peninsula, the Old Believers.

One of the first and most active of the Russian entrepreneurs to organize plans for a permanent settlement in the region was Grigorii Ivanovich Shelikov. Using the social connections of his upper-class wife's family and his own drive for economic success, Shelikov spent eight years organizing merchants and promoters in Irkutsk to finance trade expeditions to the Far East. In the early 1780s, Shelikov joined forces with another Irkutsk merchant, Ivan Larionovich Golikov, to form a shipbuilding company. Using three ships especially designed for travel in the North Pacific, Shelikov, his wife, and four crew members sailed from Okhotsk to the Aleutian Islands and Kodiak Island, where he built a fort at Three Saints Harbor in 1783.[4] The three primary purposes of the new settlement were (1) to save time and money for the Shelikov-Golikov Company's trading efforts; (2) to assist the company in fully exploiting the area; and (3) to establish a headquarters for all future Russian settlements on nearby islands and the Alaskan coast. Shelikov also built forts and established tiny settlement nodes on Afognak and Atka islands and in Kenai Inlet (Dmytryshyn, Crownhart-Vaughan, and Vaughan 1988, xlv). Shelikov is recorded to have been the first to baptize Alaskan natives in the Orthodox faith at Kodiak. His residency among the native people of the island greatly influenced his later plans for the development of the region, and when he returned to Irkutsk in 1787, he had established his design for Russian settlement in North America. His goals included giving a single company a monopoly on hunting and trade with the obligation to provide education and missionary work among the native people (Dmytryshyn, Crownhart-Vaughan, and Vaughan 1989, xxxi–xxxii).

A fascinating sidelight to the story of Shelikov's carefully orchestrated plans for Russian expansion in North America involves his efforts to secure funding for meeting these ambitious goals. Shelikov traveled to St. Petersburg in 1788 to join Golikov in requesting financial backing for development in Alaska from Czarina Catherine. The ruler denied them her support for their dreams of establishing a monopoly on trade and commerce in North America. Despite the financial failure of these first efforts in St. Petersburg, however, while waiting for his appointment with the empress, Shelikov paid a visit to the monks at the Valaam Monastery at Lake Ladoga. Shelikov made a donation of ten shares of the Shelikov-Golikov Company to one of the priests at Valaam in exchange for promises of support in the building of churches and continued missionary activity on the island. In addition, Shelikov falsely told the monks at Valaam that he had already built them a beautiful Orthodox church at Kodiak and that he would pay all expenses to transport them to the new mission. Although all of Shelikov's promises were based on false information, they ultimately set the stage for the diffusion of Orthodoxy throughout much of coastal Alaska and neighboring islands.

Several years of lobbying by Shelikov's agents in St. Petersburg and numerous letters to the government from Irkutsk resulted in Catherine's revised decision in 1793 to support the proposed plan. His earlier request for missionaries from Valaam (and promises of their support) for the North American mission was granted as a part of a larger package of support from the Russian government. Volunteers from Valaam had been selected for the long trip. They were led by Valaam's Archimandrite Ioasaf. Accompanying him were priest-monks Iuvenalii, Makarii, Afanasii, Nektarii, and Stefan, and the monks German (Herman) and Ioasaf.[5] These first Orthodox missionaries to North America arrived at Kodiak in 1784, and according to Veniaminov, "This mission was fitted out with everything, and even more than was necessary, by Shelikov and Golikov and other well disposed donors. Departing from St. Petersburg in 1793, they arrived at Kad'iak in the following year in the autumn, and commenced their task" (1836, 234).

Despite the financial support provided by Shelikov for travel and temporary lodging at Kodiak, the missionaries found conditions in the settlement very different from Shelikov's glowing description at Valaam many years before. No chapel had been constructed; nothing whatsoever had been done to prepare for their arrival. Despite the difficult climate and lack of facilities, the Valaam group began to organize their efforts to convert the native people of Kodiak. Their experiences at Valaam and the trip east across Siberia had prepared them for facing the Kodiak challenges. According to Oleksa,

> Their own monastic community had been founded on the northwestern frontier of the empire at a time when the nomadic tribes of the region professed only a shamanistic religious identity. They themselves had crossed central and eastern Siberia where monastic communities had been more recently established among shamanistic tribes. In traversing Asian steppes and forest lands, the Valaam monks reviewed the missionary history of the Orthodox Church from the Urals to the Pacific. (1987, 7)

Despite Oleksa's optimistic account of the work at Kodiak, there can be no doubt the Russians faced many difficulties in communicating their faith to the island's native peoples. To say the least, cultural and spiritual differences between the Russians and the Kodiak people were dramatic and divisive. Differences in language, stories of human origins, concepts of space and time, and worldviews made religious conversion difficult.

Despite these numerous challenges, the first Russian Orthodox church in Alaska was constructed at Kodiak in 1794. The Holy Resurrection Church has had an active congregation of believers since that time, and it remains salient in the 1990s. Within several years, a school for native children was established by the church on Kodiak, and two of the priests left to do their missionary work elsewhere in the Russian territory. Makarii went to the Aleutian Islands, and Iuvenalii went into the Alaskan interior. In the meantime, the monk Herman, the last surviving member of this first group of Alaskan Orthodox missionaries, spent the rest of his life practicing his beliefs on remote Spruce Island.

Although it is recognized that the Valaam contingent worked hard to bring Orthodoxy to the people of Alaska, other cultural and economic factors also contributed to their acceptance of new religious beliefs. Even though the religious backgrounds of the two groups were very different, their belief systems did have several things in common. The candles, incense, and mysticism of Orthodox churches undoubtedly attracted people who had long practiced a form of mystical worship. They had lived for centuries believing in a series of superstitions, rituals, and structure of behaviors that would increase the likelihood of success in life. Many of the spiritual beliefs of the native Americans resembled the beliefs of the Orthodox missionaries. The belief in a creator, the immortality of the soul, other worlds (heaven and hell), and the existence of good and evil spirits united the two groups (Mattson 1985, 24). A type of spiritual syncretism took place when Orthodox beliefs were superimposed on this in some ways similar native belief system. One significant difference between the approach used by Orthodox missionaries and that of other Christian groups in other places was their willingness to allow converts to keep many of their old beliefs. The Orthodox did not feel it necessary to deny the authenticity of this pre-Christian Aleut religious experience (Oleksa 1987, 12).

And perhaps even more important, the initial success of the ten missionaries from Valaam must be at least partly attributed to economic and social pressures, as Russians increased their economic and political hold on the region. The readiness for conversion might also be attributed to fears of the *promyshlenniki,* whose atrocities affected native life almost daily. During the second stage of Russian settlement in North America (to be discussed in the next section), the often punitive requirements of the Russian-American Company also influenced the total numbers of believers. These laws required all employees of the company to accept the Russian faith. Native Americans were also given complete freedom from paying taxes with conversion to Orthodoxy.

Russian Settlement in North America: Stage 2

Although Catherine had initially denied Shelikov's request for the establishment of a monopoly on Alaskan development and trade by his company, her son Czar Paul I formally approved the plan in 1799 with the merger of several companies in Irkutsk. This change of policy marked the beginning of the second stage of Russian expansion and settlement in North America. The newly merged organization was officially named the Russian-American Company, a term that was to become synonymous with Russian expansion in North America to the end of the frontier era.[6] Paul granted the company total control over the economic and spiritual development of the Russian colonies. According to Dmytryshyn, Crownhart-Vaughan, and Vaughan, "From its formation in 1799 to its demise in 1868, the Russian-American Company was never a private enterprise as that term is applied, practiced, and understood in the West. Rather, the Company was an important auxiliary of the Imperial Russian government" (1989, xxxiv).

Russian documents on the Russian-American Company list American land deeded to the company with its charter (Pierce 1976, 21–22). Its territory included

- all land, buildings, and forts at the islands of Afognak, Baranof (Sitka), Unalaska, and Atka;
- forts at Kenai Peninsula, Chugach Bay (at the harbor of St. Constantin and Elena), Nuchek Island, and Cape St. Il'ia;

- fort and small settlement of Slavorossiya at Yakutat;
- forts of St. George and St. Paul in Kenai Bay;
- fort and redoubt at Delarov Harbor in Chugach Bay.

Government control over Russian economic development and settlement in North America included complete control over the territories listed above and all activities of the Orthodox church. Even though Shelikov died before the official formation of the Russian-American Company, his plans for an Orthodox missionary outreach were fulfilled. With no separation of church and state in Russia, the company (as an agency of the government) was required to build churches in the new colonies, spread the Orthodox faith throughout the region, and pay for all church-related expenses. Several major provisions in the charter mandated that the Russian-American Company would care for the spiritual needs of its employees and convert native Americans to the Eastern Orthodox religion.

As discussed earlier, religious conversion of the region's native population was linked closely to the economic demands of the Russian-American Company. The vitally important role of native workers in the successful functioning of the Russian-imposed economic system in North America cannot be overstated. Russian hunters were never comfortable with sea life, since their origin in continental Siberia provided no experience with maritime work. Thus, Russian successes in hunting fur-bearing animals that inhabited ocean waters near islands and coastlines depended entirely on native labor. Consequently, the Aleuts and other indigenous people of the region were virtually enslaved by the Russians. After 1799, all males over the age of eighteen and under fifty had to work for the Russian-American Company. At least 80 percent of the Aleut population was lost during the first and second generation of Russian conquest (Gibson 1980, 129–30).

Treatment of employees of the Russian-American Company, whether Russian, native, or mixed, was generally very poor. There can be no doubt, however, that the most unfortunate subjects of the new colony were the Aleuts, the first native groups to be subjugated by the Russians. Because these residents of the Aleutian Islands were skillful *baidarka* (kayak) hunters, they were often separated from their families and sent on hunting expeditions to distant places. The valuable role of the Aleuts and other native people in the economic development of the region is summarized by Dmytryshyn, Crownhart-Vaughan, and Vaughan:

The Aleuts were superb sea hunters, especially of the sea otter. The Company could not have maintained its operations without them. In addition to this, the Company assigned Aleuts to cut timber, build dwellings for the Russians, build warehouses and other structures, fish, make bricks, and after 1850, cut ice for the Company to sell in San Francisco.

The Company also employed elderly Aleuts, both men and women, and Aleut children, to garden, tend livestock, pick berries, prepare fish, sew garments, gather birds' eggs, and perform other chores. (1989, xlvii)

From 1799 to 1819, the new governor of Alaska' and head of the Russian-American Company, Aleksandr Baranov, made plans to extend Russian influence southward. In 1799, he established the settlement of New Archangel (Sitka) on Baranof Island in the tidal channels of an archipelago of small islands off the coast of the Alaskan panhandle. This settlement node soon evolved into an economic base for furs and timber and an administrative center for the Russian-American Company and the Russian Orthodox church. It also served as a deterrent to American and English traders venturing onto the southwest coast of Alaska.

From the beginning, the settlement was challenged by hostility from native Americans in the area, the Koloshes. Despite frequent skirmishes between the invading Russian settlers and local residents, by 1817, New Archangel had a multiethnic population of 190 Russians, 182 mixed-blood Creoles, and 248 Aleuts (Gibson 1976, 10).

Abusive treatment of the Alaskan native population was especially harsh during Baranov's years as chief manager of the Russian-American Company (1790–1818). Numerous letters were sent to St. Petersburg after 1795 protesting the verbal abuse and physical harassment inflicted on the native residents of the colony and on the missionaries themselves. The priest Makarii even left his post suddenly in 1796 to carry missionary complaints to St. Petersburg. Finally, in 1804, the church sent Gideon, a monk, to evaluate conditions between the natives and the Russians on Kodiak and the Aleutians. Gideon spent two years observing life in Alaska, and his final report detailed and verified many of the abuses recorded by Father Herman in letters sent to Russia from Kodiak.

Russian Settlement in Frontier America: Stage 3

The third stage of Russian expansion and settlement in North America (1819–40) was a time of corporate reorganization, a reorientation of settlement northward and inland, decreased native hostilities, and increased foreign competition (Gibson 1976, 15). This era witnessed a new type of administration in the colonies as Baranov was replaced by a "kinder, gentler" style of leadership. Native American abuses, although still a problem in remote areas, decreased as more and more priests, teachers, and doctors arrived from Russia during this period. The push to settle new parts of the Alaskan interior and northern islands was due, at least in part, to American and British pressures to the south and the depletion of furs in previously settled areas. All of these problems laid a foundation during this stage of settlement for the later sale of the North American Russian colonies.

Despite abuses recorded in official documents and letters from the Alaskan missionaries, the charter of the Russian-American Company was renewed by the Russian government in 1821. It did, however, contain specific provisions that significantly improved conditions for native Americans in the region. The new charter also insisted on increased company support for future Orthodox missionary efforts. An additional incentive for spiritual support came from increased church enthusiasm for "spreading the word" about Orthodoxy in Russia itself. As new church decrees were sent throughout the empire, missionaries in Siberia, Kamchatka, and the Alaskan territory were exhorted to learn native languages and instruct native clergy to carry on the work with their own people.

In the early 1820s, frontier Russian America was divided into four main districts, Sitka, Kodiak, Unalaska, and Atka. Each was under the rule of a general manager of the Russian-American Company, and each was the headquarters of an Orthodox church for the surrounding area. To the Church of Archangel Michael in Sitka, built in 1808, belonged two redoubts near Sitka and Fort Ross in California; the Kodiak church administered church work to the island of Kodiak, Kenai, Nuchek, and the redoubt on Nushagak; to the church on Unalaska, built in 1825, belonged the Aleutian, Fox, and Pribilof islands and the redoubt on St. Michael's Island (Yukon area); to the Atka church, built in 1830, belonged Amelia, Bering, and Copper islands along with the Near and Kurile island groups. In 1840, the total number of Orthodox Christians in Alaska was estimated at 706 Russians, 1,295 Creoles, and 8,312 native Americans (Oleksa 1987, 43).

The religious administration of these four districts required more priests. One of these priests, John Veniaminov, known today as the "Apostle of Alaska," distinguished himself as the best known of the Alaskan Orthodox missionaries. Veniaminov spent forty-four years as a missionary in the North Pacific, working on both the Asian and American sides of the ocean. Upon his arrival at Unalaska, Veniaminov followed the new requirements of the church to the letter, translating native languages into a written form, translating sacred church materials, and training native clergy. He was reassigned to New Archangel (Sitka) in 1834 and thereafter became the most respected and best known of the Orthodox leaders in the region. Veniaminov was rewarded by the church hierarchy for his good work with a promotion to the position of bishop of the new Kamchatka diocese (and renamed Innocent). He was appointed metropolitan of Moscow in 1868.

Under Veniaminov's leadership, the importance of the Orthodox church in Alaska expanded significantly. He believed that the only way to spread the Orthodox faith throughout the entire region was to train native clergy. He also encouraged the religious training of non-Russian laymen who could conduct weekly worship services and other important ceremonies. The decision to educate new converts in church doctrine and ritual appears to have been a major factor influencing the long-term survival of Orthodoxy in the North Pacific (Smith 1980a, 5).

Due to the efforts of Veniaminov and other missionaries in Alaska and the Aleutian Islands, the number of churches, chapels, and converts to Orthodoxy continued to increase during this second stage of Russian settlement. Most churches were built and missions established at sites occupied by the Russian-American Company. Missionaries even followed the company into the southwestern Alaskan interior in an attempt to win converts among native people in that remote area. In Bishop Innocent's report for the year 1850, nine churches, thirty-seven chapels, nine priests, two deacons, and about fifteen thousand converts are listed (Gregory 1987, 292).

Russian territorial expansion during this third stage of settlement also included Baranov's efforts to seize control of the Sandwich Islands (Hawaii) because of their strategic location on major trade routes that linked Asia and North America. Russia's attempt to establish farming and military dominance on the islands is vividly described by Pierce in *Russia's Hawaiian Adventure, 1815–1817* (1965). Using documents originally copied in St. Petersburg for Hubert Howe Bancroft and later translated and housed in Bancroft Library, Pierce has collected a significant number of letters and diary entries that summarize the story of the early Russians in Hawaii. A few enduring landscape evidences of the Russian presence on the island of Kauai remain. The foundations of Russian Fort Elisabeth are still visible at Waimea on Kauai. Although it is beyond the scope of this book to discuss this dramatic story, Baranov's efforts to send the German surgeon and adventurer Georg Anton Schaffer to conquer the Sandwich Islands for the Russian-American Company tell an exciting and often incredible story and offer further evidence of the Russian concept of Manifest Destiny.

Another expression of Baranov's expansionist policies remains on the northern California landscape, where Russian settlement extended southward. The Russian-American Company sent an expedition to visit the Spanish in San Francisco in 1806 "to secure much needed provisions for the Russian colonies in Alaska" (Essig 1933b, 191). Rezanov, the leader of this California expedition, had big plans for Russian control of all land from San Francisco Bay to the Columbia River.

The Russians were received warmly by the Spanish upon their arrival in San Francisco. Many of Rezanov's crew members were amazed at the warm and hospitable lifestyle of the Californians. According to Rezanov's accounts of the visit, "The excellent climate of California, the abundance of breadstuffs there as compared to our lack of them, and the prospect of facing starvation again in the future were the hourly subject of conversation among our men. We noticed their inclination and desire to remain permanently and took measure against their desertion" (1972, 6).

Not all Rezanov's crew members could be restrained. It is reported that two members of the Russian crew, Mikhailo Kalhanin and Peter Polkanov, probably jumped ship and became San Francisco's first permanent Russian residents (Tripp 1980, 16).

Upon his return to Alaska, Rezanov strongly advised the establishment of a small village just north of San Francisco Bay, which would facilitate trade with the Spanish and which might serve as a focal point for eventual control of all land between Bodega Bay and the Columbia River. Based on his recommendations, between 1808 and 1812 four voyages were sent to California under the leadership of Ivan Kuskov, who had become the new head of the Russian-American Company. The ships returned to New Archangel with stories of warmer and more productive land to the south and places entirely unoccupied by other Europeans. They also brought back inspiring shiploads of skins from California's seals and sea lions.

In 1808, the Russian ship *Kodiak* anchored at Trinidad to investigate the possibility of establishing a settlement in the area (Bunje, Penn, and Schmitz 1937, 3). Lingering in this vicinity for at least several weeks, the Russians placed an iron plaque marked "Lands of Russian Possession" at the harbor at Trinidad before sailing south to Bodega Bay (Heckrotte n.d., 21). Attracted by the idyllic California climate and landscape, five members of the Russian expedition apparently jumped ship before it left Bodega Bay for New Archangel (Bunje, Penn, and Schmitz 1937, 3), adding to the small nucleus of Russians residing in San Francisco.

In the spring of 1812, the Russian expedition chose a site for their new settlement near Port Rumyantsev (Bodega Bay) on a bare plateau high above the Pacific Ocean about eleven miles south of the Russian River (map 8). This location was the site of an ancient Pomo village. At the time of Russian settlement in California, the Pomos occupied the coastal hills and valleys from the Guala River to an area just south of the Russian River. With the arrival of the Russians, the Pomos agreed

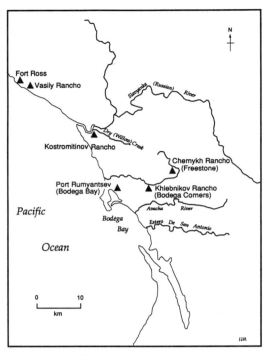

Map 8. Russian settlements in frontier America, 1800–1910. Redrawn, by permission, from Gibson 1976.

to a deed of land cession after an exchange of gifts. The native Americans no doubt thought the Russians would provide a safety barrier between them and the ever-encroaching Spanish (Schwartz 1979, 38). After the Russian stockade was completed, the Pomos resettled in the area immediately surrounding it. Except for several negative accounts of Russian treatment of the native Americans at Ross recorded in Ferdinand Wrangell's 1833 report, Russian-Pomo relations were apparently more harmonious than those between the Russians and native peoples of Alaska and the Aleutians.

The construction of a fort and compound began immediately at the new settlement with the first cutting of the coast redwood trees. The Russians built a stockade, commander's house, windmill, forge, chapel, tannery, cattle sheds, and cemetery for their new settlement. It was officially called Ross, from the root word for *Russia,* although the site was also known as Slavyansk and Slavyano-Ross by local Russian and Slavic visitors. The Spanish and English, recognizing the defensive strength of the settlement, called it Fort Ross. A report to the Russian-American Company by Kyrill T. Khlebnikov summarized its appearance:

The Ross colony presently consists of a small wooden fortress with seventeen small caliber cannon. Within the fortress, there are the administrator's home, an office, barracks, a two-story warehouse and several other buildings. Those who live in the fortress work at various jobs; all are in the Company service. There are fifty persons in addition to the Aleuts who are periodically sent out on sea otter hunts. Of the 30 promyshlenniks there, 12 are engaged in agricultural pursuits, mostly by their own volition rather than by obligation. (1976, 130–31)

The total population of Russian California varied over time, but it never included over one hundred Russians or five hundred people total (table 2). After twenty years of Russian residence at Ross, only fifty Russians, seventy-two adult Pomos, eighty-three Aleuts, and eighty-eight Creoles lived in the settlement (Schwartz 1979, 39). Residents primarily engaged in agriculture, shipbuilding, fur hunting, pottery making, wool production, brick making, flour milling, and lumbering. The first of the millstones from their efforts to produce wheat flour is still visible at Ross, as are restored buildings from this early period of Russian settlement in California. These landscape evidences, now a part of a state park, remind modern visitors of the long-term Russian presence in California. The stockade and cannons at Ross are also reminders of Russian military interests in the area. Unfortunately, these artifacts amplify already negative perceptions of Russians as a military presence in frontier America. Even though motivations for the settlement were economic, not military,

Table 2
Population of Russian-American Company's Colonies, 1833

Administration	Russians		Creoles		Natives		Total
	Males	Females	Males	Females	Males	Females	
New Archangel office	343	36	163	144	60	76	882
Kodiak office	90	13	118	121	3,282	3,325	6,949
Unalaska office	22	8	113	73	568	714	1,498
Atka office	40	1	71	75	280	313	780
Ross office	45	6	33	44	64	61	253
Northern office	6	—	12	22	99	99	238
Kurile district	17	—	1	1	57[a]	20[a]	198
					52[b]	50[b]	
Total	563	64	511	480	4,462	4,658	10,738

Source: Khlebnikov 1833, cited in Gibson 1972, 8.
[a] Aleuts.
[b] Kurilians.

the most common image of early Russians in California is often based on the assumption that Russians came only to conquer and invade. The corruption of the toponym *Ross* to *Fort Ross* further exaggerates this recurring image of the Russians as an alien, uninvited ethnic group in North America.

There were two primary economic reasons for expanding Russian settlement south into California, fur hunting of marine animals and agriculture. Furs rapidly became depleted as *baidarkas* with their Aleut hunters gathered the skins of thousands of sea otters, sea lions, and seals all the way from San Francisco Bay and the Farallon Islands to their oceanfront at Ross. The rapid depletion of furs, their inferior quality and color, and disputes with the Spanish hunters all lessened the long-term success of fur hunting as an economic base for the California settlement. As furs became depleted, the Russians at Ross increasingly turned their attention to raising food for the Alaskan settlements.

Mutual trade agreements with the Spanish encouraged the earliest development of agriculture at Ross. The Spanish supplied the Russians with livestock, horses, fruit tree cuttings, and grain in the first years of settlement at Ross. Khlebnikov's journals reported that peach, apple, pear, and cherry trees and bergamot were also imported from the Spanish at San Francisco and Monterey and that grapevines were brought in by a visitor from Peru. His records also noted that the Russians planted watermelons, other melons, and pumpkins, as well as cool-climate vegetables such as potatoes, beets, cabbages, turnips, radishes, lettuce, peas, and beans, during these early and optimistic years at Ross (Blok 1850).

There is considerable documentation in various travel journals, diaries, and government records that Russian and Californian ships enjoyed a mutual trading network and extensive intraregional travel in northern California during this period. Especially intriguing to a historical geographer was a visit to the Presidio and Mission Dolores in San Francisco by two expeditions of Otto von Kotzebue and his ship, the *Rurik*. The first of these visits was in 1816. Kotzebue and his crew, with German naturalist Adelbert von Chamisso and zoologist Johann Friedrich Eschscholtz, spent a month exploring the San Francisco Bay region. During his short stay, Chamisso collected a sample of the California poppy (now the state flower), which he eventually named *Eschscholtzia californica* after his colleague aboard the *Rurik* and the new land they had visited.

Kotzebue returned to the bay area with Eschscholtz eight years later on his second around-the-world voyage. During this follow-up visit, the travelers explored the bay region, the delta of the Sacramento and San Joaquin rivers, and the north coast. Especially significant was their trip up the Sacramento River, where they traveled at least as far as today's small town of Freeport (Dana 1939, 44). Kotzebue gave an enthusiastic account of the delta as a potential site of Russian settlement: "The many rivers flowing through this fruitful country will be of the greatest use to future settlers. The low ground is exactly adapted to the cultivation of rice; and the higher, from the extraordinary strength of the soil, would yield the finest wheat harvests. The vine might be cultivated here to great advantage" (1830, 143–44).

Kotzebue's exploration of the Sacramento delta was significant for three reasons. First, it provided Russians at Ross with their first information about other, more potentially productive parts of northern California. The fact that Russian-American Company officials overlooked the possibility of expanding Russian settlement in California into the delta or at least into the fertile Napa Valley much closer to Ross is one of those fascinating historical mysteries. Undoubtedly, Spanish control of much of northern California limited Russian expansion inland, although this vast region remained largely unsettled in this era.

The second reason for the importance of Kotzebue's trip up the Sacramento River is found on the first map drafted of the city of Sacramento by a Spanish cartographer in 1833. This map was printed first in *Grimshaw's Narrative*, a field account of the Sacramento region used as background for Thompson and West in their book *The History of Sacramento County*, published in 1880. On this early map, the American River is labeled with a Russian name, Rio Ojetska (land of the hunter). Similarly, the first Mexican land grant issued in the entire Sacramento Valley in 1834 to American John R. Cooper was called Rancho Rio Ojetska.[7] It is suggested here that a thus far undocumented Russian hunting expedition may have followed Kotzebue's lead and explored the delta sometime before 1833, assigning this first Russian toponym to a place in the Sacramento Valley.

The third reason Kotzebue's trip up the Sacramento River is significant is the prophetic nature of his written records. Crops mentioned in his account are now highly valued products of the Sacramento Valley. His recommendations for growing rice and planting vineyards are perfectly in tune with modern agricultural development in the region.

Other Europeans visited the colonies of Russian America in the nineteenth century. Duhaut Cilly, for example, a French traveler who visited Ross in 1823, described it as a European-looking settlement with "all the conveniences which Europeans value and which are still unknown in California" (Duhaut-Cilly 1946, 10).

Mexican independence and the secularization of mission farmland resulted in decreases in agricultural production in northern California. It

Figure 4. The Orthodox chapel at Fort Ross has been completely restored to its original design in recent years. Photo by D. G. Holtgrieve.

thereafter became more and more difficult for the Russians at Ross to purchase grain from other farms, and they expanded their acreage of cultivated land around their settlement at Ross.

Several Russian farms were developed in the 1830s, including Khlebnikov Rancho near today's Bodega Corners, Kostromitinov Rancho on Willow Creek, Chernykh Rancho near Freestone, and a small rancho on the Estero Americano.

As the Russian colony in California evolved into a more diversified settlement, religion provided its multiethnic residents with a cohesive identity. Although services were held irregularly at the tiny Orthodox chapel inside the stockade, Russian–native American marriages, baptisms, and other special ceremonies were carried on by visiting priests as necessary (fig. 4). Local residents conducted prayers almost every day at the chapel. Without expectation of ever having a resident priest at the settlement, the Russians nevertheless built a chapel inside the stockade in the mid-1820s. This was the first Orthodox building established in North America outside of Alaska (Watrous 1991b, 17). St. Nicholas Chapel, as they named it, was never officially consecrated by the Russian church because the site was not viewed as completely "Russian" by the church hierarchy.

In 1836, Alaska's Father Veniaminov was asked to visit Ross. During his visit to California, he was especially fascinated with the Franciscan missionaries, with whom he could converse in Latin. During his two-and-a-half-month stay in California, Veniaminov kept a diary of his impressions. He recorded the total population at Ross as 154 males and 106 females, with 120 Russians, 51 Creoles, 50 Kodiak Aleuts, and 39 converted native Americans (Gibson 1971, 60). Veniaminov's comments about the chapel at Ross reveal his disappointment with its simple, unadorned interior. The priest noted that

The chapel is built of planks, like almost all houses here, with a rather small, plain bell tower; all its interior adornments comprise only two small icons in silver mountings, so that in resplendence it cannot compare at all to the chapel on St. Paul Island belonging to the Unalaska Church (where almost only Aleuts live and no more than 30 families), but the chapel here has almost no income whatsoever from parishioners; besides, the Russians very rarely visit it. (Gibson 1971, 60–61)

Despite Veniaminov's lack of enthusiasm about the chapel at Ross, he did spend over five weeks there. According to Steven Watrous of the Fort Ross Interpretive Association, Veniaminov managed to hold a public prayer service for the czar, to consecrate the waters of Fort Ross Creek, and to hold a festive procession of the Cross around the inside of the stockade during his residency at the California settlement (Watrous 1991b, 18).

The church headquarters at Sitka continued to expand during this period of settlement. After Veniaminov was reassigned to Sitka, the importance of the settlement as a spiritual center increased. The first cathedral in the Alaska diocese, St. Michael's, was designed by Veniaminov and completed in 1848. The original church building was constructed almost entirely of Sitka spruce, and even the clock in its bell tower was designed and built by Veniaminov himself. In 1845, the New Archangel Missionary Seminary was also completed to train native clergy to carry on missionary work throughout Alaska. True to its founders' commitment to native rights, the school had classes in three languages other than Russian—Aleutian, Eskimo, and Tlingit. Despite this seemingly egalitarian approach, however, the Tlingits were excluded from services in the beautiful new cathedral. Instead, they worshiped in a church across the straits from Sitka where services were conducted in the native language (Watkins 1961, 45).

Unfortunately, the beautiful Sitka spruce cathedral was destroyed in a fire in 1966. Using photographs of the church's interior and exterior, a new plan for the reconstruction of the church was developed later that same year and the design was reconstructed from its ashes. Today, St. Michael's onion-shaped dome set against the snow-capped mountains and its four-story bell tower remain true to the original design.

Russian Settlement in Frontier America: Stage 4

The final stage of Russian settlement in frontier America, 1840–67, marks the end of Russian occupation of the region. The serious depletion of furs, decreasing support from Russia, and more and more advances from other nations that, by this time, were actively involved in the region's economic development, ultimately brought an end to Russia's colonial empire in North America. A number of events and decisions by Russia and other world powers contributed to this outcome.

Although the Russian government had renewed the Russian-American Company's contract for another twenty years in 1841, the company's leadership gradually changed from aggressive entrepreneurs who were committed to profit and economic development to administration by less aggressive government officials and politicians. This change, along with the Russian-American Company's increasing commitment to developing the fur industry in Asia (Kamchatka, Sakhalin, and the Amur Valley) and a serious depletion of the maritime fur supply in North America, led to a much less successful economic system in the North American colonies.

Promulgation of the Monroe Doctrine by the American government in 1824 limited the boundaries of Russian settlement in North America to 58 degrees, 40 minutes north latitude. This intensified the isolation of the Russian colony in California. President James Monroe proposed his doctrine in 1823 to guarantee the nations of the Western Hemisphere protection against European interference "for the purpose of oppressing them or controlling them in any other manner than their destiny." The Monroe Doctrine also stated that "from henceforth the American continents were not to be considered as subjects for future colonization by any European powers" (Commager 1973, 236).

Nor were things going well in the Russian colony in northern California during this fourth stage. Russian efforts never made Ross a successful settlement because Rezanov's dream of an agricultural base in California was never realized. Furs were soon depleted, and agricultural production failed miserably on the foggy California coast. Further decreasing the importance of Ross, the Russian-American Company had signed an agreement in 1839 with the Hudson Bay Company, guaranteeing provision of food to the settlements in Alaska. This made the California settlement's economic function obsolete.

Fort Ross was eventually sold to Sacramentan John Sutter in 1841. Early that year Russian settlement in frontier California left a last geographic mark on the map of the region. Russian scientist I. G. Vosnesensky and his colleague G. Tschernikh climbed to the top of the highest peak in the region adjacent to Ross, naming it Mount St. Helena. According to Thompson, "[Vosnesensky] named it St. Helena in honor of his imperial mistress, the Empress of Russia and, planting a post on its highest point, he nailed to it a copper plate inscribed with the name he had given the mountain, his own name and that of his companion with the date of the ascent and the word 'Russians' repeated twice, once in Russian and once in Latin" (1896, 34).

An exciting story, but there are actually many legends regarding the naming of this mountain by Russians. Gertrude Atherton suggests that Commandant Alexander Rotchef climbed the mountain first and named it for his wife, Princess Helena, niece of the Russian czar (Atherton 1893, 60). Difficulty in documenting the real story behind the naming of Mount St. Helena was exacerbated by the destruction of the Russian copper plate in the earthquake and fire of 1906 in San Francisco, where it had been housed in an historical museum.

Sutter's purchase of Fort Ross ended Russian frontier settlement in California. The purchase included all outbuildings, animals, and harvested crops, and even the Orthodox chapel. The Russian ship *Constantin* (renamed the *Sacramento*) was also included in the purchase agreement. The ship was used to make frequent trips between Ross, Bodega Bay, and Sacramento, transporting all the movable property bought by Sutter that could be used in Sacramento (Thompson 1951, 23).

Russian dominance in Alaska continued until it was sold to the United States in 1867. Russia had been grossly overextended in North America almost from the beginning. As the locationally advantaged American, Spanish, and British settlements grew and prospered on the west coast of the continent, New Archangel became more and more isolated from the center of economic and political activity. In addition, the Russian government was increasingly preoccupied with problems at home. The Crimean War, the transfer of power from one czar to another who had radically different ideas about the future of Russian America, and the renewed interest in developing the Russian Far East rather than supporting expansion in North America all contributed to the Russian decision to sell its Alaskan colonies to the United States.

The initial impacts of this decision were shocking and immediate. By 1870, only Kodiak, Unalaska, and Sitka had Orthodox churches and clergy who were still actively working for the perpetuation of the Russian faith. The Treaty of Cession to the United States assured the Russian Orthodox Greek Catholic church that it could legally retain its property in Alaska and continue its mission. Bishop Innocent's (Veniaminov's) appointment as the metropolitan of Moscow in 1868 also revived the church's commitment to maintaining Orthodoxy in Alaska. After 1870, Alaska became its own diocese, although the official center of this West Coast diocese was transferred to San Francisco in 1872.

Although Bancroft and other historians insisted that the Russian church was a failure throughout most of Russian America, more recent analyses of historic church records have established that Orthodoxy in Alaska survived the shock of political separation from Russia and continued to grow into the early years of the twentieth century (Bancroft 1886, 704; Smith 1980a, 8). According to Smith,

From a nadir in 1870, when only a few clerics served four churches, the Alaska mission grew by 1906 to include 16 priests and 15 readers, serving 15 churches, and several dozen chapels. Not only had old churches been revived, but new ones had been founded—at Afognak, Belkovsky, Nuchek, Kilisnoo, and Pavlosk (present day Chuathbaluk on the Kuskokwim River, near the site of Kolmakovsky Redoubt). (1980a, 8)

Map 9 illustrates this wide distribution of Orthodox churches in Alaska in 1906. Smith summarizes the long-term success of the church in Alaska as the result of four major factors: (1) the use of lay leadership; (2) the establishment of schools and literacy; (3) the role of the church as an advocate of native rights; (4) the acceptance and retention of sacred values of the native cultures (1980a, 10–13). Table 3 summarizes data found in an 1895 issue of the *Russian Orthodox American Messenger*. These figures establish further evidence of the lingering importance of Orthodoxy after the sale of Alaska to the United States. In 1867, according to census figures, there were at least 576 Russian men and 206 Russian women in forty-three communities in Alaska. Church services were being conducted in Russian and the Aleutian language in nine Russian Orthodox churches and thirty-five chapels, many of which still remain today (Wertsman 1977, 6).

Alaskan natives and lands were undeniably Russified. Evidences of the Russian language and social customs linger today. Nowhere is this Russian-American connection more evident than in the retention of the Russian Orthodox religion in the region. Native people still play the

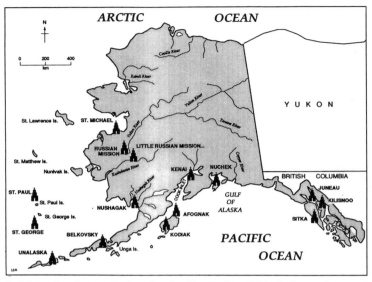

Map 9. Major Russian Orthodox churches in Alaska, 1906. Redrawn, by permission, from Smith 1980.

Table 3
Orthodox Population of Alaska, 1895

Town	Members
Unalaska	970
Nushagak	2,919
Kuskokwim	1,484
St. George Island	88
Juneau	228
Kadyak (Kodiak)	1,118
Athognansk	652
Belkovsky	515
Kvikhpakh	4,204
St. Paul Island	197
Sitka	844
Kilisnoo	376
Kenai	1,017
Nuchek	452
Total	15,064

Source: Russian Orthodox American Messenger, 27 December 1897.

balalaika and cook Russian foods. According to the director of the Aleut Corporation of Alaska, "It [the culture] permeates their whole existence as few outsiders can understand" (Davids 1984, 4).

Recent studies take the influence of Russian Orthodoxy in Alaska one step further by insisting that the church actually improved native life after the sale of Alaska. Although there can be no doubt that Russian occupation inflicted great suffering and economic and cultural deprivation on thousands of native people in the region for over a century, long-term benefits of their conversion to the Eastern Orthodox religion cannot be denied. After the sale of Alaska to the United States, life in Alaska for many years was dictated by a strict military government. Much of the success of the American system was a direct result of previous work accomplished by Russians in the area, particularly in terms of educational attitudes and antecedent systems. The church also helped maintain native culture and prevent community disintegration during this period of readjustment. Anthropologist Gerald Berreman describes the role of the church in an Aleut village in the 1950s:

Map 10. Russian Orthodox churches in Alaska, 1990. Based on telephone and city directories, interviews, church records, and Straight 1989, 22–23.

The Russians participated in the Aleut culture and so had an opportunity to demonstrate their ways in a context familiar to the villagers. The Russians did not try to make the Aleuts over into Russians. Socialization of children was left in the hands of villagers. After 1820, when the Orthodox church became active in the Aleutians, efforts toward Russianization were limited to matters of direct concern to the church. The church is the most impressive structure in the village, and they are justly proud of it. Its Russian origin is well known, but it is considered by villagers to be part of the "Aleut" ways. Aleut ways were to a remarkable extent preserved. (1955, 51)

Map 10 locates major Orthodox churches in Alaska in 1990. The large number of congregations is another indication of the lingering importance of Orthodoxy in the region. In recent decades, native-heritage groups in Alaska continue to celebrate their Russian connections with festivals, exhibits, and other cultural-awareness activities. The important role of the Russian religion in the preservation of native culture and identity in Alaska during the American period is an important part of native peoples' search for information and appreciation of Alaska's Russian heritage. It also provides a fascinating backdrop for a discussion of subsequent eras of the settlement of other Russian religious groups in western North America.

FOUR

Changes and Challenges: Russian Migration and Settlement from 1867 to 1987

FOLLOWING THE INITIAL era of Russian frontier expansion, four waves of Russian migration and settlement swept into the region. This chapter examines the three waves following the sale of Alaska to the United States in 1867: 1880 to 1917, 1917 to 1945, and 1945 to 1987.

The First Wave: 1880–1917

Russians migrated to the Pacific Rim of North America for religious, political, and socioeconomic reasons. Thrust into the American mainstream by problems at home and drawn into California, Oregon, Washington, and British Columbia by promises of an improved lifestyle for themselves and their families, almost fifty thousand Russians had resettled in the region by the beginning of the Russian Revolution in 1917. Among these newcomers were large groups of religious sectarians as well as Orthodox believers. They have made lasting imprints on the life and landscape of the region.

THE ORTHODOX

At the sale of Alaska to the United States in 1867, the Treaty of Cession stated that Russian residents of Alaska had two choices for their residency. They could either return to Russia and keep their Russian nationality or remain in Alaska and enjoy all the rights and privileges of citizens of the United States. A number of those who chose to stay in Alaska traveled to San Francisco to begin new lives as Americans, as travel and trade increased between the regions following the signing of the treaty. These Alaskan émigrés found other Orthodox Russians who had come

75

to the area after the sale of Fort Ross in the 1840s and the Gold Rush in the 1850s.

Economic opportunities in California's largest city encouraged Russian residences and businesses to locate near the downtown. City directories document evolving Russian location patterns in San Francisco during these early years. Although Russian businesses and residences tended to cluster in a distinct pattern between 1860 and 1900, an analysis of surnames in city directories reveals that a variety of other ethnic groups also lived and worked among the Russians in the city's increasingly heterogeneous neighborhood.

During this same period the first Russian-language newspaper in the United States, *Svoboda* (*Alaskan Herald*), was published from 1868 to 1871. Agapius Honcharenko, the paper's editor, envisioned a publication that would combine information on business opportunities with Russian and American legal and cross-cultural differences and with sketches on Russian life and history (*Alaska Herald*, 1 March 1868, 1). Information provided by Honcharenko, a liberal and sometimes cynical journalist, is one of the best sources of data on Russian settlement in San Francisco immediately following the sale of Alaska. His paper helped bridge the gap between the Russian population and the rest of the English-speaking residents of the area (Wertsman 1977, 7).

The sale of Alaska to the United States also marked an important point in the history of the Russian Orthodox church in North America. The church began a missionary effort in western North America, redefining itself in a very different system that separates church and state. The prospect of new missionary work among European immigrants and non-Orthodox Americans coupled with failing social and economic conditions in Alaska encouraged the spread of Russian Orthodoxy southward. Orthodox believers in San Francisco organized a Greek-Russian-Slavic Orthodox Church and Charitable Society in 1867 to promote and preserve the Orthodox faith (Tarasar 1975, 33). From 1868 to 1872, the multiethnic Orthodox church in San Francisco was called the Prayer House of the Orthodox Oriental Church and was located on Greenwich Street. After seven moves between 1868 and 1909, the small prayer house grew into today's All Holy Trinity Cathedral, rebuilt on the corner of Green Street and Van Ness Avenue after the 1906 earthquake. Adding strength to the Orthodox presence in the city, the Russian Orthodox church headquarters was transferred from Sitka to San Francisco in the 1870s. Records from Archbishop Vladimir's residency in the area from 1888 to 1891 indicate that 350 of the 700 Orthodox believers in California resided in San Francisco (Tarasar 1975, 30). As the number of Greek Orthodox immigrants in the city increased in the last decade of the century, they made plans to form their own ethnic parish. This separation of Greek members of the parish in 1900 led to the eventual withdrawal of all non-Russian members of San Francisco's first Orthodox church after 1900. This trend toward maintaining the exclusively Russian identity of the church occurred throughout the region in the early twentieth century, as increasing numbers of Greeks, Serbs,' and other Orthodox groups formed their own parishes.

Russian Orthodox settlement during this period also concentrated in other urban areas where economic opportunities were maximized. Russians had first settled in Oregon's largest city in the late 1880s and early 1890s. Most early Russians in Oregon worked for logging companies, for the railroad, and in sawmill and craft industries (Cole 1976, 17). The first Orthodox congregation in Portland, Oregon, was started in 1890 by an Alaskan of mixed native American–Russian heritage. This first Orthodox church in the Pacific Northwest was finished in 1894. Its fledging membership consisted of two Russians, six Arabs, and four Serbs. Despite the small membership, the church was officially blessed and dedicated by Hiermonk Sebastian, a Serb, who had been sent as a missionary to Seattle and the Northwest by the bishop of Alaska. He later blessed Seattle's first Orthodox church, St. Spiridon, in 1896 (Tarasar 1975, 16),

The St. Spiridon parish in Seattle was founded in 1892 by a combination of Russian and Greek immigrants in a joint agreement encouraged by an offer from the Russian government to provide a bilingual priest if the two groups would purchase one church building (Tarasar 1975, 35). The church's Greek membership formed its own parish in 1918.

A visitor to Portland from St. Spiridon noted in 1900 that there were fifty Orthodox believers in Portland, even though their chapel was in disrepair and ethnic factions were regularly disrupting services. The Orthodox chapel was abandoned in 1910 and remained closed until a new wave of Russians settled in Portland after the Russian Revolution ended in 1922.

Seattle's beautiful St. Spiridon church later became mother church to the chapel in Portland, to Holy Trinity Chapel in Wilkeson, Washington, and to missionary outreaches in Victoria and Vancouver, British Columbia; Clifton, Black Diamond, and Cle Elum, Washington; Astoria, Oregon; and other scattered settlements in the Pacific Northwest (Cole 1976, 21). The chapel in Wilkeson is especially notable for its longevity. Built in 1900 for a parish of forty-two members, the same building has been in use ever since (Tarasar 1975, 36).

During this same period of activity in the Pacific Northwest, Russian mass migration began in the eastern United States as well. In 1882, the

Russian population in the United States exceeded 16,918, and by 1899, it reached the highest total for any year in the nineteenth century, with 387,416 émigrés from Russia living in the country (Davis 1922a, 8). These statistics, of course, represent only an estimate of the total number here in any one year. Fear of identity, lack of language skills, and confusion regarding the census takers' definition of "Russian" all affected the accuracy of census counts. Figures presented here as in other parts of this book, therefore, undoubtedly underestimate the actual number of total Russians.

At the beginning of the twentieth century, peasants and laborers from all over Europe began to feel the consequences of industrialization at home. Many also heard about the "golden land of opportunity across the sea." As economic conditions improved in the United States and worsened in Europe, new influxes of immigrants succeeded one another decade by decade. New industries needed cheap labor. American agents, shipping companies, and improved modes of transportation also encouraged the emigration of millions of people out of Europe during this period. The majority were of peasant origin socially and occupationally, and most came seeking a more prosperous way of life for themselves and their children. Many brought their religious beliefs as a vitally important part of their cultural baggage. Among the Russians, Orthodox religious beliefs and language separated them from other immigrants and other Americans. The church, therefore, became their social as well as their religious center. About one-sixth of all Orthodox churches in the United States, in fact, were established in the first two decades of the twentieth century (Paraskevas and Reinstein 1969, 84).

Russian immigration into western North America was also encouraged by the turbulent situation in Russia caused by the loss of the Russo-Japanese War and by the completion of the Trans-Siberian Railroad at the turn of the century. This transcontinental link made migration from European to Asian Russia possible and opened up economic and cultural connections between the North American Pacific Rim and northeast Asia. Tens of thousands of Russians had settled in Harbin, Manchuria, during construction of the railroad and then stayed on (*Christian Science Monitor*, 12 Feb. 1985, 1). In 1896, Russia had obtained the right to build a trans-Siberian railroad through Manchuria. Because of its administrative function for the Chinese Eastern Railroad, the city rapidly became an international crossroads (Moser 1985, 67). Russia had also signed a secret defense treaty with the Chinese to keep the Japanese out of Manchuria. Russian settlers were thus encouraged to remain there as permanent residents (Lee 1983, 27).

Cohesive Russian neighborhoods had evolved in Harbin after the completion of the railroad. Russians living in China developed a distinctive Sino-Russian dialect; over 120,000 Russians resided in Harbin by the end of the Russian civil war (*Sacramento Union,* 8 July 1985, B1). Russians in this Chinese city maintained a strong religious and cultural identity, despite sometimes disruptive political issues. They built twenty-two Orthodox churches, sponsored a large orchestra, and even opened a Russian university during these years. A retired Orthodox woman in West Sacramento remembered her adolescent years in Harbin fondly:

Oh, it was such a beautiful city. We Russians had many, many large buildings and churches and an excellent symphony and university and much contact with each other. We rarely spoke with the Chinese people there because there were so many Russians. Our part of the city was on a floodplain near the big river. There were thousands and thousands of good Russian people in Harbin when I left. (A. Rubinaw interview, West Sacramento, 29 December 1985)

The cities of Vladivostock and Harbin subsequently became major embarkation points for Russians on their way to the west coast of North America (map 11). The vast majority were Orthodox believers who hoped to begin more prosperous lives in the United States and Canada. Most of these early-twentieth-century émigrés chose to resettle in San Francisco, but a significant number gravitated to Seattle and Vancouver, British Columbia (C. Padick telephone interview, 17 April 1983).

Emigration out of eastern Russia and Manchuria was amplified in the early twentieth century by the decision of the United States Board of

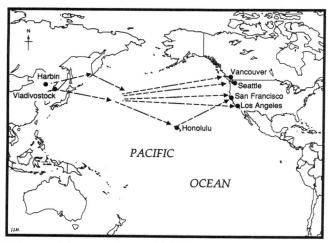

Map 11. Early twentieth-century Russian Orthodox migration to western North America

Immigration in Hawaii to recruit hundreds of Russian workers from Manchuria for labor in the Hawaiian sugarcane fields (Nordyke 1977, 33). These workers were encouraged to leave eastern Siberia between 1909 and 1912 by Hawaiian agents who promised them large salaries for work in the fields. According to now elderly Russians who came to northern California by way of the cane fields, they were actually "paid only half the rubles we had been promised back in Siberia" (P. Domasky interview, West Sacramento, 9 November 1983). Disappointment with financial conditions and dissatisfaction with difficult working conditions encouraged most of the Russians in Hawaii to resettle in coastal California.

An interesting sidelight to this Russian-Hawaiian connection was remembered by a retired married couple who were born in San Francisco after their parents settled there following their migration via Hawaii. Mr. and Mrs. Raymon Vessell (Vesselleroff) remember an ethnically mixed group of musicians who played in San Francisco in about 1925, known as the Hawaiian Cossacks. Mr. Vessell, a piano player in a Russian club in San Francisco in those years, recalled: "It was really strange to be sitting at the piano and have a Japanese man come up and begin speaking perfect Russian with no accent at all. He said he had worked with all Russians in Hawaii and had been forced to learn the language" (R. and L. Vessell interview, West Sacramento, 19 September 1985).

THE DOUKHOBORS

The Doukhobors, a sectarian group long persecuted by the Russian government and the official Orthodox church, were the first Russian religious group to migrate to North America en masse. Up to the time of their arrival in the study area, Russians had migrated and settled here individually, rather than in large groups. Doukhobors also constituted the single largest group of immigrants ever to arrive in Canada up to that time (Dawson 1936, 7). This migration of over seven thousand Doukhobors to Canada in the late nineteenth century is even more amazing when considered in light of the circumstances they had to overcome to organize and fund it.

Despite their economic successes in the difficult environment of the Caucasus Mountains, things had not gone smoothly for the Doukhobors after the death of their leader Luker'ia Vasil'evna Gubanova. Following her death, Luker'ia's brother and uncle competed for the prestigious position of Doukhobor leader. A bitter conflict soon developed between various factions until the case was finally taken to court (Dawson 1936, 3). The outcome of the court decision, which awarded control of Doukhobor property and decision making to Luker'ia's brother, was supported by a minority of its members. At least twelve thousand people formed the "Large party" and gave support to the other candidate, Peter Verigin, the young man Luker'ia had trained to be leader. Verigin became a much respected and revered leader even though his extreme views frequently brought him into conflict with Russian authorities. He was eventually exiled to Siberia in 1887, where he continued to provide leadership and make decisions relayed via Doukhobor messengers. His decisions were often based on a real lack of understanding of the restrictions of conditions in Doukhobor settlements thousands of miles away. This resulted in yet another schism in the group, as some Doukhobors refused to follow his strict requirements. Those who implicitly obeyed his rules refused to eat meat or to bear arms, held regular fasts, and strictly obeyed the words of their esteemed spiritual leader. Eventually, the four thousand members of this "Fasting party" were severely flogged and dispersed to tiny villages throughout the Tiflis, Georgia, area (Dawson 1936, 4).

Despite spatial and spiritual separation and the banishment of their leader to Siberia, the Fasting party began organizing a plan for mass emigration from Russia. Inspired by books and letters from Western Protestants, Verigin advised the group to change its name from Doukhobors to the Christian Community of Universal Brotherhood to make it more acceptable to the authorities.

After several years of letter-writing campaigns and meetings with government authorities, the Doukhobors finally gained permission to leave their homeland. The English Quakers were the first to take up the Doukhobor emigration cause. Along with the support of the English Society of Friends (Quakers), who raised over $200,000 for Doukhobor emigration from Russia, author and pacifist Leo Tolstoy added financial support by contributing the royalties from his book *Resurrection* (Elkinton 1903, 3). In 1899, approximately 7,363 Doukhobors departed to lands unknown to begin their new lives. About two-thirds of the Doukhobors, those who had not been as extremely persecuted for their beliefs, remained in Russia.

Choosing a suitable place for resettlement was a difficult and often confusing issue. It was important for the Doukhobors to locate in a place with enough isolated agricultural land for them to live in a large group. They also needed to find a government willing to tolerate their need for complete separation from outsiders. After the funds were gathered for their departure, Tolstoy suggested four considerations for resettlement: Cyprus, Manchuria, the Sinkiang province of China, and Texas. The idea of Texas especially appealed to Tolstoy, since several communal settlements of French and Russian socialist groups had been attempted there (Woodcock and Avakumovic 1968, 119). The isolation and openness of the "wild West" doubtless also influenced his positive feelings about Doukhobor migration to Texas.

Tolstoy continued to work toward establishing the Doukhobors somewhere in the United States until late 1898. His final recommendation was for migration to Hawaii. As mentioned earlier, Hawaiian sugarcane plantation agents had been actively recruiting Russians. Tolstoy's idea was based on communication with these agents.

Despite these ideas about American settlement, the Doukhobors' final decision was to migrate to a place that was a part of the British Empire. The British not only had taken the lead in raising funds for their emigration from Russia but also had remained supportive throughout the entire process. The Doukhobors finally selected Tolstoy's last choice, the island of Cyprus, which was a part of the British Empire at the time.

Despite reports brought by preemigration Doukhobor scouts of poor soil and a hot climate, once the decision was made, resettlement of the Doukhobors on the island proceeded quickly. The first group of 1,126 arrived on the island in August 1898 (Woodcock and Avakumovic 1968, 125). They proceeded to build a small agricultural village, constructing homes of Russian-style mud bricks and preparing the soil for planting vegetables. By fall, however, various disagreements had developed about the value of communal versus individual farming and other social and economic issues. Lack of leadership and adjustment to the new physical environment also took its toll on any potential Doukhobor success. Many continued to live in damp tents; those who did live in houses were forced to exist in extremely crowded and unsanitary conditions. These poor living conditions and a limited diet (vegetables were not ready for consumption for months after planting, milk was available only in condensed form, and eating meat was against religious requirements) caused outbreaks of serious illness among the weakest of the new settlers. Two months after the arrival in Cyprus, the first two deaths occurred. Many others lingered in a sick and weakened state. The Doukhobors remaining in Russia decided on a new destination for their group, a place where the climate was more like that of their homeland. In April 1899, Doukhobors from Cyprus sailed to Canada to join their fellow sectarians to begin yet another new life on the Canadian prairies.

Two large groups of Doukhobors had already arrived in North America before they were joined by the Cyprus survivors. Accompanied by teachers, assistants, and a Russian scholar (who later documented the experience) and his physician wife, the first Doukhobors had arrived at

Halifax, Nova Scotia, in the early spring of 1899 (Foster 1935, 332). Their arrival must have been a startling sight for local Canadians. According to one account,

No one had ever witnessed such a landing as when the ship *Lake Huron* plowed into Halifax harbor on a bitterly cold January 24, 1900. Here was an aggregation of black-suited men and scarved peasant women, many with children, carrying packs as if they were beasts of burden, singing the while and praising the Lord. Thirty-two precarious days at sea had only raised their hopes that the millennium must be near. A group of Quakers, on hand to welcome them, were overwhelmed when they saw the burdened Russians bow down to them with foreheads touching the ground. Then, at a signal, they arose and sang their angelic hymns, bowed to one another, saying "Slava Bohu." (Bach 1961, 191)

Anxious to populate prairie lands with proven agriculturalists, the Canadian government provided support for Doukhobor settlement in several ways. First, the Dominion Lands Act granted free land to male heads of families. Second, the special Hamlet Clause of the act, passed fifteen years earlier to accommodate Mennonite settlement, allowed homesteaders to live in villages within three miles of their land. This made a communal lifestyle possible and encouraged ethnic and religious homogeneity on the Canadian prairies. The Canadian government also accommodated Doukhobor needs when it passed section 21 of the Dominion Military Act in late 1898, exempting Doukhobors from military service.

Doukhobor settlement in Canada was originally to be located in three blocks of land in today's province of Saskatchewan, an area then known loosely as the Northwest Territories. These three sites included Rosthern Colony, North Colony and South Colony, and an annex called Good Spirit Lake in the Assinoboia District (map 12). Although Verigin had hoped for mutual sharing and complete economic and social connections between groups, Doukhobors from various villages in Russia settled together in specific villages in Canada (Gale and Koroscil 1977, 59). Despite Verigin's plans, some of the settlements were strictly communal, while others operated on an individual basis.

Doukhobor settlements in Canada were designed almost exactly like those they had left in Russia. Following a village plan sent in a letter from their still-exiled leader, one- and two-story sod or log houses were constructed for each family. Most of the houses had fenced yards with trees and a garden. Large barns serving the entire settlement were built behind the houses in communal villages in North and South colonies. In more individually owned Rosthern Colony, barns were attached to the

Map 12. Early Doukhobor settlements in Canada, 1900

rear part of the house, with granaries constructed in front yards. All villages also had public bathhouses, and some had meeting houses for church services (*sobranya*) (Gale and Koroscil 1977, 60–61).

Despite the harsh conditions of life on the prairie, enthusiasm and support for the Doukhobors' religious principles were at a high level in the first years after arrival in Canada. Left without a leader (Peter Verigin was still in Siberian exile although he wrote regular letters of advice and support to the Canadian settlers), local groups soon developed their own concerns and issues. Many were disappointed that the climate of Canada's prairie provinces was too extreme for raising fruits and vegetables. The severe winters were especially disappointing. The vast majority of men and adolescent boys worked away from the farm villages every summer in order to survive financially. Most worked for the Canadian railroad, building the tracks across the Canadian prairie, while women and girls stayed behind to work farmland. One of the most vivid memories of early non-Doukhobor residents of Saskatchewan was watching strong Doukhobor women harnessed to plows, breaking up the land.

Railroads brought land seekers and speculators into Doukhobor villages. These new settlers eventually caused the Canadian homestead law to be changed to allow the settlement of non-Doukhobors among Doukhobor farmsteads. The culturally disintegrating effect of contact with foreigners worried Doukhobor leaders, and many considered moving to a more remote part of Canada to establish exclusively Doukhobor villages. The eventual migration of almost six thousand Doukhobors to British Columbia was a response to this concern.

Other factors entered into the decision to relocate in British Columbia. Doukhobors had long refused to legalize their rights to Canadian land. Their aversion to taking oaths, their fears of possible military service if they became involved with the government, and their lack of leadership added confusion to decisions about owning land. After Peter Verigin ("Peter the Lordly") arrived in Saskatchewan in 1902, he registered Doukhobor lands in the name of the entire community. But the law now required that land had to be owned by individuals and that all owners must take the Canadian oath of allegiance. Since Verigin's concept of community was based on collectivist principles and because the Canadian government had originally promised to respect the Doukhobor wish for communal living, Verigin refused to cooperate (Avakumovic 1979, 32). Many problems developed. As a result of the confusion over land records, one hundred thousand acres of land, some of it already developed, was taken from the Doukhobors by the Canadian government (Foster 1935, 334).

Verigin decided to move the Doukhobors who had lost their land to a new place. After his decision to relocate these Community Doukhobors to British Columbia, many Independents made the decision to stay on their land in Saskatchewan as free and independent people. Most of the Community Doukhobors decided to go to British Columbia with their leader, and by 1914, about five thousand had resettled west of the mountains (Gale and Koroscil 1977, 64).

During these years of uncertainty and adjustment, several small parties of independent Doukhobors from Saskatchewan also explored the possibility of resettling in the western United States or Mexico. Families traveled to Mexico, the Sacramento and San Joaquin valleys, and even to North Dakota in search of a more free and productive place to settle. Most never returned to Canada (M. Chursenoff interview, Orangevale, California, 1991; Chursenoff 1969, 10).

Verigin's choice of British Columbia was a reflection of his desire to take his followers to a place where no previous settlements existed, where they could practice their communal lifestyle and follow their religious beliefs without interruption. And the fertile land near the confluence of the Columbia and Kootenay rivers reminded the settlers of the rich Milky Waters area of their Russian past. Verigin first bought a tract of land in the Columbia River Valley and in the boundary region near Grand Forks.

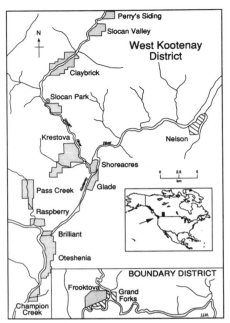

Map 13. Doukhobor settlements in British Columbia, 1920. Reprinted, by permission, from Gale and Koroscil 1977, 66.

Soon four settlements were in place: Grand Forks, Glade, Brilliant, and Pass Creek (map 13). By 1916, Doukhobors owned nineteen thousand acres of mostly virgin land in British Columbia.

Verigin had big plans for the design of these new settlements in British Columbia. His distinctive "double house" was one of the most observably unique features of the Doukhobor cultural landscape (fig. 5). By the early 1930s, a total of 128 of these large double structures had been built (Gale and Korosch 1977, 65). Designed as 2 two-story buildings connected by a one-story U-shaped building wrapped around an inner courtyard, these double houses were planned to accommodate up to one hundred people. Unfortunately, most of these distinctive homes have been destroyed in protests by radical members of a subgroup of the sect, the Sons of Freedom.

Doukhobors in British Columbia soon diversified their economy, moving beyond a system based entirely on agriculture. As fruit trees matured, a jam factory was built to mass produce the soon-famous Doukhobor product. All seemed to be going well for the new British Columbia settlers. However, their refusal to register births, deaths, and marriages and

Figure 5. This typical Doukhobor double house in Grand Forks, British Columbia, is no longer in use. Photo by Pamela Posey.

to send their children to public school became an ever increasing problem between the Doukhobors and the Canadian authorities.[1] Tensions between the sectarians and the Canadian government intensified after World War I. School burnings and public protests by the most radical of Doukhobor subgroups, the Sons of Freedom, increased in the early 1920s. In 1924, Doukhobor leader Peter Verigin, his traveling companion, and several other passengers were killed when their train was blown up at Farron, British Columbia. Investigations never pinpointed the exact cause of the explosion. Repercussions from the tragedy rippled through Doukhobor communities, adding fuel to their discontent. After the funeral and period of mourning ended, school fires again became an issue. When the new Doukhobor leader, Peter P. Verigin ("Peter the Purger") arrived in Canada from the Soviet Union in 1928, his support of education and increased contact with the outside world smoothed tensions for a short period of time (Foster 1935, 337).

But disturbances soon began again, as the Sons of Freedom organized burnings and nude protests. This radical group had first developed in protest of the policies of Peter Verigin. They claimed that their inner light shone brighter than the inner light of their divine dictator (Bach

1961, 195). These Freedomites had moved far into the mountains and built their own village, Krestova. To the outside world, they appeared insane much of the time. Marching naked through towns in protest of school attendance and other government policies, the "Mad Douks" tarnished the reputation of the entire Doukhobor population. They felt themselves to be the only true Doukhobors, the ones who were most willing to follow the divine scheme of things. The participation of the Sons of Freedom in radical protests was seen by them as their mission in life and as a part of a God-directed plan. According to an active participant in these protests,

We know we are crazy. Just like birds sitting on a wire. When one goes, we all go. I met at a place where he said. Six of us got into the car. I didn't know where we were going or what we would do. But soon I found out we were going to Brilliant, then I knew we were going to burn. Oh, it was awful the first time we took our clothes off, with all those people looking. Something just made us do it. We can't promise what we will do tomorrow or next week. We don't know what God might tell us to do. (Hawthorn 1955, 167)

By 1932, it was obvious to the authorities that something had to be done to gain control of the situation. The Canadian Parliament expanded the requirements of its criminal code, announcing that it was now unlawful for anyone in Canada to appear naked. Eventually over three hundred Doukhobor men and women were arrested for this offense. Most were sent to prison for three-year terms.

The challenges of the Depression along with the erratic leadership and lifestyle of "Peter the Purger" caused great financial and spiritual hardships for the Doukhobors in the 1930s. Their organization, the Christian Community of Universal Brotherhood, was forced to declare bankruptcy in 1937 (Avakumovic 1979, 32). By the end of the 1930s, it was clear that the Doukhobor *Gemeinschaft* was falling apart. Economic problems and internal disagreements divided the group even more firmly into Independents who stayed on their own land and became acculturated into Canadian life, the Sons of Freedom who lived mainly in the valleys and plateaus of the Kootenay Mountains and resisted Canadian culture entirely, and the Orthodox Doukhobors, who remained somewhere between individualism and collectivism, materialism and spiritualism, assimilation and isolation (Avrich 1962, 268–69).

From the 1930s through the 1950s, the activities of the Sons of Freedom remained one of British Columbia's most serious problems. Even though more than twelve thousand Doukhobors had become fully Canadianized, the reputation of this subgroup continued to be a problem for them all (Bach 1961, 199). A small percentage of the poorest and least educated of all Doukhobors belonged to the Freedomites. Some left their mountain village of Krestova in 1947 and formed a communal settlement on Vancouver Island near the town of Hilliers. There a group of about sixty Freedomites hoped they could practice their collective lifestyle in peace (Turyk 1950, 18–19). All possessions were shared by the group. Even husbands, wives, and children were shared by all as members of a common family. The decision to give up the exclusivity of marriage was "the supreme test of selfishness and lack of envy and lust" (Herbison 1955, 183). This supreme willingness to follow their goals and commitment to decisions based on spiritual principles ultimately ended in the failure of the Vancouver Island Doukhobor settlement, with most of its residents returning to Kootenay area settlements.

The government in British Columbia finally decided that the only way to solve the "Doukhobor problem" was to force the group to become educated in Canadian culture and law. Toward this goal, the authorities removed all school-age Sons of Freedom children from the Krestova area to a boarding school in Denver, British Columbia. After a renewed wave of bombings, burnings, and public protests, and threats to leave Canada and return to Russia, the group finally accepted the inevitable.[2] By the time Doukhobor children returned home from their boarding school "prison" in 1959, conditions between the Sons of Freedom and Canadian authorities had improved considerably.

By 1951, there was no formal pattern of communal living of the almost twenty thousand Doukhobors in Canada (Gale and Koroscil 1977, 68). Although some remain in original settlement nodes in British Columbia and Saskatchewan, in a trend common to most other immigrant groups in North America, most of the younger generation have moved to larger cities, especially Vancouver (P. Gritchen and S. Babakaiff interviews, Grand Forks, British Columbia, August 1991). Employment opportunities, the search for economic and personal amenities, and a disbelief in Doukhobor spiritual principles has diluted Doukhobor cohesion in recent years (M. Chursenoff interview, Orangevale, California, 1991). Twentieth-century Canadian census records show a continuous increase in the number of Doukhobors despite their continuing spatial dispersion (table 4). A more detailed discussion of post-1960s Doukhobor acculturation experiences is presented in chapter 6.

THE MOLOKANS

Soon after the resettlement of Doukhobors in Canada, a second large Russian sectarian group began making plans to leave their homeland. The Molokans formed a major part of the substantial increase in the

Table 4
Doukhobors in British Columbia and Saskatchewan

Year	British Columbia	Saskatchewan	Total in Canada
1901	—	8,700[a]	8,775
1921	5,074	7,166	12,648
1951	8,170	4,536	13,175
1971	6,720	1,675	9,165
1981	5,065	1,065	6,700

Source: Canadian Census of Population, "Religions," 1901, 1921, 1951, 1971, 1981.
[a]Includes Assiniboia (Northwest Territories).

number of Russians in California after 1900. Most of this early-twentieth-century Russian migration to North America was due to economic, social, and political issues that intensified during the Russo-Japanese War and the first Russian civil war of 1904–5.

The largest of the affected early-twentieth-century sectarian groups, the Molokans left Russia between 1901 and 1911, settling mainly in East Los Angeles. Inspired by their prophets and encouraged by earlier migrations of Doukhobors to Canada, the Molokans who migrated to western North America were primarily from the Transcaucasus region, as the Doukhobors had been. Molokans were given in 1839 a fifty-year exemption from military service by the czar if they agreed to leave central Russia and resettle in the Transcaucasus. When the exemption expired, Molokan leaders petitioned the government for release from required military service and for permission to emigrate (Moore 1973, 7).

It took more than the worry of obligatory military service and persecution from church and state for the Molokans to make the final decision to leave their homeland. Also important was the power of numerous prophecies warning of future disasters for the group if they remained in Russia.

A major emigration (*pokhod*) out of Russia had been predicted by Molokan Pryguny and Maksimist prophets for many years before the actual departure for the United States. No one knew the exact time or place of the predicted refuge, but Molokan songbooks still contain songs written about the long-hoped-for place. These words are from a typical song of pokhod:

Is it not time for thee Zion to prepare thyself for
Pohod? From this terrible menace that is coming so soon,
From this northern land it is time for thee to escape
To a far southern country, a wilderness of peoples
There is the refuge for members sealed to be there.
(Berokoff 1969, 14)

These prophecies began to take form as early as 1852, when a young boy wrote down a list of three events that would precede the pokhod from Russia. This young prophet waited more than forty years for them to occur. The three significant events were the gathering of people for midnight prayers, a light flashing across the sky at night, and a special song being sung at night by Molokans in villages located in a linear pattern spreading from east to west (Berokoff 1969, 15). In the early years of the twentieth century, these three events seemed to the Molokans to occur within a matter of months.[3]

To prepare for the prophesied journey, Molokans first sent three elders to visit the Doukhobors in Canada to evaluate land and life in North America (Berokoff 1969, 19). The elders returned to Russia and expressed their dissatisfaction with the cold Canadian climate, advising their people to settle in the United States. In 1900, four younger Molokans visited Canada, then traveled south to Los Angeles to work for the Pacific Electric Railroad Company. The warmth of the climate and the similarity of the topography of southern California to their homeland encouraged this small advisory group to recommend Los Angeles for Molokan settlement (Young 1932, 12). Three of them returned to Russia with "a glowing account" of their life in California, its glorious climate, and an abundance of work for willing hands as compared to severe winters and poorer living conditions in the old country (Berokoff 1969, 20). The promise of the United States government to offer the Molokans perpetual freedom from conscription was also vitally important in their decision to settle in California (Story 1960, 15).

The beginning of the Russo-Japanese War and imminent military service forced the issue. The night before the war began, a large group of Molokans quickly and quietly began to undertake their emigration to North America. Migration routes varied. Some traveled to Germany, sailed to New York or Galveston, Texas, and then took trains to California. Others traveled on less direct routes, some even going through South America, crossing the continent from east to west, and sailing north to California from Chile (map 14).

Most of the Molokans who came to North America left between 1904 and 1912. Many remained behind, however, believing their true pokhod was in other places. Large numbers of Pryguny believed their elders, who preached that the true land of exile was in the Middle East at the base of Mount Ararat. Those who stayed behind got caught in the restrictions of the First World War. Some eventually escaped to Iran and Syria, resettling in the United States in the 1950s. Less than 3 percent of all Molokans left Russia before the Revolution (O'Brien-Rothe 1989, 3). By 1911, there were at least a thousand Molokans living in San Francisco and over five thousand living in southern California (Young 1932, 22).

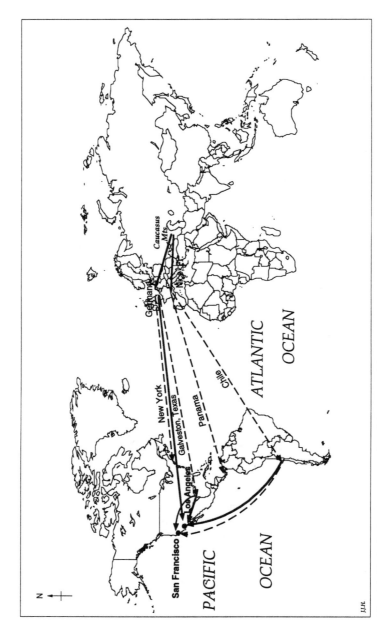

Map 14. Typical migration routes of Molokans to California, 1904–12

The number of their descendants in America now is estimated to be at least twenty thousand, with most residing in California and Oregon (O'Brien-Rothe 1989, 3).

Three subgroups of Molokans migrated to California from the Transcaucasus area. The Pryguny settled in Los Angeles, while the Postoiannye migrated to San Francisco. Because the Pryguny, especially the Maksimisty, were more persecuted by church and state in Russia, many more of them emigrated to California. From the outset, then, the Los Angeles Molokan community was much larger than the one in San Francisco. The next largest community developed in the San Joaquin Valley near the town of Kerman, west of Fresno. Molokans have also settled in other small towns in the San Joaquin Valley, in the Willamette Valley in Oregon, and in Washington, Arizona, Mexico, and Australia (map 15).

Molokan settlement in Los Angeles concentrated in an ethnically diverse area east of the city's downtown in a neighborhood known locally as the Flats. The first settlement node concentrated in the area between the Los Angeles River and Boyle Heights in downtown Los Angeles (map 16). Settling near lumber and railroad yards, industrial plants, and other places of potential employment, Russian men found work as unskilled laborers almost immediately. Women worked as domestics. Some picked fruit in nearby orchards. Molokan families rented single-family homes rather than rooms in tenement buildings, in an effort to avoid contact with outside groups. Several Molokan families usually shared one house, and conditions were often crowded and difficult. The following descrip-

Map 15. Molokan churches in California and Oregon, 1992

93

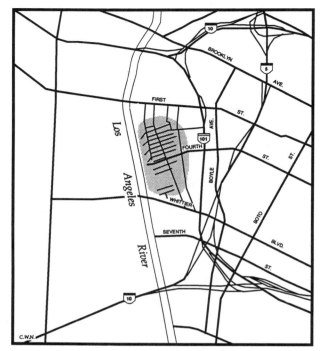

Map 16. Early Molokan settlement core in Los Angeles, 1920. From A. J. Conovaloff interview, 1 March 1991.

tion of the neighborhood provided by sociologist Pauline Young illustrates the challenging living conditions:

The atmosphere of the Flats is heavy. Factories, warehouses, small industrial plants of all kinds and descriptions contribute their share of pungent smells. Feed, fuel, and livery stables, a wholesale drug company, a cooperative bakery, a firecracker factory, a granite-works establishment, a creamery, a garment-manufacturing concern, are some of the varied types of industrial establishments which hem in the district to the north, south, and east, while the railroads define the west boundaries. Noisy engines, clanking over a maze of tracks, puffing steam in spirals, and emitting volumes of black smoke, spread a pall over the region. A network of railway tracks stretches along the dry bed of the Los Angeles River, which is a reminder of the rare occasions when the river runs. (1932, 17)

Even though Los Angeles, with a population of 102,000 in 1900, was much smaller than it is today, this urban atmosphere was alien and extremely stressful to the Russian sectarians who had spent their entire lifetime in isolated, rural villages. But despite the stresses of urban life, the majority of Molokan families purchased their own homes within a few years, immediately constructing a traditional Russian *banya* (sauna) in the backyard. By 1906, there was also a Molokan grocery store and meat market in the neighborhood. Meat from local Jewish slaughter-houses was sold to Molokans, who attempted to maintain their strict Old Testament dietary laws (Berokoff 1969, 35).

In the 1920s, other ethnic groups, notably blacks and Mexicans, moved into the Flats, displacing the Russians. As city redevelopment projects and low-income housing units were built in the neighborhood, Molokans began to disperse outward. Older residents moved to Boyle Heights immediately east of the original cluster. Younger families moved to the suburbs, settling in Montebello, Cudahy, and Monterey Park (Moore 1973, 22). Despite this continuing suburban dispersal, Los Angeles remains the spiritual center of Molokan life in southern California. New churches were built as a response to population shifts and as a solution for community factionalism. Differences in interpretation of church rituals were at the heart of most disputes. Since various groups of Molokans from widely scattered villages in the Caucasus had con-ducted their services in slightly different ways, it was difficult for them to agree upon one right way. When these communities settled together in Los Angeles, much energy and thought was given to arguing the merits of one interpretation against another (Moore 1973, 25). As the only institution shared by the group, churches became a forum not only for discussing spiritual issues, but also for the resolution of political and social issues in the community.

The typical Molokan church in North America is difficult for outsiders to identify. As shown in figure 6, all churches are plain buildings sur-rounded by a fence and gate, and most are unmarked. Urban churches are on residential streets, and rural churches are on remote country roads. Services in most Molokan churches are conducted in Russian, although a new and growing Reformed Molokan movement in Wood-burn, Oregon, uses English except during the singing of psalms from the Russian Bible and Molokan songbook. Some songs are also sung in English to traditional Molokan melodies.

Despite the relative economic success of Molokans in Los Angeles, many of the church leaders began to have reservations about the city's desirability as a permanent residence. Molokans were basically rural people, accustomed to a slower pace of life in a safer, more homogeneous environment. A few Molokans returned to their villages in Russia, but most began to search for a suitable agricultural area in the American West. In 1905–6, the first group to leave Los Angeles went to Hawaii. Another larger group, consisting of fifty families, bought thirteen thou-sand acres of land in Mexico's Baja California, sixty miles south of the

Figure 6. This Molokan church in East Los Angeles has a typical chain-link fence and locked gate. Photo by D. G. Holtgrieve.

border. They formed the largest, most successful, and longest-lasting communal attempt by Molokans in North America. Up to one hundred families farmed over twenty-three square miles until the 1940s.

A typical Russian village, known as Colonia Rus, was constructed almost immediately at Rancho Guadalupe. Houses were built in a central village layout, with individual farmers working their own fields in outlying areas. Houses in the village were arranged side by side along a straight, tree-lined road where every family had the same-sized strip of land along the main street (Muranaka 1988, 4). Houses were constructed in a simple two-room design with rear kitchens, much the same as those in rural Russia. One major difference in Guadalupe construction was the use of adobe bricks rather than wood for home exteriors.

Geographer Oscar Schmieder, in an early visit to Guadalupe in the 1920s, described an economic system much like the one practiced in the Transcaucasus, including crop choices, livestock management, and land tenure (1929, 419–21). Russians depended on four main cash crops in Guadalupe—wheat, grapes, tomatoes, and alfalfa. They also grew a wide variety of garden crops for household food (Story 1960, 31).

The most important aspect of the Molokans' village life was their desire to withdraw from all outsiders whenever possible. This desire had spatial as well as social manifestations. Villages were built as far away from non-Molokan residents of the area as possible. It was, in fact, the arrival of Mexican squatters in Rancho Guadalupe in the 1950s that caused most Molokans in the area to return to California. The completion of a new road in 1958 brought in not only Mexicans, but also Jewish, Japanese, and Chinese settlers, changing the isolated character of the town (Muranaka 1988, 12). Some Molokans returned to Los Angeles to take advantage of higher-paying jobs during the war. Others had returned to California because of fears of upheaval during the Mexican Revolution and the subsequent economic effects of the *ejido* system (collectivization of agriculture). However, enough Russians remained in Colonia Rus in the 1950s for a new church to be built in 1955 (Story 1960, 60, 127). In the 1990s, only one family of Russians remains, along with several intermarried Mexican-Russian families. In today's Molokan settlements in California and Oregon, many middle-aged and older Molokans born in Guadalupe are trilingual, speaking fluent Spanish, Russian, and English.

Other smaller groups of Los Angeles Molokans sought their rural *pokhod* in other places. About twenty families went to the Hawaiian island of Kauai, thinking they had bought a sugar plantation. When they arrived on the island, the terms of their contract said they were actually workers on the plantation, rather than owners. Many returned to Los Angeles, disillusioned with the American system of business (Berokoff 1969, 43–44).

Arizona was also seen by some as a place of refuge during these early years of settlement. Drawn by promises of fertile soil and the availability of irrigation water from the new Roosevelt Dam, a group of Molokans left Los Angeles in 1911 to settle in Glendale, Arizona. Molokans also went to Glendale directly from Russia, and by the end of World War I, the town's Russian population had grown to over one hundred families.

Irrigated farming methods were new and challenging for these Arizona colonists. Attempts at raising sugar beets failed after years of effort. The fields were then successfully planted in alfalfa. Other Molokans turned to dairy farming. The Glendale Molokan settlement depended on dairying and alfalfa until the early years of World War I. The war created a tremendous demand for cotton, and thousands of irrigated acres in Arizona and in other parts of the West were planted in this cash crop. Borrowing money to convert their fields to this new and suddenly prosperous enterprise, Molokans in Glendale spent the war years in financial bliss. Unfortunately, the "economic crash that followed the end of the war shut off the supply of easy credit resulting in the collapse of the price of cotton and bankrupting eighty percent of Molokan families"

(Berokoff 1969, 58). All but about twenty-five Molokan families returned to Los Angeles to establish themselves all over again.

But the search for a more rural pokhod continued. As the problems of adjusting to urban life in Los Angeles intensified, so did the quest for an agricultural lifestyle. Some moved north into the San Joaquin Valley after 1913. There they formed nodes of settlement in Kerman, Shafter, Delano, and Porterville. Some settled even farther north in the town of Hartline in eastern Washington, where they raised wheat in an environment much like the one they had left in Russia. Despite initial economic success, Molokans in Washington returned to Los Angeles after several years of drought, as did other small groups who had bought land in Park Valley, Utah.

Of all the rural Molokan settlement nodes, the town of Kerman in the fertile San Joaquin Valley of California has been the most economically successful. Molokans first planted grape vines there in 1915, and grape production has continued to expand ever since. Kerman now has three active Molokan churches as well as a busy schedule of religious and cultural activities, including Russian-language classes at the newly constructed United Molokan Church Association building.

Molokans also settled in San Francisco in a small neighborhood on Potrero Hill (Dunn and Dunn 1978). The neighborhood, now a rapidly gentrifying part of the city, was at the time of their arrival a grassy knoll in view of the city's downtown. The new émigrés built wooden steambaths with metal chimneys in their backyards for Saturday-night baths. They also constructed a church in 1929, the only two-story Molokan church in North America, which has remained a focal point of the community despite continuing residential dispersal (Tripp 1980, 157).

Inspired by utopian promises of the Russian Revolution, several Molokan families from San Francisco returned to the Soviet Union in 1922. Disillusioned with their new lives in the Soviet system, they all returned to California by 1927.

Other San Francisco Molokans also searched for a more rural environment for their children and themselves. In the 1920s, some formed a small colony near Mount Lassen, California; others moved to Klamath Falls, Oregon. These Molokans resettled within a few years in the Sacramento Valley towns of Sheridan and Elmira and have remained there. The Molokan church in Sheridan is still used by local residents.

Molokans from both Los Angeles and San Francisco also were inspired to make a pokhod to Oregon's fertile Willamette Valley. In 1953, the first Molokans settled in the small town of Woodburn, and since then, several hundred other Molokans have "come north." Molokan settlement in Oregon's Willamette Valley was to become a magnet for the arrival of Russian Old Believers and Pentecostals in later decades. The

Figure 7. This Molokan couple has just finished Sunday morning services held in a historic farmhouse near Gervais, Oregon. They are members of the new Reformed Molokan congregation. Photo by author.

photograph of a Reformed Molokan couple dressed for Sunday services in Woodburn in figure 7 was taken in 1991.

Molokan emigration from the Soviet Union after the Revolution was completely halted by government authorities. It was not until the end of World War II that new Russian Molokans settled in California. The story of more recent Molokan migration, settlement, and landscape continues later in this chapter.

THE BAPTISTS

Russian Baptists established churches in San Francisco, and in small settlement nodes in West Sacramento, Los Angeles, Seattle, and California's rural Sonoma County during the early years of the twentieth century. In San Francisco, Russian Baptists first began to have services together as early as 1911 (Tripp 1980, 160). One of the first pastors of their small church on Potrero Hill was Siberian Ivan Efimovich Voronaev, who later was converted to Pentecostalism in New York City and became Russia's first Pentecostal missionary. Voronaev also preached to tiny Russian Baptist congregations in Los Angeles and Seattle during his stay on the West Coast.

Not all Russian Baptists on the California coast preferred urban areas. Several months after arriving in San Francisco, a group of about a hundred Baptist colonists living on Potrero Hill near the Baptist church began searching for a tract of rural land for permanent settlement along the northern California coast. By June 1912, the group had rented land formerly used for lumbering at Del Mar (Sea Ranch) and moved all their possessions there by boat from San Francisco. Within a few months, the colonists had planted about a thousand acres of vegetable crops (*Point Arena Record,* 6 December 1912, 3).

With the ranch's fertile, well-drained soil and the isolation needed to maintain their Russian religion and culture, the Baptist congregation at Del Mar seemed to have found the perfect place for permanent settlement. They even built a small church in 1912 and invited community residents to attend its dedication (*Point Arena Record,* 13 December 1912, 3).

A series of discouraging misfortunes eventually drove the group back to the relative safety of their Potrero Hill neighborhood. The first major setback happened in September 1912 when a few Russian men tried to transport their newly imported steam-driven traction engine from Point Arena to Del Mar. While the engine was being driven across an old bridge that crossed a deep coastal ravine, the bridge collapsed, and one of the men was crushed between the engine and the falling bridge (Clark 1990, 146). The burial of thirty-eight-year-old Nicholas Podsakoff on the bluff overlooking the foggy Pacific Ocean marked the first official ceremony of the new settlement.

Despite the difficulty of transporting machinery into the ranch, Russian First Farm prospered. Susan Clark's thesis on the settlement of Del Mar ranch summarizes the following major achievements of the group's first six months (1990, 150–51): (1) Besides establishing a secure refuge for the open practice of their religious beliefs and the successful construction of a Russian Baptist church, the colonists developed a positive relationship with their non-Russian neighbors. (2) They built their own school and brought in a teacher who spoke both Russian and English. (3) Their economic situation seemed to be stabilizing. First Farm had begun to provide enough fruits and vegetables to support all the Russian families in the community.

Then serious financial problems turned the tide. In late 1912, pleased with their progress, Russian leaders of the colony decided to ask the Del Mar Development Company about purchasing the land. By the time the deed was signed, possibly due to language difficulties or cultural miscommunication, the Russians had agreed to pay six times what the land was worth. Constant hard work on the farm during most of 1913 was not enough to make the monthly payments on the expensive property. In the early fall of 1913, giving up with great regret and disappointment, the Russians sailed back to their Baptist and Molokan neighborhood on Potrero Hill (Clark 1990, 153).

At about this same time, the West Sacramento Land Company began to take advantage of Russian immigrants by sending promotional letters written in Russian to the Russian neighborhood in San Francisco. This promotional effort was an attempt to encourage Russians to buy newly drained land in West Sacramento. In some cases, lots were purchased, sight unseen, on land still not completely reclaimed for settlement from the seasonal flood water of the Sacramento River. Letters in the historical file of the West Sacramento Land Company, dated 1914, indicated that they had successfully convinced the Russians to buy property in West Sacramento. Once several Russian families became well established in the neighborhood along the Sacramento River, chain migration brought other Russians into the area from San Francisco (table 5).

The majority of these early residents recall their original feelings about the area as centering on the cultural-symbolic amenities of living near the Sacramento River. "It looks exactly like the Russian Volga" was a frequent comment during field interviews I conducted. Some interviewees had been born in European Russia near the Volga River, but most had never even seen it. The majority of Russian residents in West Sacramento came from Siberia or Manchuria, thousands of miles east of the Volga River. However, memories and fantasies of life on the "beautiful Volga"

Table 5
West Sacramento Russians Naturalized before 1930

Name	Date of Naturalization	Birth Place
Goodoshinkoff, Basil and Anna	1906	Harbin
Ukrapina, Chris	1907	Serbia
Kristoff, William	1910	Harbin
Shevchinko, John and Irene	1910	Harbin
Svetchnikoff, Paul and Vera	1916	Harbin
Nasaroff, John and Natalia	1916	Vladivostock
Samborski, Anton and Dorothy	1912	Omsk
Skobavda, Anna	1922	Harbin
Sidelnicoff, Alexander	1923	Irkutsk
Mikhaeltsoff, Victor and Maria	1926	Armavir
Shilin, Nicholai and Maria	1927	Harbin
Dobrosmisloff, Boris	1927	Orel

Source: Yolo County Naturalization Records, 1900–1930.

remained strong in their shared perception. Songs and stories about the "beautiful river Volga" abound in Russian culture. Virtually all of the early Russian immigrants in California knew the words to this folk song:

From places far way, the river Volga flows.
The river Volga flows, it flows on endlessly.
Through fields of golden grain,
And 'cross the snowy plain.
The river Volga flows, and I am seventeen.
And mother said, life can bring many things.
You may grow weary of your wanderings.
And when you come back home at journey's end,
Into the Volga's waters, dip your hands.

This well-known folk song resonates with symbolic and cultural undercurrents for Russian immigrants. Their symbolic baptism in the Volga, representing their deep connection with Mother Earth, remains a strong symbolic bond to their Russian homeland.

The following comments collected during interviews with longtime residents of the Bryte suburb in West Sacramento speak to the Russian attachment to the river (fig. 8):

The river was always the best thing about our house in Bryte. It flowed right by the home we built on Riverbank Avenue. That was before the levee was built, and what a perfect place for a Russian to live. The flowing Volga could not have even been a better place to be. (N. Planteen interview, West Sacramento, 19 September 1985)

We Russians have always loved the river here because it is so much like the Volga. In Russia, living beside the beautiful Volga meant so much to so many of us . . . we can never forget its waters. (P. Domasky interview, West Sacramento, 2 March 1983)

My father grew up about five hundred miles from Moscow right along the Volga. Wasn't he lucky? He said Bryte looked just like home to him when he first saw the river in 1914. We Russian people always love the river most. (L. Vessell interview, West Sacramento, 22 October 1985)

We had our houses near the big river in Harbin too. Rivers are very important to our heritage, that is for sure. (A. Karakozoff interview, West Sacramento, 1 November 1985)

This common feeling about the importance of the river illustrates that the initial magnets for Russians to settle in West Sacramento were both cultural and economic. Shared feelings about the neighborhood's close

Figure 8. The Sacramento River flows past the suburb of West Sacramento, where most of the early Russians in California's capital city settled. Photo by author.

proximity to the Sacramento River established a close bond between the land and people during these early years of settlement.

After the land was fully reclaimed in 1914, a concentration of Russians congregated in the small Sacramento River suburb. Subdivider D. W. Hobson and his West Sacramento Land Company continued to encourage only "desirable" white European people to invest in property here, thereby intensifying the Old World European ambience of the neighborhood (H. Fisher interview, West Sacramento, October 1983). Naturalization records summarized in table 5 reveal that the majority of the area's Russian settlers came from eastern Russia or Manchuria with a typical migration pattern from Harbin, China, or Vladivostock to San Francisco. Many lived in San Francisco Russian neighborhoods during their first years in the United States, relocating to West Sacramento for permanent settlement after several years.

The Second Wave: 1917–1945

At the end of the Russian civil war in 1922, thousands who were fleeing the Soviet regime arrived in the United States and Canada. Many had left their homeland to escape religious persecution. The vast majority of these post-1917 émigrés were Jews who had left Russia to escape religious and political persecution.

A large percentage of Russians who emigrated during this wave came from the aristocratic classes or were professionals, military officers, Orthodox clergy, and others opposed to the Soviet regime (Day 1934, 8). While their military training or aristocratic background had served them well in their homeland, they often found it difficult to achieve social status in the United States. Most newcomers had to accept employment at the lowest level when they first arrived, thus making adjustment to their new lives difficult. During these stressful early years, newcomers often turned to the Russian church for comfort and cultural connections.

Russians came to the North American Pacific Rim during and after the Revolution via three main routes (map 17). The great majority of them filtered across Siberia to Harbin and into the Sinkiang province in China. Most eventually migrated by way of Shanghai or Hong Kong, then settled in San Francisco, Vancouver, Seattle, or Los Angeles after a brief stay in China. These eastern routes, in particular, brought thousands of Russians into California, Oregon, and Washington as anti-Bolsheviki moved into east Asia in the turmoil of the post-Revolution years. Russians from Harbin and Shanghai in particular settled in Los Angeles, San Francisco, Portland, and Seattle in large numbers in the 1920s. Many of these new Russians were wealthy and educated.

The second group left Odessa, Feodosiya, and other ports on the Black Sea and took refuge temporarily in Constantinople. Many waited there for several years hoping for political change at home that would enable them to return to Russia. The third group, arriving via the European route, were military officers who had served in the czar's army in the Russian division in France during World War I. The government had given this division to the Allies during the war, and they remained in France after the war was over. Hundreds of these officers came to the United States and Canada and began new lives as civilians after the war. A large number ended up in West Coast cities.

Many Russians found their way to the North American Pacific Rim via eastern and midwestern cities. Settling initially in Toronto, New York, Philadelphia, Chicago, and other major urban areas, these Russians eventually migrated to the West Coast for permanent settlement (Day 1934, 8). These political and religious refugees settled in well-established Russian neighborhoods in Los Angeles, San Francisco, and Vancouver, a trend that was common throughout the region (map 17).

Los Angeles experienced a particularly large influx of new Russians immediately following the Revolution. Most settled initially in Holly-

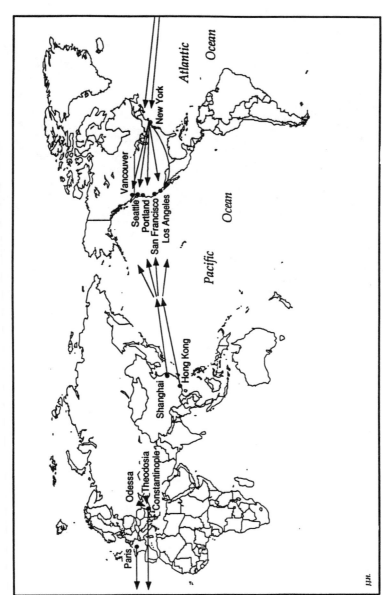

Map 17. Russian migration routes to North America, 1917–39

Figure 9. This Russian Orthodox church on Micheltorena Street in Los Angeles was built in the 1920s by the first Russian Orthodox residents of the city after the Russian Revolution. Photo by D. G. Holtgrieve.

wood just west of the earlier Molokan enclave. Others settled in other parts of the Los Angeles area, including Santa Monica, Venice, and Long Beach (Day 1934, 3). Russian cultural centers, language schools, art clubs, and restaurants held the community together and helped maintain Russian culture. The first Russian Orthodox edifice in southern California was built on Micheltorena Street by these 1920s era immigrants (fig. 9). This church and other Russian mediating institutions created a buffer between American and Russian life in an increasingly multicultural city.

Thousands of refugees in this second wave also gravitated to the Pacific Northwest. Most of this group came from Harbin, where they had fled during the Revolution. Many were drawn to Vancouver and to Seattle, where there was an active Orthodox community under the leadership of St. Spiridon's church. In 1922, a rector of the Orthodox church in Harbin arrived in Seattle. He was sent to Portland to renew regular religious services at the now defunct Holy Trinity Chapel (Cole 1976, 38–39).

Because of his work, by the time new Russian refugees arrived in Portland in 1923, a sense of community among the older Orthodox members of the community had been restored.

But divisions soon developed within the Portland Orthodox congregation. They reflected broader schisms within Orthodoxy that reverberated throughout the region in these turbulent post-Revolution years. Until 1917, the Russian Orthodox church in North America had been supported and governed by the official Orthodox church in Russia. All financial control and all decisions regarding leadership in North America had been controlled by the hierarchy of the Russian Holy Synod. Thus, from its beginnings in Alaska in 1794 through 1924, the North American Orthodox movement was connected with the church in Russia. After the Revolution, this system fell apart. Instead, various church factions in Russia supported various political systems. Some supported the causes of the Revolution, some were decidedly anti-Bolshevik, some had more moderate viewpoints. In the early years of the Revolution, a council of the Russian Orthodox church agreed to restore the official patriarchate that had been abolished two hundred years before by Peter the Great. This decision effectively separated church and state for the first time in two centuries. After the Bolsheviki came to power, numerous church officials were imprisoned, including the patriarch of the newly defined church. This threw Orthodoxy into renewed confusion. Eventually, the Fourth All American Sobor in Detroit in 1924 removed Orthodox churches in North America from the jurisdiction of the Russian church, declaring them "temporarily self-governing" (Tarasar 1975, 187). The Orthodox church of America then developed its own dioceses and parishes and became completely independent from the Russian church.

These issues and conflicts affecting Orthodox church unity spilled over into North American Orthodoxy, causing numerous divisions that remain in the 1990s. One dramatic example of this growing disunity in Orthodox life happened in Portland in the mid-1920s. Older, pre-Revolution Russian émigrés in Portland supported continued secularization of the Orthodox chapel, while new arrivals insisted on keeping it a religious center. A major rift between Russian groups occurred, typical of Orthodox churches in other parts of the country. According to David Cole,

Tempers flared and matters came to a head Easter Sunday, 1924. On that date, the antichurch group assembled outside Holy Trinity Chapel and attempted to disrupt the Paschal Liturgy by shouting loudly and banging on the door. The men inside, mostly newcomers and still unfamiliar with their new homeland, remained silent and unmoving. But one brave soul would have nothing of this sacrilege; she was Elena Sprawkin, wife of Paul, one of the oldtimers who had helped reestablish Orthodox church life at the chapel. When the disrupters attempted entry of the chapel, she turned past the unmoving worshipers and drove the opposers out of the chapel with her umbrella! Given heart, the men joined her in restoring peace. (Krivoshein and Cole n.d., 3)

Angry members of the antichurch group convinced the fire marshal to close the Orthodox church in 1925 because of its poor physical condition. This event, coupled with the forced departure of the now pro-Bolshevik priest, practically shut down Orthodox services in Portland during these turbulent years.

After the closure of Portland's original Orthodox chapel, an active group of Russians organized a fund-raising campaign to purchase a new church building. Purchasing a former German Protestant church building in the Albina district of northeast Portland, the official Saint Nicholas Russian Orthodox Church of Portland, an active constituent of the Orthodox church of North America, was opened in 1927.

The 1920s also brought many changes in Russian life in San Francisco. The cosmopolitan city, with its well-established Russian neighborhoods and port of entry for most transpacific émigrés, initially attracted large numbers of post-Revolution Russians. By 1923, the number of Russians there had increased to between eight and ten thousand. By 1928, the number had reached at least fifteen thousand (Tripp 1980, 93). The confusing politics brought on by the Revolution coupled with the arrival of thousands of new émigrés from diverse places in the eastern Pacific Rim brought many changes to San Francisco's Russian community.

The divisions that plagued Orthodox churches in Portland, Seattle, and other parts of the United States also affected Russian churches in San Francisco. Holy Trinity, the original Orthodox diocese, split off from the Moscow patriarchate in 1926, later holding services in an old Episcopal church on Fulton Street and naming it Holy Virgin Cathedral (Tripp 1980, 105). This church, later rebuilt on Geary Boulevard, has remained a part of the Russian Church outside Russia (formerly known as the Russian Church Abroad). Continuing problems with leadership in the church resulted in a visit by an archbishop from Moscow in the mid-1930s to establish St. Nicholas Cathedral on Divisadero Street. The numerous divisions contained in the confusing story of this one church typify the chaos within the Russian Orthodox church, brought on by the political differences of Russian immigrants arriving in North America during this wave (map 18).

In California's capital city, meanwhile, a less divisive Russian Orthodox congregation was developing. The 1920s brought a substantial expansion of the fledging Russian neighborhood in West Sacramento's

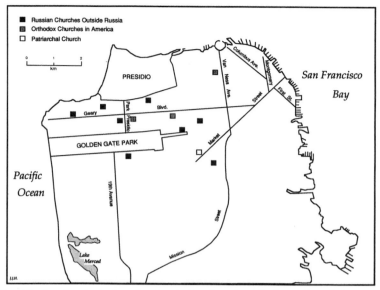

Map 18. Russian Orthodox churches in San Francisco. Redrawn from Tripp 1980.

suburb of Bryte, where earlier Baptist and Orthodox émigrés had first settled along their beloved Sacramento River. New immigrants built modest houses on recently drained land in this Central Valley community. After the settlement wave of these post-Revolution Russians, a church and several commercial establishments were constructed in the heart of the neighborhood. By the early 1940s, Bryte had a Russian-owned gas station, two grocery stores, a "speakeasy," and a Russian Orthodox church (map 19).

The Orthodox church is the older of the community's two churches. It is a small wooden structure, topped with two domes with Russian crosses on top. Cypress trees stand at the fenced entrance to the church and social hall. Orthodox Russians in Bryte had to attend services in downtown Sacramento at the Greek Orthodox church in their earliest years of settlement in the area, or they traveled the ninety miles to Holy Trinity Cathedral in San Francisco (Kondratieff 1976, 1). Building their own church in Bryte was a significant step in ethnic self-identification with the growing Russian neighborhood in the 1920s.

Orthodox services were first held in a small Russian food store, but in 1925, Russians in Bryte secured permission from Archbishop Alexis in San Francisco to organize their own parish. A Russian student drew the architectural plans for the church in his high school drafting class,

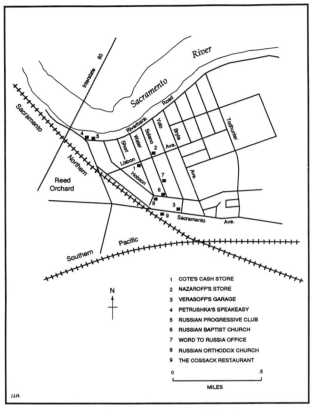

Map 19. Russian cultural landscape in West Sacramento (historic and present-day)

and women did most of the actual construction of the church building (Larkey and Walters 1987, 81). Their husbands contributed labor on their days off from work at the Southern Pacific Railroad yards in nearby Sacramento. Chandeliers, candle holders, crowns for wedding services, and a small ceremonial tomb were constructed in the railroad machine shops for use in the chapel. According to one participant in the work crew: "The first church bell was donated by the Southern Pacific administration from an obsolete locomotive; scrap metal was salvaged from old steel pipes and straps were used for chandelier, crowns, or candle stands" (Kondratieff 1976, 2).

The Saint Myrrhbearing Women Russian Orthodox Church, now known as the Holy Myrrhbearers American Orthodox Church, was officially consecrated in 1927 after several years of labor by members of the small parish. Mapping of the residences of today's eighty-five members of the church reveals that 75 percent of them reside in neighborhoods near the church in West Sacramento. The remaining members, who live in other parts of the sprawling Sacramento urban area, testify to the continued importance of the old original church as a symbolic institution of Russian identity.

Other Orthodox parishes were formed in northern California as a result of this second migration wave. A new parish of Orthodox believers was formed in Santa Rosa, California, in 1936, and a monastic center was built by San Francisco Russians in Calistoga in 1942 (Tarasar 1975, 216). The small town of Calistoga, located in the heart of the California wine country, has since become a gathering place for Orthodox retirees from the San Francisco Bay area.

Russian settlement in the United States and Canada slowed in the 1930s and early 1940s as restrictions in the Soviet Union and in North America limited the possibility of resettlement. In the USSR, Stalin's repressive policies effectively curtailed out-migration for several decades. In the United States, restrictive immigration laws were passed in 1924 and became effective in 1929. The National Origins Act established the annual immigration quota at 150,000, with total number per country dependent on percentages of populations already living in the United States. Since figures used in these percentage calculations were based on the 1920 census, and large numbers of Russians had settled in this country after 1922, the total number of people permitted entry from the Soviet Union was minimized. Between 1930 and 1944, the United States Immigration and Naturalization Service recorded only 14,016 Russian immigrants from the Soviet Union (Eubank 1973, 73). Mass migration of Russians, both individually and as part of religious groups, would not occur until changes in the refugee laws enacted after World War II made their entry possible. A detailed discussion of American immigration law is presented in chapter 5.

The Third Wave: 1945–1987

A variety of Russian religious groups arrived on the North American Pacific Rim after World War II. Especially significant in this era were the thousands of Russian Orthodox, Old Believer, Baptist, and Pentecostal immigrants who had fled Russia during its civil war years. Settling primarily in Harbin and the Sinkiang province, these White Russians had been forced out of China in the late 1940s because of the emerging dominance of the new Communist government.

The dramatic story of the numerous migrations of Russian Old Believers from China is discussed later in this chapter. Several years before the Old Believer migration began, during the Chinese civil war from 1946 to 1949, tens of thousands of the other Russians who had been living in China were also forced to leave the country. As White Russians, they had no other option but to emigrate somewhere other than China or the Soviet Union (G. Tokmakoff interview, Sacramento, 5 February 1983). Many escaped to China's coastal cities, seeking exit visas for emigration to other countries. They went in all directions—to Western Europe, South America, Australia, the United States, and Canada. Some ended up in the cities of the North American Pacific Rim, relocating most often in well-established Russian neighborhoods in Los Angeles, San Francisco, Sacramento, Portland, Seattle, and Vancouver, thereby renewing ethnic and religious identity in these now stable enclaves.

But their migration to North America was not without its complications. A month prior to the Communist takeover of Shanghai in May 1949, close to fifteen thousand Russians were transported to Tubabao, a former military base in the Philippines, by the International Refugee Association (M. Lokteff interview, West Sacramento, 16 September 1984).

Many Russians now living in California clearly remember the experience of leaving China. A member of one family who settled in California during these years vividly recalls:

We left our village in China in 1948 to escape the Communists once again. We traveled towards coastal Shanghai in a wagon train, and I remember how frightened we kids all were because the Chinese could have killed us at any time. It took a whole year to get to Shanghai, and when we got there, we found out that the Americans no longer were going to let us into their country. After a lot of waiting, we were taken to the island of Samar in a big boat. It was a very Russian place after we were there for about a year. We had Russian churches and schools and little grass houses to live in. Finally, many of our group became stir crazy waiting there so long, and they left to go to South America or Australia. My family stayed until 1950, when we were finally able to come to America. (M. Lokteff interview, West Sacramento, 10 March 1978).

Collective memories of this Russian migration from China to the Philippines to California reveal that the camp in Tubabao was a very Russian place. Russian churches, schools, medical clinics, and tent "neighborhoods" were constructed during the early months of the refugees' residence in the Philippines.

Leaving the camp on Samar would prove difficult. Due to the restrictive United States immigration laws, Russians could not qualify as immigrants for admission into the United States. Senator William Fife Knowland of Oakland, California, was asked by the refugee organizations to intervene on their behalf in order to allow Russian entry into this country. After visiting Tubabao, Knowland sponsored a bill in Congress that expanded the United States refugee quota to include Russians. This was accomplished amid massive anti-Communist hysteria in this country during the early McCarthy years. Because of these changes in American immigration restrictions, Russians came to this country in large numbers in 1950 and 1951. Conditions for entry were much more difficult than they had been in earlier migrations. Each Russian family needed a documented and signed affidavit from an American citizen assuring that they would be met on arrival, lodged, and assisted with employment for at least one year (Tripp 1980, 109–10). Members of church congregations were particularly sought as sponsors as was the Tolstoy Foundation in New York and other charitable organizations.

New Russian churches were built in many cities of the Pacific Rim as a direct result of this wave of settlement. Russian Baptist churches were organized in San Diego, Santa Ana, Los Angeles, Fresno, San Francisco, Sacramento, and Seattle. Pentecostal groups were formed in California in Montebello, Alhambra, Hesperia, San Francisco, San Mateo, and Sacramento. They were also built in Hubbard and Portland, Oregon; Seattle and Bellevue, Washington; and Vancouver and Vernon, British Columbia (map 20). These Russian Protestant congregations became magnets for glasnost-era settlement nodes in the early 1990s.

Post–World War II Russian migration also brought new vitality to Orthodox parishes on the west coast of the United States and Canada. Two nuns from China built a small chapel in Calistoga in 1949, and two years later, an Orthodox retreat was founded near San Rafael at scenic Point Reyes National Seashore, as a monument to all who had died in the Second World War. Numerous other new parishes were established in California, with new churches built in Walnut Creek, Menlo Park, San Anselmo, San Francisco, Sacramento, Los Angeles, Oxnard, Pasadena, and San Diego (Tarasar 1975, 217, 252).

Energy from this renewed era of construction and dedication also affected the growth of Orthodoxy in Alaska. The rebuilding of St. Michael's Cathedral in Sitka, the organization of a new and active parish in Anchorage, and the canonization of Father Herman of Alaska as the first saint of the Orthodox church in America in 1970, marked the beginning of a new era of expansion of Russian Orthodoxy in Alaska that continues today.

Orthodox, Baptist, and Pentecostal Russians were not the only religious groups who benefited from changes in the quota system. Molokans who had refused to leave Russia during the first migration wave into California finally had their second chance. Escaping to Turkey, Syria,

Map 20. Russian Baptist and Pentecostal congregations on the North American Pacific Rim

and Iran during forced Soviet agricultural collectivization in the 1930s, they made contact with relatives in the United States in 1946 after a Russian Baptist immigrant arrived in Los Angeles the year before and contacted a Molokan family to give them the address of their relatives in Iran (Berokoff 1969, 39). Only then did California Molokans discover that this group had been trying desperately to emigrate to the United States since the 1930s. Molokans in Los Angeles and San Francisco became sponsors for these Molokans for admission into the country. As with the earlier settlement, the majority were Pryguny, and so they established residency in East Los Angeles. Postoiannye chose San Francisco, revitalizing the somewhat stagnant ethnic community there and energizing their church. About two hundred Molokans who settled initially in San Francisco in 1949 moved to the agricultural towns of Wheatland and Sheridan, northeast of Sacramento, for permanent settlement several years later. These Russians are now successfully involved in raising wheat and rice and have built a small church and cemetery in Sheridan. These "Persian" Molokans have added vigor and growth to Molokan life in California's heartland.

OLD BELIEVERS

As discussed in chapter 2, Old Believers separated from the Eastern Orthodox church during the Great Schism of 1666, insisting on remaining faithful to the original teachings of the church. Because they refused to follow the seventeenth-century reforms of Patriarch Nikon and Czar Alexis, the Old Believers were driven out of their Russian homeland. Tens of thousands migrated east into remote Siberian villages. Others moved west, resettling in Romania, Bulgaria, Poland, Turkey, and Iran, hoping to maintain their faith in a more tolerant place.

After the Russian Revolution, rural villages were collectivized, and farming was controlled by the state. To escape socialist control of their land and lives, thousands of Old Believers migrated across the Sino-Soviet border. Groups living in Siberia and the Far East escaped into mountains near Harbin. Those in the Asian region of Altai fled across the border into the Tien Shan Mountains in the Sinkiang province. Small groups settled wherever they could find land to farm.

By the end of World War II, Soviet forces had moved into the border lands of China, and many Old Believers were forced into trucks and driven back across the border into the Soviet Union. In 1949, the Communist takeover in China resulted in the collectivization of thousands of Old Believers into villages once again. Their plight drew the attention of the World Council of Churches, which secured visas and funds to help them emigrate.

Old Believers from Sinkiang and Harbin came together in Hong Kong and prepared to resettle in Australia, New Zealand, Brazil, Argentina, and Uruguay. The majority went to Brazil and resettled on land donated by the Brazilian government. As one elderly member of the group recalls: "These were very hard years and it was very hot in Brazil. We could not grow potatoes or beets, and so we had no borscht. So what is life without borscht?" (anonymous Nikolaevsk interview, 1990).

In addition to problems with traditional agriculture, the newcomers could not supplement their farm income with handicrafts because of local economic restrictions. Fears of the spread of communism from nearby Chile also worried them. With the sponsorship of Molokans and others in the United States and the financial assistance of the Tolstoy Foundation, most of the Brazilian Old Believers migrated to the United States in 1964.[4]

Old Believers from Brazil settled in a region of rich farmland in the Willamette Valley of Oregon in and near the town of Woodburn. This religious group had first heard of "beautiful, green Voodburn" from Russian Molokans who greeted their ship, passing through the Los Angeles harbor on the way to Brazil from Hong Kong. The Old Believers were told about other Russian Molokans who had settled in Oregon in the Marion County area (Hall 1969, 5). Earlier Molokan residents of Woodburn, in fact, sponsored Old Believer families in the 1960s, encouraging Russian chain migration to Oregon. These connections established important ethnic linkages and added vitality to the well-established Russian cultural landscape in the Willamette Valley.

At the same time, another group of Old Believers who had been living in Turkey for many generations also emigrated to the United States. Settling first in New Jersey, this community of sixty households resettled in Oregon's fertile Willamette Valley near the town of Gervais in 1965. Map 21 shows the complicated migration routes taken by Old Believers after they left Russia.

At first, the three distinct Old Believer groups from Manchuria (Harbintsy), Sinkiang (Sinzyantsy), and Turkey (Turchane) lived separate lives in Oregon, identifiable to outsiders by their distinctive dress and customs. Their religious beliefs, however, were basically the same. During the past two and half decades, the three groups have begun to come together through marriage and community contact.

The Willamette Valley region now has over five thousand Old Believers with six different congregations (*sobors*). Churches are mostly new buildings, but services were held originally in converted chicken houses and migrant workers quarters (Smithson 1976, 36; fig. 10). Some Russian houses are distinguishable by the large number of sunflowers growing around them and by the bright-colored paint inside. One Molokan family in Woodburn who sponsored the first Old Believer family in the area recalls the custom of painting with bright colors:

It was so irritating really. When they first arrived here, we rented them the house next door to us. I painted and cleaned everything before they came from Brazil. The first thing they did was to paint all my nice white walls in bright colors. Of course, their religion demands that they make everything pure and clean after other people have lived in a house, I understand that. (V. Kostiakin interview, Woodburn, Oregon, 9 March 1991)

Although Russian families live among other residents of the area on small farms and in quiet neighborhoods, the older generation continues to keep the old traditions and live culturally and religiously apart from the community. Daily contact with American children at school and in the community worried Old Believer parents soon after their resettlement in this quasi-rural part of western Oregon. These fears and the belief that complete avoidance of mainstream culture was the only way for their religion to survive, caused five Harbintsy families to leave Oregon for Canada and Alaska in 1968. They settled along the Plat River in northern Alberta and on the tip of the Kenai Peninsula in Alaska. Today, at least ninety families live in Alaskan settlements, with over fifteen hundred people living in seven small villages. Some live amid the thick spruce forests, others in fertile agricultural valleys, and some on windswept peninsulas, bluffs, and remote islands (map 22).

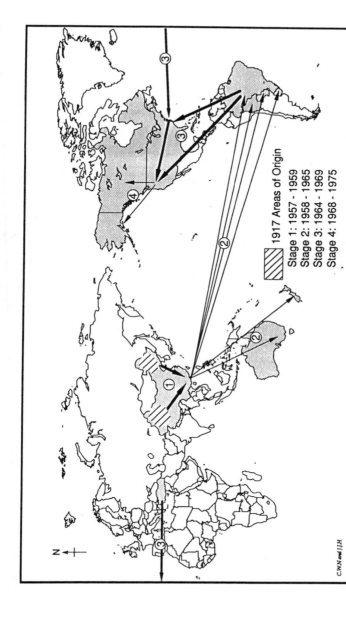

1917 Areas of Origin

Stage 1: 1957 - 1959
Stage 2: 1958 - 1965
Stage 3: 1964 - 1969
Stage 4: 1968 - 1975

Map 21. Mid-twentieth-century Old Believer migration routes to the North American Pacific Rim

Figure 10. This typical Old Believer church in Woodburn, Oregon, has adapted traditional Orthodox church architecture. Photo by author.

A loan from the Tolstoy Foundation helped Old Believers purchase 640 acres of government land on the Kenai Peninsula. Their original village, Nikolaevsk, named for the important Orthodox saint St. Nicholas, grew and prospered for fifteen years as more families moved north from Oregon. Homes, roads, fences, and a state-funded school were built in the cleared spruce forest. Early settlers worked in nearby Homer fish canneries, at the marina at Kachemak Bay, and on small construction crews. Today, commercial fishing is the dominant economic activity, with at least 90 percent of Alaskan Old Believer men earning their living from fishing (Gay 1988, 25). Having learned the woodworking industry in Oregon, most Old Believers build and maintain their own boats, naming them *Amur, Volga, Zion, Ural,* and *Terminator* (fig. 11). Most are drift gill-netters in Cook Inlet, Bristol Bay, or Prince William Sound, although some fish for halibut in the Gulf of Alaska.

Old Believers prefer independent work with their own people. Fishing is thus especially appealing to them, since it not only is lucrative but also allows them the freedom not to work on holy days. Because religion is a part of everything they do, Old Believer workers and school children are absent from work and school on specified holy days. Old Believer's

Map 22. Old Believer settlements in Alaska

use the old Julian calendar, which is thirteen days behind the Gregorian calendar generally used in North America.

Religion is the binding force that holds together all Old Believer groups. At baptism, children are given a colorful, handwoven belt to be worn all their lives, signifying their tie to Christ. Women are required to wear scarves on their heads in public, and men may not shave. Outsiders are considered unclean and are not allowed to eat in the same room or from the same dishes as members of the religious community. All food and drink consumed must be prepared at home. These beliefs and customs are shared by all three groups of Old Believers regardless of their place of origin, although, as will be discussed in chapter 5, these strict requirements of the faith are beginning to break down among the younger generation.

Old Believers originally from Harbin, Sinkiang, and Turkey live together in Nikolaevsk. Many of the younger generation were born in Nikolaevsk or in Oregon. One teenager described his mobile family: "I was born in Alaska, but my parents were born in China, and they both lived in Brazil when they were young. They met and fell in love in Woodburn and moved to Alaska in the 1970s" (I. Kuzmin interview, Kodiak, Alaska, 11 July 1990).

According to the principal of Nikolaevsk school, children from the

Figure 11. The harbor at Ninilchik, Alaska, is filled with Russian Old Believer fishing boats with names like *Volga, Meteor,* and *Interceptor.* Photo by D. G. Holtgrieve.

various groups mix well in school activities, although they remain conscious of their family's place of origin:

Sometimes I even get the kids' names mixed up because, even though most of them were born in Oregon or Alaska, they still call each other names according to their family's geographic connections and place of origin . . . kids from Brazil are called "monkeys," kids from Harbin are called "bears," those whose families came from Sinkiang are "fish", and the ones coming from Turkey "turkeys"! (B. Moore interview, Homer, Alaska, 6 July 1990)

But life has not been this peaceful among some of the adults of Nikolaevsk. Due to a religious schism in 1982, there are now four settlements growing nearby: Dolina, Rozdolna, Vozkrecenka, and Kachemak Celo. Today, there are more Russian Old Believers living in these villages at the head of Kachemak Bay than in their original settlement at Nikolaevsk (*Anchorage Daily News,* 19 July 1990, A12). Old Believers also live in a small village in the Matanuska Valley north of Anchorage as well as on remote Raspberry Island near Kodiak.

The division in Old Believer unity originated with the issue of priests and general church leadership. The division actually began many centuries ago in Russia. After the Great Schism of 1666, no monasteries existed to train priests, so one group of Old Believers, the Bezpopovtsy, have been practicing their religion with lay leaders for several centuries. In the late 1970s, however, several of the Russians in Nikolaevsk decided to send one of their young men to an Old Believer monastery in Romania. Upon his return to the village, a difference of opinion developed among residents of the community about his role in the church. Some wanted to be baptized by the priest and follow his teachings, while others rejected the whole concept of priests. In 1982, opinions became so extreme that violence in the community brought in Alaskan state troopers to calm the situation. A local judge closed the Old Believer church until a resolution could be found. A new church was built across the street from the original church for the dissenting group. One year later, a fire destroyed the old church. The two groups blamed each other for the disaster, and many began to move away. Today, after fires, threats, and the rebuilding of the original church, village residents seemed to have reached a truce. But many Russians from Nikolaevsk have since moved to other villages and formed their own congregations. According to an eighteen-year-old girl from Nikolaevsk, "It is just a terrible mess. My husband's family goes to one church and my family goes to the other. Because I am married to him, it is a real problem for me and my children" (anonymous Nikolaevsk interview, 1990).

Russians who have relocated to villages beyond the original Alaskan settlement at Nikolaevsk have also been drawn away by nonreligious reasons. Many have moved up Kachemak Bay and onto Raspberry Island to further isolate themselves from the outside world, since the majority of the more recent Old Believer settlement nodes are accessible only by boat, horseback, or all-terrain vehicles. They believe Nikolaevsk has become too large and too susceptible to American ways. According to a teacher at Nikolaevsk school, "Our Old Believer kids don't want to go back to the old ways. When one of their thirteen-year-old female classmates was planning to get married, they were very upset. 'Oh, please, don't let us all go back to the old way ever again,' they pleaded in my office one day" (P. Chitty interview, Homer, Alaska, July 1990).

A smaller group of Old Believers from Oregon settled near Edmonton, Alberta, in 1973. This community was formed by Harbintsy and has grown slowly over the last two decades (Smithson 1976, 279). Old Believers in Alberta grow wheat and cold-climate vegetables and are employed by lumber companies. Most live on individual farms and see each other only at religious services.

The widely scattered Old Believer settlements in North America, in a sense, form one North American religious "community." Dispersed Russian residents continue to communicate with each other through kin and friendship networks. According to anthropologist Richard Morris,

There is continual travel back and forth in both directions. The smaller settlements have become additional, albeit distant, villages, each with a different resource base. Continual contact and exchange has many mutual advantages. Alaskan kin bring down salmon and other fish and take back berries, fruit, and preserves. Oregon families travel to Alaska in the fishing season to help relatives with the catch. Alaskans and Canadians come to Oregon in the winter to work in the woods. The young people visiting back and forth are consciously on the lookout for eligible marriage partners. (1981, 53)

Conclusion

After the sale of Alaska to the United States in 1867, Russian religious migration and settlement on the North American Pacific Rim found foci in both rural and urban areas in the region. Early Orthodox Russians settled in four major nodes in the region—San Francisco, Los Angeles, Seattle, and Vancouver—laying an ethnic foundation for the later inmigration of other Russian religious groups.

These four core areas became irresistible magnets for thousands of Russian émigrés in the early part of the twentieth century. As political, economic, and religious conditions in Russia deteriorated, tens of thousands of new immigrants came to the west coast of North America, via European and Pacific Rim routes. Many were members of persecuted religious groups who were seeking freedom of religion and spatial isolation. Orthodox Russians surged into West Coast cities immediately after the Revolution, arriving individually or in small family groups. Orthodox church memberships increased substantially in the 1920s as new parishes were formed and new religious buildings were constructed in well-established Russian neighborhoods. After the Russian Revolution ended in 1922, politically inspired schisms within the Orthodox church divided church memberships. Numerous Orthodox churches were built to accommodate these new splinter groups. The vast majority of these Orthodox Russians remained urban residents, with some spillover to smaller cities. Secondary migration streams subsequently stretched out from San Francisco to West Sacramento, from Seattle to Portland, and later from Vancouver to Vernon, British Columbia.

The first large group of Russian sectarians to arrive, the Doukhobors, avoided urban nodes altogether, seeking isolation in the vast prairie lands of western Canada. Soon after their settlement in Alberta, they relocated in eastern British Columbia, where they built distinguishable and distinctive villages that reflected their religious beliefs about common landownership.

In contrast, sectarian Molokans, arriving a decade later, congregated in East Los Angeles, drawn there by climatic amenities and employment opportunities. They also settled on Potrero Hill in San Francisco. Many of the Molokans, unaccustomed to multicultural urban life, preferred the periphery and yearned to escape to a more rural environment. Numerous Molokan families subsequently resettled in isolated, rural nodes in other parts of the American West and northwestern Mexico. Los Angeles and San Francisco, however, have remained the spiritual and cultural hearths of their life in North America to the present day.

Russian Baptists also came to San Francisco in the first decade of the twentieth century, settling among the Molokans in their Potrero Hill neighborhood and building their church several blocks from the earlier Molokan church. Baptists soon after resettled in rural Sonoma County and in an emerging Russian node in West Sacramento. Their numbers increased significantly in the early 1950s, as Russians from China emigrated to western North America by the thousands. This decade witnessed large increases in both Russian Baptist and Orthodox populations and churches in Vancouver, Seattle, San Francisco, Sacramento, Fresno, Los Angeles, and San Diego.

Ignoring urban areas by choice, Russian Old Believers arrived in the region in the 1960s, searching for their preferred social and spatial isolation to preserve their religious beliefs and customs. Settling in the fertile Willamette Valley of Oregon, Old Believers at first felt they had made a wise choice. Only a few years after their arrival in North America, however, a small group relocated in even more remote places in Alaska and Canada, hoping for more isolation to protect their children from the influences of American culture.

FIVE

God and Glasnost

 Yuri

He seemed almost relieved to talk about all that had happened to him. Yuri and his wife Regina and two-year-old daughter Abigail were one of the first Russian Pentecostal families to arrive in San Francisco from the Soviet Union during the glasnost era. They came to California in the summer of 1989, full of enthusiasm for this "great country of America" (Y. Menekh interview, San Francisco, 19 November 1989). But when questioned about religious freedom in the United States, Yuri was quick to point out that, in many ways, it had been easier for him to be a believer in the USSR than in California. Life here depended on making so many decisions. Among so many choices, what if he made the wrong one? In the Soviet Union, it seemed all the important decisions had been made for him.

Memories of his former life were always with him. Economic conditions had been terrible when they left. Food was rationed, good health care almost nonexistent, and employment difficult. As a university graduate, Yuri had worked for the Academy of Sciences as a physicist, but career advancement was impossible for him because of his religious beliefs. Even his parents had turned against him because of his "spiritual tendencies." In fact, they were certain he had gone mad.

This madness began when he was eighteen years old after a friend's mother loaned him her Bible. Yuri had been raised in a conventional Soviet atheist family and had never heard of God. He began to read and study the old, worn book carefully. Yuri's usually somber eyes light up as he recalls his sudden and dramatic conversion to Pentecostal Christianity. Somehow, participating in the Komsomol had never made him feel this secure.

Two months later Yuri was speaking in tongues for the first time. "It was a miracle. But my parents thought I had gone crazy for sure." Hearing their son speaking in an unknown language and seeing him sing and dance wildly in spiritual ecstasies, Yuri's father had him committed to a mental hospital. After his release, his parents enlisted him in the Soviet army, hoping time away from home would cure him permanently of this unacceptable "social disease."

He remembers those years in the military as a time of great struggle and great sacrifices in order to maintain his religious beliefs. Yuri spent much of his time composing Christian songs and evangelizing among the other soldiers. He also began to think about finding some way to leave his country.

Now Yuri is living in San Francisco. The decision to emigrate was a difficult one, but when the KGB came to his house in Vilnius and suggested he leave, he knew it was time to go. Encouraged by his church friends and financially supported by the Tolstoy Foundation in New York, Yuri, Regina, and Abigail resettled in Salt Lake City. Finding life in the desert unbearable after their former lives in a cooler, greener place, the trio boarded a Greyhound bus and headed west. Now they are living in a small flat in a multicultural neighborhood of San Francisco. Many new decisions lie ahead.

Life is not easier now, but Yuri faces different problems each day than the ones he faced at home. Religious freedom is no longer an issue, but employment, English-language skills, and fears for the safety of his wife and daughter haunt him. His involvement in one of the city's two Russian Pentecostal churches has become the focus of his whole existence. Several of the songs Yuri composed during his years in the Soviet army have recently been recorded by an American evangelical record company. His music, his church, and his family are Yuri's only lifelines in a new and often frightening city.

Yuri's story, like the stories of other Russians in this book, is true. His experiences in the former Soviet Union and in California represent the experiences of thousands of other recent Soviet immigrants in the western United States and Canada. Their decision to leave the USSR was difficult. Even though economic, political, and social conditions were miserable, it was difficult to imagine life in any other system. Despite these challenges, more than one million people have emigrated from the Soviet Union since 1948.

Push Factors

The reasons for this mass exodus are complex. Numerous push factors were behind Yuri's decision and the decisions of other Russian Christians to leave home permanently. Economic conditions deteriorated rapidly in the 1980s, bringing the economy to a virtual standstill in the early 1990s. One of the most challenging problems of this worsening economic situation has been maintaining an adequate food supply. For years, purchasing food and other necessary consumer goods has been a daily struggle. Waiting in long lines, finding food store shelves empty, spending hours every day searching for affordable bread, tea, cucumbers, and even beets had been exhausting (fig. 12).

Because of the shortages, ration coupons were issued by the government once a month, limiting food purchases to below the most basic levels. Meat was particularly difficult to find. And it was not just the difficulty of finding enough, it was the poor quality of food. Only the "good, dark Russian bread" remained abundant during the years of massive national shortages.

Political restructuring has not, to date, solved these severe economic problems. After the formation of the Commonwealth of Independent

Figure 12. Empty shelves in a food market in Moscow in 1991 leave this shopper frustrated and afraid. Photo by author.

States in early 1992, food shortages continued. And nutritional deficiencies have not been the only problem. Most other consumer products have also been in constant short supply. It has not been unusual, for example, to wait six or seven years for a telephone to be installed in an apartment, or to wait ten years for the apartment itself. Purchasing other consumer goods, such as automobiles, clothing, shoes, and more frivolous things like cosmetics, has been almost impossible.

The struggle for economic survival was bad enough, but the almost constant persecution for their religious beliefs had caused the greatest grief for immigrants now in North America. Before the glasnost era, people known to be Christians were persecuted at every level. School children were taken aside by their teachers and scolded for their "stupid, meaningless beliefs." Later, most were barred from college and university admission. Limited to secondary school educations, many became carpenters, plumbers, or other skilled, blue-collar laborers. A few attended trade schools; however, job advancement was impossible. One Pentecostal immigrant now living in California remembers being told at his graduation from four years of study in a trade school in Russia to "take his pick . . . a Bible or a diploma" (*Sacramento Bee,* 23 Nov. 1989, A1). According to another recent immigrant, "Once our church building was confiscated. If we complained too loudly, they could take our children away and put them in an orphanage. There was constant pressure to denounce our religion" (*Sacramento Bee,* 23 Nov. 1989, A11).

So the most overwhelming problems had not been the limitation of material possessions. Always, it was fear of greater persecution that haunted these new North American residents most. Obsessive thoughts about their family's safety and their own well-being filled them with anxiety. Throughout the day, fears of what had happened in the past and what lay ahead ran over and over in their minds. Even after conditions for religious believers began to improve in 1987, memories of their own or their parent's imprisonment and daily persecution because of their beliefs remained clear. As one recent immigrant in Everett, Washington, recalled: "What if the new system should fail? They had made promises before and nothing ever changed. No one in the government could be trusted. This Gorbachev is a Communist, of course, just like all the others. Why should we think that it will really be different this time?" (anonymous interview, Everett, 15 November 1990).

National policy changes had not altered local government attitudes toward these non-Communists. A recent Russian migrant to the Sacramento area, Valerie Razumov, recalls with horror her experiences as recently as 1989. Local police in her village would regularly break up prayer meetings and Sunday schools and conduct house-to-house searches on Sunday mornings. According to Valerie, "They would check through the clothing, bedding. If there was anything religious—hymns, Bibles, literature—they would confiscate it. They would tear everything apart" (*Sacramento Bee,* 27 September 1990, A20).

Decades of oppression had created a large group of people afraid to trust anyone except one another. The bonds of their faith grew stronger, both faith in God and trust in other believers. Eventually, church friends and family became their only social network. Over the years, these networks tightened with each new round of persecution. This distrust of everything Soviet was expressed by another recent immigrant: "I just did not want to play their games anymore. Always lies . . . You pretend you trust someone and they pretend they trust you. Both of you know what you are really thinking" (Samuel L. interview, Davis, California, 4 June 1991).

These fears grew out of decades of often violent and painful persecution. Ivan Poonka, a Baptist minister from the Siberian village of Prokopyevsk now living in Sacramento, emotionally recalled his imprisonment for Christian beliefs during the Stalin era. After a sharp blow to the genitals, prison guards warned him, "Here we will teach you not to propagandize against our government." Reverend Poonka was then stripped of all clothing and locked in a dark room with a concrete floor covered with icy water. Sixteen months later, he was brought to trial and sentenced to five years of hard labor. Working in a coal mine and living on one meal of watery soup a day, his weight dropped from 165 pounds to less than 80 pounds. Finally released in 1949, Poonka returned to his ministry, preaching first in Frunze, capital of Kirghiz, and then resettling in Sukhumi in Georgia. The Poonkas migrated to Sacramento in 1989 (*Sacramento Bee,* 27 Sept. 1990, A20).

The first formulation of a plan for Russian Christians to emigrate from the Soviet Union began after World War II, as Pentecostals in particular began to consider a mass exodus from their homeland. According to Ludmilla Alexeyeva, "They believed that the Lord's cup of wrath must some day spill over on that godless country and that before that happens, God will lead the Jews, the chosen people (whose emigration had already begun) and the righteous from the sinful land. But before God's will is fulfilled of itself, it is the duty of true Christians actively to seek to emigrate" (1987, 220).

Efforts intensified in the mid-1960s. A Pentecostal leader, Vasily Patrushev, submitted to another Pentecostal in Vladivostock a list of believers who wished to emigrate. The list eventually reached the Western world via a Japanese entrepreneur who was visiting Vladivostock. Both Pentecostal leaders soon thereafter served Soviet prison sentences, thereby discouraging any efforts to emigrate. Their efforts did, however, mark the beginning of active involvement of Russian Christians with the Moscow-based human rights movement in the 1970s. Early work by Pentecostals in Nakhodka in the Far East and Chernogorsk in the Krasnoyarsk region was boosted by similar efforts in the Krasnodar region. Problems with the KGB and the Soviet government in general continued, but when Jimmy Carter, a Baptist, was elected president of the United States in 1977, the Soviet emigration movement was encouraged to continue its efforts. Prayer hours and letter-writing campaigns to Washington, DC, were organized. According to Alexeyeva, "Pentecostals from the Rovno and Brest regions, from the Caucasus and the Rostov regions, from the Ukraine and from Estonia, from near Leningrad and from Chernogorsk, wrote to 'their' President Carter to ask him to request the Soviet government to allow them to emigrate to the United States and to intercede on their behalf with Breznev" (1987, 225).

By 1977, thirty-five hundred Pentecostals and Baptists had filed emigration papers. But the struggle for human rights continued, as persecution of believers in the Soviet Union intensified in the late 1970s and early 1980s. Eventually, over ten thousand Jews and Christians risked their lives by signing a petition requesting freedom to leave the country. One signature usually represented whole families. Although a few families did manage to emigrate to the United States, including the now famous Siberian Seven discussed in chapter 4, no large-scale exodus occurred until the late 1980s.

A decade after Carter's presidency and the first period of massive Pentecostal and Baptist emigration efforts, Mikhail Gorbachev rose to power in the USSR. Hope for a mass departure from the Soviet Union had grown extremely dim during these ten years. In 1987, as a part of his efforts for glasnost and perestroika, President Gorbachev met with President Ronald Reagan to discuss emigration and human rights issues. Following their meeting, Gorbachev made the startling announcement that residents of the USSR were free to leave. This announcement triggered the first large-scale emigration from the Soviet Union since the early years of the socialist revolution. Effects of this decision would have major ramifications in cities along the Pacific Rim of North America. It is interesting to note that Russians today do not give credit for their freedom to Gorbachev, but to Reagan. Distrusting Gorbachev, Russians credit Reagan's policies for ending the Cold War and making emigration possible. According to Vladimir Kebets, "We are grateful to everyone. From President Reagan, who started it all, to President Bush, who has continued it. Without them we would not be here" (*Sacramento Bee*, 23 Nov. 1989, A9).

Along with encouragement from the American government, Soviet emigration policy was also changing at home. As a part of the general process of political reform, the Supreme Soviet gave preliminary approval to a new law in 1989 that made emigration legal for all Soviet citizens. After the passage of this law, people wishing to leave the country found their processing greatly simplified and bureaucratic red tape lessened considerably (Heitman 1991a, 5).

Pull Factors

Accompanying these changes in Soviet emigration law in recent years have been parallel changes in American immigration policy. Although the United States has had a long and turbulent history of changing immigration law, a long-term concern for the plight of refugees suffering religious and political persecution has been reflected in policy. Due to our long-standing politically hostile relationship with the Soviet government, particular concern and support for émigrés from the USSR has been codified into immigration law in recent years.

North America has been viewed as a land of opportunity and of religious and political freedom ever since the first European immigrants settled this vast continent in the early 1600s. For centuries, the United States and Canada have welcomed people escaping persecution and injustices elsewhere. Since the great majority of recent Russian immigrants have come to the United States rather than to Canada, this section details United States immigration law that led up to the present conditions.

Preferences for migrants from certain parts of the world became law in 1882 with the passage of America's first immigration act, the Asian Exclusion Act, limiting entry of almost all Chinese immigrants. This decision was followed by the denial of permission to any Japanese laborer to migrate to the United States, in the Gentlemen's Agreement with Japan passed in 1907. The Immigration Act of 1917, with its confusing "literacy test" requiring all applicants over the age of sixteen to read a short passage in any language, was the first comprehensive law affecting people from all nations. This law did little to limit the total number of immigrants entering the country; in 1920, over eight hundred thousand people from other nations settled in the United States.

Not until the 1920s were laws passed by Congress limiting the number of non-Asian refugees permitted entry into the United States. The law controlling the number and selection of Soviet émigrés who were permitted to resettle permanently in the United States has its foundation in these earliest immigration laws. Since then, requirements of immigration law have been changed many times.

In 1924, quotas were established for each country of the world, based on the population of the United States as counted in the 1920 census. This meant that, the more members of a nationality living in the country at the time of the 1920 count, the more new people would be admitted from that country. This blatantly racist law limited immigrants from eastern and southern Europe and Asia, although the number of people admitted from Western Hemisphere countries was unrestricted. Of the 154,000 people permitted entry into the United States by the passage of this law, almost 66,000 were assigned to Great Britain, 26,000 to Germany, and 18,000 to Ireland, leaving only 44,000 for the rest of the world (*Oregon State Refugee Program* 1990, 15). The foundation for limiting national quotas established by this law was to dominate American immigration policy for four decades. Even the passage of the Displaced Persons Act in 1948, which permitted the admission of Eastern European victims of World War II, continued to use national quotas established in the 1920s as the basis for charging against future admission the total number of people permitted entry. In 1950, the Displaced Persons Act was changed to authorize financial support for the resettlement of refugees from the Second World War, although total numbers admitted from each country continued to be mortgaged against future admission ceilings.

Two years after the amendment of the Displaced Persons Act, the Immigration and Nationality Act was passed by Congress. Despite loud protests from President Truman, who attempted to veto this law because of its negative political implications, the bill was approved by a large majority in Congress. Restrictions on total numbers of immigrants from all but Western Hemisphere countries continued to be an important part of the "new" law, which still used national quotas based on the 1920 census. A product of the early years of the Cold War and the widespread concern for national security, the 1952 law denied admission, for the first time, to all Communists and Fascists.

In 1965, Congress repealed these quotas based on country of origin and replaced them with laws aimed at reuniting families and permitting entrance of immigrants with particular job skills. However, a different type of "regional favoritism" grew out of the revised law. Since that time, 85 percent of all new immigration has come from two areas—Latin America and Asia (*Congressional Quarterly* 1990, 48:2519).

The Immigration Act of 1975 established a preference system for immigrants granted permission to enter the United States. It gives this order of preference:

1. unmarried sons and daughters of United States citizens;
2. spouses and unmarried sons and daughters of permanent residents lawfully admitted to the United States;
3. members of the professions or persons of exceptional abilities in the sciences and arts;

4. married sons and daughters of United States citizens;
5. brothers and sisters of United States citizens and their families;
6. skilled and unskilled workers in short supply;
7. refugees

(*Oregon State Refugee Program* 1990, 22).

Decisions regarding the admission of the final category, refugees, have been severely tested since the passage of this law. The aftermath of the war in Southeast Asia brought more than four hundred thousand refugees from this devastated area into the United States between 1975 and 1980. It became evident that the restrictions of the 1975 law had to be addressed.

The Refugee Act of 1980 was passed to clarify policy for refugees from all over the world. Along with officially defining the term *refugee* for the first time, a ceiling was established of fifty thousand refugees admitted into the country from around the world. Confusing the requirement of the new act was the arrival in Florida of masses of illegal entrants from Cuba and Haiti in 1980. Thousands were transported there by boat. Refusing to consider these sudden arrivals as refugees, the federal government gave them a special classification, *entrant status,* which classified them for access to public social and employment programs.

In the uncertainty of these numerous changes in immigration policy, the decision to completely restructure the process was made at about the same time Gorbachev was permitting the emigration of tens of thousands of Soviet citizens in the late 1980s. President Bush signed the comprehensive revision of former policy, the Immigration Act of 1990, into law on 9 November 1990. This law significantly revised the seven-level preference system and established new categories for employment-based, family-sponsored, and diversity-based immigration. It also established an annual total of 700,000 entries for 1992 through 1994. After 1994, total legal entries will be reduced to 675,000 and will include only visas related to family sponsorship, employment, and the new diversity category.

The great majority of Russians admitted to the United States under this revised law will be a part of the family preference system. Most new immigrants admitted from the Soviet Union after 1992 will qualify for the second preference level of this four-level system. Some will undoubtedly also be admitted under the employment and diversity system. Visas granted under this category will be allocated according to the following preference levels:

1. unmarried adult sons and daughters of United States citizens;
2. spouses and minor children of permanent residents and unmarried sons and daughters of permanent residents;

3. married sons and daughters of United States citizens;
4. brothers and sisters of adult United States citizens (over the age of twenty-one)

(Bean 1989, 18).

Despite the restrictions of these numerous immigration laws, prior to 1987 it had long been the policy of the United States government to encourage human rights in the Soviet Union. Pressing Soviet leaders for changes in freedom of movement for potential emigrants and demanding Soviet religious freedom have been cornerstones of American attitudes and foreign policy at least since World War II. Gorbachev's decision to change emigration law was therefore first met with enthusiasm and relief by American refugee policymakers. But the United States and Canada have not been the emigrants' only destination. Between 1948 and 1990, Germany and Israel admitted more Soviets than did the United States (table 6). There was a major increase in the number of Jews emigrating to Israel, ethnic Germans migrating to Germany and ethnic Greeks returning to Greece (Heitman 1991a, 2). The vast majority of ethnic Russians who emigrated to the United States in the most recent wave of settlement were categorized by our government as refugees.

To be granted refugee status, a person must be escaping political, religious, or racial persecution by the government of their home country. Economic deprivation is not considered a justifiable basis for granting refugee status. The Refugee Act of 1980 brought the United States legal definition of refugees into conformity with international law. It also codified other refugee policy decisions that had first been agreed to under the 1967 United Nations Protocol on the Status of Refugees (Bean 1989, 19).

To qualify as a refugee, a person must be the victim of immediate persecution, that is, a serious threat to life or freedom. Discrimination may also be defined as being persecuted because of religious beliefs. Even though someone may not have suffered persecution to date, he or she may be admitted if there is reasonable fear of persecution in the future. Refugees must also establish that their persecution is due to their association with a particular group, and that they suffer harsher discrimination than the general population in their country.

The total number of people granted this status is determined by the president of the United States, and the number changes often. When Ronald Reagan was president, he repeatedly expanded the number of people admitted from the Soviet Union and Eastern Europe and lowered the numbers for Latin America. Refugee arrivals from Latin America, for example, peaked at 6,700 in 1980 and were as low as 173 in 1986

Table 6

Destinations of Soviet Emigrants by Nationality or Religion, 1948–90

	Jews			Germans[b]	Armenians			Greeks	Evan. & Pent.		Others
Years	Israel	U.S.	Other[a]	Germany[b]	U.S.	France	Other[c]	Greece	U.S.	Canada	U.S.
1948–89	191,900	170,800	28,300	266,400	63,800	12,000	1,500	10,000	14,000	200	200
1990	181,800	6,500	13,000[d]	148,000	6,500	—	300	14,300	4,100	100	2,600
Totals	373,700	177,300	41,300	414,400	70,300	12,000	1,800	24,300	18,100	300	2,800

Sources: Totals in Heitman 1991b, 7. Tallied from United States Department of State; Israeli Embassy, Washington, DC; German Ministry of Interior, Internationale Gesellschaft für Menschrechte, Frankfurt-am-Main; Hebrew Immigrant Aid Society; Armenian informants.

[a]Other places where Jews have resettled include Canada, Europe, Latin America, and Oceana.

[b]Figures for Germany include emigrants who settled in both the FRG and the GDR.

[c]Other places where Armenians resettled include the Middle East, Greece, and the Netherlands.

[d]This figure comprises 6,000 Jews who resettled in Germany and 7,000 who went to other countries—see note d above.

(Bean 1989, 95–96). The view that Soviet refugees are victims of political, religious, or racial persecution and that Latin American refugees are victims of economic persecution consistently favored Asian and Soviet and Eastern Europeans during and after the Reagan years. Since the late 1970s, Southeast Asia has been granted the largest number of spaces for refugees. Since then, at least half the refugees admitted each year originate in Southeast Asia (Siegel and Canter 1991, 10–12). President Bush increased total Soviet refugee admissions to fifty thousand a year beginning in 1989.

Every refugee applicant must have a sponsor living in this country before his or her paperwork can be approved by the Immigration and Naturalization Service. Although people may establish without a doubt that they are escaping persecution in their homeland, they cannot be granted asylum or refugee status if they have already been admitted to another country.

A second category of potential émigrés is *asylees*. People in this category do not need American sponsors for their resettlement, and they cannot qualify as an asylee until they have reached the United States. Spouses and children younger than twenty-one are granted Accompanying Relative Status, automatically qualifying as approved refugees or asylees. There is no annual quota for the total number of asylees, but they must also be the immediate victims of a fear of political, religious, or racial persecution. If an émigré is already living in the United States, he or she may also seek political asylum. Before arriving in this country, however, one must have fulfilled the requirement of continuous flight. In other words, a person must have come directly to the United States without stopping in another country en route. Trips from the Soviet Union to the United States by boat or air almost always meet this requirement, but émigrés who traveled by land (and who stopped in other countries on their way here) sometimes may find themselves denied asylum status by the Immigration and Naturalization Service. People seeking asylum are much more prone to economic hardships when they arrive, since they have no guarantee of support from an American sponsor.

Refugees must prove they can pay for their own transportation to the United States and have a sponsor to support them when they arrive. Sponsors may be individuals, church congregations, or refugee assistance organizations. Applicants for asylum do not need to prove their financial viability. Today's immigration policy has four major objectives:

1. the reunification of families of citizens and legal permanent residents;
2. the admission of workers, some as permanent residents and some for temporary stays;

3. the resettlement of those of the world's refugees who are of special interest to the United States for foreign or domestic policy reasons, or for humanitarian reasons because of their suffering and the desperation of their situation; and
4. the accommodation of temporary stays of a variety of people, from tourists to diplomats, whose movement across borders is part of the political, economic, and social practice of most contemporary societies

(Bean 1989, 25).

It is obvious that categories 1 and 3 are of the greatest significance for émigrés from the Soviet Union. The first encourages spouses and children of those already admitted to emigrate. The reunification of families, in fact, is one of the primary goals of American immigration policy. In the earliest years of glasnost-era Soviet immigration into the United States, most came under category 3. Since 1990, however, the majority of new arrivals have been family members of those already admitted. The law encourages a strong chain migration pattern to develop in North America, as family members join residents already in place.

The most recent change in immigration law, HR 4300, was being debated in Congress as this book went to press. Bruce A. Morrison of Connecticut, sponsor of the bill, is hoping the law will encourage more diversity of regional categories and admit more people with special talents. HR 4300 keeps a priority for relatives of people already living in the United States but increases the number of job-related visas available (*Congressional Quarterly* 1990, 48:2519). Currently, about five hundred thousand immigrants settle in the United States per year. The new bill, if approved, would increase the annual number to eight hundred thousand.

The Resettlement Process

After Gorbachev made his almost unbelievable announcement legalizing emigration from the Soviet Union, thousands of people began the scramble to secure exit visas from the Soviet government. The American embassy in Moscow was almost immediately in chaos. A system of departure had to be developed to handle the more than one million requests for emigration that came in by the end of 1990.

The first procedure involved transporting émigrés to American-run refugee camps outside Rome and Vienna. Soviet Jews and Christians were flown from Moscow to Vienna to Rome, where their paperwork by the United States Immigration and Naturalization Service was completed. In the early years of this process, many thousands of Christians left the Soviet Union on Israeli visas. This charade was first tried by several Pentecostal families in 1985 who obtained photographs of visas used by Soviet Jews for emigration to Israel. The Pentecostals applied to emigrate to Israel at the Dutch embassy in Moscow, which acted as a proxy for the Israeli government. These petitions were approved by not only Dutch but also Soviet and Israeli authorities, and the Pentecostals left the USSR as a part of the Jewish group (Heitman 1991b, 18–19). Upon reaching the camps, American Christian resettlement organizations changed the visas to allow entry into the United States. By 1989, over fourteen thousand Pentecostals had left the USSR via the Vienna-Rome pipeline under these conditions (Heitman 1991b, 19). Jewish applicants were unhappy with this procedure because the non-Jewish refugees used the majority of the allowed Israeli applications. One recent Jewish émigré recalls: "It was really a terrible problem for us. The other people took all the Israeli visas before our family could get them. So we had a very hard time getting out of the USSR. My mother and sister and I did manage to get visas, but my niece is still waiting there in Kiev. We were very, very angry with those people for doing that to us. They don't like Jews in the USSR, you know" (Samuel L. interview, Davis, California, 15 April 1991).

The weary migrants spent several weeks to several months in the resettlement camps. They were taught survival techniques for adjusting to life in America and strategies for getting along with American people. Sometimes the training was confusing. Nikolai Ivannik remembers being told that Americans are extremely punctual people. One lecturer said that American dinner guests expected food to be on the table the precise minute they arrived. Ivannik discovered after arriving in Sacramento that this information was highly overstated (*Sacramento Bee*, 5 July 1990, 6).

Sacramento émigré Vladimir Kebets also vividly remembers his international migration experience. The move for him and his family in 1989 was supported by World Relief and accomplished in a series of stages. After leaving almost everything they owned behind at their home in Sukhumi, Georgia, the large Kebets family traveled to Vienna, to Rome, and finally to the United States. Vladimir Kebets's memories of fear of the future and uncertainty and his experiences are typical of those who left during the earliest years of glasnost-era migration (*Sacramento Bee*, 23 Nov. 1989, A9).

Eventually, the overwhelming number of émigrés made maintaining the Rome and Vienna resettlement camps difficult and expensive. To ease the burden of paperwork and the expense of processing such a large number of people, the Washington Processing Center of the Immigration and Naturalization Service opened in Arlington, Virginia, in October

1989. At the same time, the American embassy in Moscow stopped handling émigré paperwork. This complicated job was taken on by the Soviet/Pan Am Travel Effort (SPATE), under contract to the International Organization for Migration. All medical exams and travel arrangements to the United States have since been handled by the SPATE office in Moscow. In addition, a direct line was established between Washington and SPATE to update refugee case information.

The Washington Processing Center has become a massive operation. Over thirteen hundred pieces of mail are sent out each week. In addition, more than four hundred phone calls are received each day, many from the Soviet Union. As of August 1990, the Washington Processing Center had received 299,000 applications and entered 43,000 cases (150,000 individuals) into their database (Carl Pihl, Lutheran Social Services memorandum, 6 August 1990). Between 1975 and 1990, a total of 221,069 Soviet refugees migrated to the United States, with at least 50,000 more predicted for 1991. Soviets in the nonrefugee category increased from a total of 19 people in 1985 to 4,147 in 1989.

This complicated emigration process does not always operate smoothly. The personal experiences behind these statistics tell a more complete story. One of the many challenges applicants face has been qualifying for refugee status. Under current immigration law, the United States admits only fifty thousand Soviet refugees per year. As discussed earlier, those with refugee status must have American sponsors and are eligible for welfare benefits upon their arrival here. They also receive government loans for reduced airfare expenses. However, quotas and frequent errors in paperwork have resulted in tens of thousands of applicants being turned down for refugee status. Several thousand of these nonrefugee applicants have managed to emigrate to the United States every year since 1988, as parolees and on tourist visas. Parolees have been denied refugee status. They must pay their own way and do not receive welfare benefits upon arrival in the United States. They are required to have sponsors who agree to support them for up to three years. Emigrés in this category often end up destitute because they do not officially belong either to the United States or to the Soviet Union (B. Robinson interview, Sacramento, October 1991).

Those who do qualify as refugees also face numerous problems. Despite efforts to make all paperwork bilingual, filling out the complicated forms is often an overwhelming experience. The time factor is also stressful. Several months after papers have been submitted to processing offices, all family members over the age of fourteen must travel to Moscow for their exit interview. They return home for a four- to six-month wait. If their case is approved, they must return to Moscow thirty days before departure to pick up their official departure papers. Since the former Soviet Union was the largest country on earth, the expense and energy required for long-distance travel often seem overwhelming. Along with this, responding to the dozens of official, often personal, questions during exit interviews can be exhausting. Boarding the flight for New York often feels almost anticlimactic.

A Russian woman still waiting for final clearance and her travel documents in the Russian town of Maloyaroslavets lamented: "It is all so difficult for us here. We do not know what to do when the mail does not come. Every day we wait for news about our departure. I wonder, when will we ever really get to America?" (anonymous interview, 1991).

Upon arrival in New York, Russians usually travel to the home of their sponsors. These sponsors are often members of evangelical churches in the United States and may be anywhere in the country. Sponsors agree to provide housing, furniture, and clothing; assist with refugee employment; and generally provide support to arriving families. Interviews with numerous recent refugees in California, Oregon, and Washington reveal that their sponsors have fulfilled these requirements at various levels.

Soon after their arrival, many make the decision to leave the sponsor's city or town and move on to a place they have selected for permanent settlement. Their choices occasionally depend on the perceived climatic and economic amenities of a particular place, but more often on information conveyed by tightly structured religious networks. The settlement pattern of recent Russian Baptist and Pentecostal immigrants, in fact, has been almost entirely dependent on religious affiliations. Letters, telephone calls, announcements at church services, and personal contacts at health clinics, schools, and stores have intensified refugee networking. Each of the major settlement nodes of recent Russian immigrants on the North American Pacific Rim is discussed below in the context of these religious connections.

American Space, Russian Place

SACRAMENTO

California's capital city has become the preferred resettlement site for the majority of Russian Christians during the glasnost era. Since the first new immigrants arrived in early 1988, over eight thousand more have settled in widely scattered neighborhoods in this Central Valley city. Several thousand more are expected by the end of 1993, as chain migration based on familial and religious connections intensifies. Although economic and climatic amenities are a major factor in the decision to migrate to central California, several other processes, primarily based on religious connections, are even more important in explaining the continued attraction of Russian Pentecostals and Baptists to the Sacramento area.

Of primary importance to their recent settlement in the Sacramento urban area have been local churches and national relief agencies. Both Russian and American churches and their congregations in Sacramento have acted as sponsors for Russian refugees and their families. Regional offices of two active Christian groups, World Relief and Lutheran Social Services, have also organized church sponsors and provide follow-up support services for new arrivals. These agencies not only supply financial support for Russian refugees but also assist them in the challenging resettlement process.

The second reason Russians are drawn to California's Central Valley in ever greater numbers is the continued viability of a well-established Russian neighborhood in West Sacramento. As discussed in chapter 4, this ethnic enclave has been a core area of both Russian Baptist and Orthodox settlement since the early years of the twentieth century. Its Russian Baptist church has been particularly active in organizing sponsors and services for recent refugees.

Another activity of the Russian Baptist church in West Sacramento is the publication of a Russian-language Christian newspaper. In production since 1966, *Our Days* is printed and mailed from a small office behind the church. Support for the publication is provided by the Pacific Coast Slavic Baptist Association, an organization of Russian Baptist churches. In addition to its wide distribution in the Soviet Union, *Our Days* is mailed to Australia, New Zealand, Germany, France, Belgium, England, Austria, Finland, Greece, Argentina, Brazil, Paraguay, Uruguay, Israel, and Korea.

Even more important than the newspaper have been the weekly broadcasts of shortwave radio messages into the Soviet Union by Word to Russia. These Russian-language broadcasts have reached thousands of Russians all over the USSR since 1972. Word to Russia's tiny office and recording studio in West Sacramento continues to record and broadcast taped Christian programs to the USSR. A small staff of musicians, ministers, and Russian children tape programs to rebroadcast from shortwave stations in Louisiana, Alaska, Ecuador, Monaco, Saipan, and Korea. In 1990, Word to Russia began broadcasting its first live radio program from a major radio station in Ukraine (M. Lokteff interview, West Sacramento, September 1990).

Numerous Russians who now live in Sacramento heard these broadcasts in their homeland and were drawn to California's capital city.

Others were told about these programs and about the Russian-American director of the effort, Mikhail Lokteff, in refugee camps in Rome and Vienna. According to one recent Russian Baptist immigrant now living in West Sacramento, "It was so exciting to finally be in this place. Sacramento is like the 'promised land' to us, you know. We all felt like we already knew Mikhail Lokteff and wanted to meet him and thank him for everything he has done for us during our difficult years in Russia" (V. Morgunov interview, West Sacramento, December 1990).

Russian Pentecostal radio programs from Sacramento also reached deep inside the former Soviet Union. Sacramento Assembly of God minister Paul Demetrus has had a large influence on the size of the city's evolving Russian community. His program, "The Voice of Truth," has reached Soviet listeners for the past thirty-six years. Supported by American missionary funding, Demetrus broadcast his messages first from Philadelphia and then San Francisco, finally settling in Sacramento thirteen years ago. Tapes were then mailed to radio stations in Manila, Korea, Portugal, Alaska, and other places with transmitters strong enough to beam the program on shortwave radio into homes in the Soviet Union. A recent Pentecostal émigré remembers crowding around the family radio every Sunday at 7:30 P.M. Moscow time with his family and other young friends to listen to the Christian programs. He recalls: "It was big, noisy, but we tried to catch the Paul Demetrus voice on radio. From my early childhood I heard his voice on the radio. When I came here to be near my brother and sister, I was very much in wonder of him. The first day at church last April I asked, 'Where is Paul Demetrus?' I was very happy when I first saw him" (anonymous interview, February 1991).

Many Russians arriving in Sacramento for the first time feel that the city is their "new mother Russia." Religious connections established prior to their arrival in California have forged strong ties among the émigrés and with the city of Sacramento.

A third factor encouraging mass Russian settlement is the area's economic conditions. Rent and living expenses in the Sacramento urban area are considerably lower than in San Francisco or Los Angeles, making it a more economically viable place for families living on welfare checks and low immigrant wages. By law, refugees were previously allowed to leave their homeland with only $90 and two suitcases, so almost all arrived financially destitute. Sacramento has numerous affordable apartments and small houses for rent, along with a moderate level of minimum-wage jobs. Enrollment in educational institutions is inexpensive as well. Many Russian immigrants have been drawn to the area by these economic advantages. According to Raisa Shved, who moved to the city in 1990 after three months in Los Angeles, "Los Angeles was too big, too much traffic, bad air too. But the real reason I am now in Sacramento is because I want to go to college and my husband is going already to mechanics school. We can afford to go to college here because there are so many cheap schools and they are close by our apartment, too" (interview, Sacramento, 6 February 1991).

The most recent factor that has encouraged Russian Christians to settle in Sacramento is the direct result of chain migration. Relatives of immigrants already there now have first priority for admission into the United States. As discussed earlier, one of the primary goals of American immigration policy is the reunification of families. Russian family members already living in Sacramento act as sponsors for relatives in Russia. These new immigrants settle in Sacramento to be near their families. According to Carl Pihl, regional director of a Lutheran agency assisting with resettlement, "You have to remember the 'second migration' phenomenon. You have to figure that, for every person we place directly in Sacramento, at least one—and probably more—comes unofficially to join relatives and friends" (telephone interview, San Francisco, May 1991).

A strong chain migration based on familial connection is thus operating in high gear in Sacramento. The first families sent word to other members of their families and home churches, and a larger community began to develop. According to Sacramento Pentecostal Ivan Krasnodensky, "We heard people saying 'Go to Sacramento. There is a good life there.' We didn't know anything about America. We didn't know about its climate or its geography. When they said to us that Sacramento is a good city with a good church, well, why not go there?" (*New York Times*, 11 September 1991, A10).

The more than eight thousand Russian Pentecostals and Baptists currently living in California's capital city have begun to change the city's ethnic and religious landscape. Especially noticeable are changes in church patterns. Before the arrival of new immigrants in 1988, the small, red-brick, 1950s-era Russian Baptist church in West Sacramento had dwindled to about thirty, mostly elderly members. The sudden arrival of new Russian Baptists has brought new vitality along with new problems to the ethnic church. Faced with increasing demands for more space, Russian Baptist families now fill almost every bit of seating space in the church building on Sunday mornings. Children have replaced the elderly as the church's dominant population.

Overcrowding is not the small church's only problem. New Russians arrive in West Sacramento with very traditional, fundamentalist beliefs based directly on Bible teachings. Many believe women should not wear makeup or fine clothes to church and insist on scarves modestly covering women's heads. Some kneel to pray, others stand. Some allow women to wear pants in their homes, others insist on skirts. With new church members from diverse regions of their huge homeland, customs, rituals, and traditions differ. Confusion over the role of the church's pastor has also become a divisive issue. Coming from a place where all decisions about religion were made by the church hierarchy, many find it difficult and sometimes impossible to make decisions based on a more democratic system.

Issues facing the West Sacramento church face other Russian churches as well. A second Baptist church near the city's Broadway district faces similar problems. Its membership also increased dramatically after 1989. Both churches are attempting to offer social and educational services for refugee families as well as spiritual guidance. English classes, employment counseling, clothing drives, and other support efforts have drained church leaders.

But less than 10 percent of the city's new immigrants belong to the two Russian Baptist churches. The vast majority of Sacramento's recent immigrants attend Pentecostal services. Almost eighteen hundred Russian and Ukrainian Pentecostals now meet for services every Sunday afternoon in one church. This congregation has grown from a small group of about sixty believers holding services on a backyard patio in 1989. More than 550 children attend Sunday school classes. The Sacramento Pentecostal Church now has the largest Russian evangelical membership of any church outside the Commonwealth of Independent States (*Sacramento Bee*, 20 May 1991, A1, A12). Its ethnically Russian and Ukrainian members come from widely scattered places in various republics, including Georgia, Estonia, Ukraine, Armenia, and Lithuania.

Members of this large church, along with those attending one of the other four Russian Pentecostal congregations now meeting in Sacramento, participate regularly in three-hour services on Sunday afternoons. Most are solemn worshipers who emphasize healing, speaking in tongues, prophecy, and baptism of the Holy Spirit. Foot washing is often included as a regular part of their communion service. This custom is taken from Christ's washing of his disciples' feet at the Last Supper. Lengthy sermons are interspersed by the reading of poetry and the singing of religious songs by children and adults. Most Russian Pentecostals are conscientious objectors. Because of this belief, many suffered imprisonment in their homeland for refusing to serve the required two years of military service.

Other day-to-day requirements based on religious beliefs form a regular part of Russian Pentecostal lifestyles. Smoking and drinking are prohibited and are grounds for excommunication. Women usually have long hair, which is covered by a scarf during worship services. Cosmetics, jewelry, and fine clothing are avoided by most women and girls. Men usually wear slacks and suit jackets to church, avoiding ties, which are considered too decorative. All have very fundamentalist Christian beliefs.

Most Russians in California believe it was their sacred duty to leave their homeland to resettle in the United States. During the Soviet coup in August 1991, Russian Pentecostals became more convinced than ever that their destiny was to leave the Soviet Union. Recent arrival Leonid Kalenyuk defines the current turmoil in his homeland as a confirmation of apocalyptic prophecies for believers. Kalenyuk recently told a *New York Times* reporter that "this coup attempt was a warning to believers that they *must* leave while they can." And in even stronger words, recent Pentecostal immigrant Grigory Krasnodensky proclaimed: "We believe these events are God's will. The time of the Apocalypse that has been predicted has not yet come. But we believe that freedom will not last long in the Soviet Union, and that when the Apocalypse comes it will affect the whole world" (*New York Times,* 11 September 1991, A10).

Another Sacramento Pentecostal, Pavel Mishin, insists these prophecies are based on the apocalyptic warnings of the Bible. According to Revelation, believers are urged to flee from Babylon before it is consumed by plagues and fire (*New York Times,* 11 September 1991, A10).

The minister of the largest Pentecostal church in Sacramento is radio broadcaster Paul Demetrus. Believing in keeping Sacramento's Pentecostals together in one church, Demetrus is searching for a larger place to hold services. Despite frequent differences of opinion, he has thus far attempted to let new immigrants organize church services according to their old customs. According to Demetrus, "Being an American, I leave hands off. All I'm responsible for is that they don't go overboard and the doctrine is correct. Salvation by grace, water baptism, partaking of communion, speaking in tongues, and living a clean, moral life" (*Sacramento Bee,* 20 May 1991, A12).

Despite efforts to unify new Pentecostal immigrants in Sacramento, at least four other churches have been formed. All are located on busy commercial streets in the city's north suburban area. This church location pattern parallels residential patterns. A majority of Baptists have clustered in the older West Sacramento enclave, near the Baptist church. Although some Pentecostals do live in the West Sacramento enclave, the vast majority have settled in other parts of the city, primarily in Rancho Cordova, Fair Oaks, and south Sacramento.

Not all recent immigrants practice their religion in formal church buildings. As discussed in chapter 4, Pentecostals in the Soviet Union often belonged to unofficial, unregistered congregations. These groups of believers preferred to meet in secret, often gathering in members' homes or outdoors. These "underground Pentecostals" also meet in Sacramento. Their story is best told through the experiences of their leader, Nikolai Ivannik.

Nick and Nadezhda Ivannik, both thirty-eight, rented a modest home in West Sacramento in 1989. Drawn by the support of Nadezhda's relatives who already lived in Sacramento, the Ivanniks and their four young children represent the stories of numerous other Pentecostal immigrants. Nick was a bishop in his unregistered home church in the Soviet Union before emigrating to the United States; he has likewise assumed a strong leadership role here. His family came from Poti, Georgia, a port city on the Black Sea just north of the Turkish border, leaving their homeland because "God told us to come here." Like other Russian immigrants, the Ivannik family abandoned their home and all their possessions when they were given permission to leave for the United States. Their emigration plans were coordinated by World Relief and the World Church Services.

Soon after their arrival in Sacramento, Nick established his independent Pentecostal congregation, conducting the first worship services in his home. More than fifty participants now hold services together on Sundays at the homes of various members. As in other Pentecostal gatherings, prayers, sermons, and singing are highly emotional (*Sacramento Bee*, 5 July 1990, 6).

Despite these numerous activities of Russian churches and home worship groups, the Russian religious landscape in Sacramento remains quietly unobtrusive. As with earlier waves of Russian settlement in North America, glasnost-era Russians prefer to remain unnoticed and unobserved. Fears of persecution, even in this land of religious freedom, continue to haunt them. Pentecostal church buildings are usually undecorated and have no sign on the door identifying their religious function. Russian Baptist churches also often go unnoticed by the casual observer. This ethnic invisibility is also evident in other parts of the region, especially in the midst of multicultural and multilingual Los Angeles and San Francisco.

Other California Settlement Nodes

Although the primary magnet for Soviet Pentecostal and Baptist immigration into California has been the city of Sacramento, other urban areas in the state have also attracted large numbers of immigrants during the glasnost era. Soviet Jews in particular have settled in the Los Angeles and San Francisco urban areas in large numbers. Their populations have swelled statistics on total Soviet refugee arrivals, especially since 1988. Although a discussion of Soviet Jewish settlement in California is beyond the scope of this book, it is important to note here that their total numbers are much larger than Soviet Christian arrivals in the state. In 1990, for example, at least 10,742 Soviet refugees settled in Los Angeles (up from only 2,896 in 1988). Only a small percentage of these southern California immigrants are non-Jewish.

California is currently the most frequent destination for Soviet refugees in the United States. In 1990, at least 60 percent of total refugee placements in the country were in California, followed by New York (20 percent), Massachusetts (6 percent), and Illinois (4 percent). Soviets are the oldest among all refugees in California, with a median age of 31.4 years of age for women and 30.1 years for men. Eight percent of all Soviet refugees in California are 65 or older. The majority of the population is, in fact, over 40 years (*Estimates of Refugees in California Counties and the State* 1991, 4).

As in Sacramento, Russian Pentecostal and Baptist refugees have been attracted to other parts of urban California by economic and climatic amenities, a generous welfare system, and an atmosphere of openness and acceptance of cultural diversity. Russian churches in Los Angeles, San Marcos in San Diego County, the San Francisco Bay area, and Fresno have sponsored refugee families much like those in Sacramento. Some of these families have stayed in the neighborhood of their sponsors, but the vast majority have resettled (or plan to resettle) in Sacramento. Numerous interviews with these Soviets immigrating to Los Angeles or San Francisco and then to Sacramento have cited bad air, too much traffic, cost of living, and fears about the safety of their children. Most of these families are adding to the pattern of the general population's white flight to California's Central Valley. Their image of the state's heartland as a safer, more homogeneous, more "Christian" region is based more on perception than on reality. Sacramento has one of the highest crime rates in the nation and has become, in recent years, a massive and rapidly growing urban area with well over a million people.

As in Sacramento, refugees in southern California and in the San Francisco Bay area tend to settle near well-established Russian churches. The location of Russian Baptist and Pentecostal churches in Monterey Park, East Los Angeles, and Hollywood in the Los Angeles area and on Potrero Hill and Balboa Street in San Francisco reflect antecedent Russian settlement patterns. Drawn to older Russian neighborhoods in these cities, refugees find well-established religious and social networks awaiting them. Many refugee families were housed in Russian church basements and other empty rooms when they first arrived in California. One such family, the Mistuks, lived in the Russian Baptist church on Balboa Street for several months before finding housing in the city. But as Branislava Mistuk remembered his life in the Soviet Union, life in a church attic did not sound so bad. He recalled:

When I was a young child, my father, who was a farmer, had his own flour mill in the Volga District near Samara. Well, because he had his own mill, the Communists thought he was a capitalist, so they sent our family to Siberia for four years. Oy, it was so bad there. They just threw us all from the train out there in the cold of winter. We couldn't do anything because there were no towns nearby, so we just dug holes in the ground to stay warm and tried to survive until spring came. After that we finally moved down to Uzbekistan. Life there was pretty good until the Muslims got nationalistic when the shah of Iran came into power. They didn't like us Russians much after that. Then we moved near to Moscow and waited for a chance to leave. This church sponsored us to come here, and we met a lot of families who had almost the same exact experiences in Siberia. We are all just so glad to be safe now. (interview, San Francisco, 11 November 1989)

An exact count of the Soviet refugees arriving in California is difficult because their migration patterns are still in flux. As stated earlier, many arrivals in California's larger cities become secondary migrants, moving into the Central Valley soon after their arrival in the state, seeking permanent resettlement in Sacramento. The most recent count taken by the United States Department of Health and Human Services lists the six counties with the most 1990 Soviet refugee arrivals as Los Angeles, San Francisco, Sacramento, San Mateo, Alameda, and Fresno (table 7).

Despite trends to leave California's larger cities and move into the Central Valley for permanent settlement, the Russian Baptist church on Balboa Street in San Francisco has increased its membership during the

Table 7
Soviet Refugee Arrivals in California, 1988–90

County	1988	1989	1990
Los Angeles	10,742	4,714	2,896
San Francisco	539	1,491	1,594
Sacramento	15	248	908
San Mateo	21	179	223
Alameda	57	192	203
Fresno	47	67	105

Source: U.S. Department of Health and Human Services, Office of Refugee Resettlement, "Report to the Congress: Refugee Resettlement Program," Washington, DC, 1990.

glasnost era from about thirty elderly members in 1987 to over one hundred in 1991. According to the church minister, A. F. Efemov, only about ten of these members speak English, underscoring their recent arrival in the United States. Other Baptist and Pentecostal churches shown on map 20 have also experienced a small but steady influx of new members in recent years. The Russian Gospel Temple in the Mission district of San Francisco, for example, has at least 150 new members. One of the first churches to experience major growth after the 1988 arrival of new refugees from the Soviet Union, this Russian Pentecostal congregation was established over thirty years ago. A recent visit to the Russian Gospel Temple as a nonmember participant observer was an experience in cross-cultural confusion.

Services, conducted in Russian with occasional rapid and incomplete English translations, are held in a large, simple, undecorated room. Approximately two hundred of the five hundred members were present. In contrast to Russian Orthodox congregations dominated by elderly women, Russian Pentecostal churches are filled with young and middle-aged couples with large families. This diversity is undoubtedly a reflection of the Pentecostal appeal for people from a variety of ethnic and economic backgrounds. Interviews with recent immigrants attending the service indicated a concern for financial security in expensive San Francisco neighborhoods and a fear of "big city" temptations for their children. One hundred percent of the Russians interviewed at the Russian Gospel Temple expressed an interest in relocating to Sacramento.

These older Russian congregations throughout the state of California are experiencing great change in the early 1990s. Not only are membership lists increasing, but numerous issues divide the older, more Americanized members and the new, unacculturated believers. At the Hollywood Baptist Church, for example, the more than one hundred new members now dominate decision making about services, lifestyle, and belief systems of the entire church. In some places, new congregations have been formed to offset these disagreements, such as the one at Harbor Terrace in the Los Angeles area. According to Tony Ahave of the Russian Baptist church in Fresno, "The newcomers have just about overrun the old timers, and no one seems to like it very much. Such a large immigration all of a sudden has confused everybody, and many groups from different parts of the USSR are splitting off to form their own congregations" (interview, 1991).

Settlement Nodes in the Pacific Northwest

Other parts of the North American Pacific Rim are also experiencing influxes of Russians. Despite recent economic problems due to the declining importance of natural resources in the region, Oregon and Washington have become important destinations.

The first Russian Pentecostal families in Oregon arrived in the small town of Woodburn, south of Portland, in April 1988. Attracted by the sponsorship of the Russian Gospel Temple, by the end of 1988 Russian Pentecostals had become Oregon's third-largest refugee group, after Southeast Asians and Romanians. By 1991, they were the state's largest incoming refugee group (table 8). In 1987, they made up only 1 percent of all refugees in the state. They were 14 percent in 1988 and increased to 55 percent in 1989 and 61 percent in 1990.

One of the first families to arrive in Woodburn was that of Lev Lyulka, a Pentecostal who is now a school custodian. After being told by authorities in the Soviet Union that he would "find himself in a class equivalent to slavery," Lev is active in church and community activities. When questioned about his future, he replied, "My real dream is that my children will be on the same level as all children in America" (*Oregonian*, 9 September 1989, 1).

Russians settling in Oregon most often choose antecedent Russian settlement nodes in the agricultural Willamette Valley for permanent settlement. Drawn to Woodburn and Hubbard by church sponsorship in the area, many have resettled in Portland. There are two Russian Pentecostal churches and one new Russian Baptist church in Oregon's largest city. By early 1992, new arrivals had settled in widely scattered neighborhoods in Portland, as well as in Woodburn, Hubbard, Salem, and Eugene.

As an example of the challenges facing new Russian immigrants in the Pacific Northwest, the Oregon State Refugee Program recently filed this summary report about one typical family in their caseload:

Victor and his family of six arrived in the United States on July 21, 1989. The father was thirty-six, the mother thirty, and their children were eleven, nine, seven, and four.

The first day they came in to their voluntary agency office to pick up their transitional checks (provided by the voluntary agency which resettles them), they were given welcome booklets in the Russian language.

At Intake I, the usual appointments were made for the family—with the Refugee Health clinic for health screening, with the Portland schools for the children's education, with the Social Security Office for social security numbers and with Adult and Family Services, the state's welfare office, for food stamps.

Pre-employment training (PET) started on August 28, 1989 for Victor. The job worker agreed that Ileana would attend PET after Victor had completed it, for children's reasons.

Victor's evaluation set his motivation level at "not very high." He also "resisted trying new activities." But the evaluator also said that Victor knew enough

Table 8
Incoming Refugees in Oregon, 1988–91.

Ethnicity	1988	%	1989	%	1990	%	1991	%
Southeast Asian								
Cambodia	26	6	129	19.3	24	4.5	19	2.1
Hmong	17	3.9	26	3.8	6	1.1	10	1.1
Mien	62	14.3	55	8.2	22	4.1	87	8.7
Other Laos	101	23.4	35	5.2	45	8.4	67	7.5
Vietnam	226	52.3	422	63.2	433	81.6	689	77.1
Non–Southeast Asian								
Afghanistan	0	0	18	2.6	6	0.3	6	0.4
Angola	—	—	—	—	0	0	8	0.6
Romania	127	62.5	78	11.2	197	10.1	193	14.9
Soviet Union	9	4.4	513	73.8	1,688	87.2	1,026	79
Ethiopia	12	5.9	15	2.1	18	0.7	31	2.4
Libya	—	—	—	—	1	0.1	0	0
Iran	22	10.8	9	1.3	3	1.5	10	0.8
Poland	17	8.4	13	1.8	4	0.2	0	0
Hungary	3	1.5	8	4.6	4	0.2	0	0
Czechoslovakia	5	2.5	2	0.28	1	0.1	9	0.7
China	7	3.4	0	0	12	0.6	1	0.1
Thailand	0	0	32	4.6	1	0.1	0	0
Pakistan	0	0	7	1.0	—	—	—	—
Iraq	1	0.49	0	0	—	—	—	—
Nicaragua	—	—	—	—	4	0.3	0	0

Source: Oregon State Refugee Program 1990.

English for essential interview skills. He had worked as a photographer and film developer in the USSR and was now referred to Pre-industrial Training.

As soon as Victor completed PET, Ileana started her training. On October 18, 1989, Ileana's evaluation said that she was ready for an entry level job where she could be trained as a supervisor.

Victor and Ileana both started full-time employment as janitors at ABM on December 26, 1989, at $5.50 an hour. Medical insurance was available after thirty days.

While trying to enroll their children for medical insurance under his policy, Victor was shocked to learn how expensive the coverage was. He decided not to enroll the children into his medical insurance due to the costs. The case manager told him the sliding-scale fee for services at the International Health Clinic was another option. Now, thoroughly aware of the high cost of living, Victor looked for better paying work and found work at Cascade General at $13.50 an hour. This is shop maintenance work which is sporadic, and Victor sensibly kept his ABM job, cutting his hours there to four per day. Later he started to work at Northwest Marine Iron Works—another unionized ship maintenance job. (*Oregon State Refugee Program* 1990, 63)

This caseworker's report capsulizes a number of important issues involved in the refugee resettlement process. The shock of facing a high cost of living in the United States, the lack of socialized medical care and employment benefits, and the individual motivation needed to succeed in a capitalistic system that does not guarantee employment as a right of all adults have stunned many Russian immigrants. These difficult issues and others facing Russian refugees in North America are discussed in detail in chapter 6.

Washington state has also had a continuous stream of Russian refugee arrivals since early 1988. Many come from St. Petersburg and other northern parts of the former Soviet Union, drawn to the cool weather and climate of the Pacific Northwest. According to one of Seattle's first Russian Pentecostal immigrants, "I come from Petersburg, you know. It is so cold and so wet there and so beautiful and green in the summer. I would miss that good wet weather if I lived in California instead of Washington. I came here and I plan to stay here because it reminds me so much of home when it is cloudy and gray outside. My husband and I also came to Seattle because there were other Russians already here. Also, it is much safer than California" (anonymous interview, Seattle, 9 March 1990).

As in Oregon, the vast majority of Russian refugees in Washington have settled in a north-south linear pattern along the Interstate 5 corridor. Drawn to small towns like Marysville, Bellingham, and Everett by the promise of employment in agriculture there and to larger cities like Seattle and Vancouver by the sponsorship of local churches, Russians

Table 9
World Relief Soviet Arrivals in California and Washington, 1989–91

Office	1989	1990	1991
San Francisco	426	213	282
Garden Grove, CA	319	151	173
Fresno	1	43	15
Sacramento	910	862	1,783
San Diego	0	0	0
Seattle	425	357	571
Connell, WA	153	226	184
Total	2,234	1,852	3,022

Source: World Relief files, Nyack, NY, 1991.

have made up an increasingly large percentage of refugees coming into Washington in recent years. In 1988, they made up only 6 percent of all refugees, but by 1991, 45 percent of all refugees entering the state came from the former Soviet Union. A microcosm of the relative migration decisions of Russian Christian refugees in California and Washington is presented in table 9. These figures were gathered by the primary resettlement agency working with Christian refugee resettlement in the United States, World Relief. Their figures for 1988–90 illustrate the growing importance of Washington and California as resettlement sites.

Russian Pentecostals and Baptists have changed the dynamics of older, well-established Russian churches in Washington much as they have in California. Many new immigrants have started their own congregations, renting space for Sunday-afternoon services from other religious denominations. The older Russian Pentecostal church and Russian Baptist church, both located in the Ballard district in northeast Seattle, continue to be dominated by older, more acculturated Russian immigrants, while more than two thousand new immigrants attend services in a distant part of the city. According to Paul Strove, a longtime member of the Ballard district Pentecostal church (and a Russian who moved from Argentina to Seattle in the early 1960s), "Our church was dying before these new people came. Membership was down to about five families, and well, even our minister quit. Now we have all these new members. It is a miracle of God for sure" (interview, Seattle, November 1990).

Three distinct congregations of Pentecostals and two groups of Baptist immigrants now meet in the Seattle-Bellevue area. Churches have also sprung up in Vancouver, Everett, and Bellingham to serve the ever-increasing refugee population. As in California, these church memberships change almost weekly. A recent immigrant from St. Petersburg, now living in Everett, recalled: "It has just been really amazing. When I first came to Washington with my husband in 1989, our Pentecostal church had about ten members. Now, here it is less than two years later, and our little group has grown ten times as big" (anonymous interview, Everett, 15 November 1990).

This same émigré, along with Southeast Asian and Hispanic refugees, is attending adult education classes at the community college in Everett. Selected curriculum materials at the school have been translated into the Russian language, but instructors there who had "never seen a Russian person in my life" before 1989 are adjusting slowly to the new demands. Similarly at the Bellingham Vo-Tech Institute, instructors are struggling to learn enough basic vocabulary in Russian to augment their new program. According to one English-language instructor, "I just feel completely overwhelmed by these new refugees from Russia. I can't believe they are here. How do you suppose they ever found our little town way up here? I really want to help them, but they don't seem to understand our system. It almost seems like they want you to do everything for them. Their motivation to achieve is just so different from ours" (P. Anderson interview, Bellingham, Washington, 17 November 1990).

Other educators have had a more positive experience with the adjustment process. According to Mary Castro of Everett Community College, "Some are engineers, chemists, engineers, and construction workers. The ones in my class are very eager and fast learners" (*Seattle Times*, 11 July 1990, F3).

Many of these engineers, chemists, and other skilled workers and their families are farm workers on berry farms along Interstate 5. Russians make up over 30 percent of the work force on a 328-acre berry farm near Everett owned by Dianna Biringer. According to Biringer, "They come in families and work in groups. We've never had Russians before. They tell me they are here to stay. I'm curious why so many of them are coming. They certainly didn't come for the Goodwill Games" (*Seattle Times*, 11 July 1990, F1).

One of the Everett farm workers, fourteen-year-old Zoya Gudev from Cherkessk, picks berries with her sister while her parents attend Everett Community College language classes. Zoya had this to say about life in the United States: "In Russia my Dad was an electrical engineer, and my Mom was a horticulturalist. When I finish high school I think I must go to work. So much I like America. I like Seattle. Some people are nice, but some are not so nice" (*Seattle Times*, 11 July 1990, F1).

Conclusions

Russian immigrants have been attracted to the Pacific Rim of North America in large numbers since emigration from the Soviet Union began in earnest in 1988. While more than four thousand Russian Pentecostal and Baptist immigrants have made Oregon and Washington their home and several thousand have settled in Vancouver, California has rapidly become the preferred destination for the vast majority of Russians entering the United States in the early 1990s. Soviet Jews have settled in the sprawling Los Angeles and San Francisco urban areas, while others have been drawn to the Central Valley city of Sacramento. Russians have been attracted to the West Coast by climatic and economic amenities, but connections with church leaders via preglasnost shortwave radio broadcasts into the Soviet Union have played an even more important role in migration and settlement decision making.

A strong chain migration effect has been in motion since the earliest arrivals in the region. The United States government has made it the priority of current refugee policy to reunite families. Immigrants already living in the United States are working actively to bring the remainder of their families here, and, in fact, the majority of newcomers from late 1991 throughout 1993 have been relatives of people already here.

Church congregations and Christian refugee relief organizations have also played an active role in encouraging chain migration into the region. Sponsorship by antecedent Russian churches in North America has created a clustering of like-minded believers in distinctive settlement nodes. These ethnoreligious nodes are characterized by both demographic and religious homogeneity, as young families and their parents settle near each other, often residing in the same street or neighborhood.

Although many immigrant groups in the United States and Canada have lived in close proximity in their early years of settlement, the tightly cohesive pattern of Russian settlement in the region is unique in its intensity and its persistent religious connections in a 1990s multicultural urban setting. Drawn to particular apartment buildings and neighborhoods by those of similar religious beliefs, Russian immigrants by choice now find themselves isolated from other ethnic groups. These ghettoized regions of containment, especially in Sacramento, may radically slow assimilation and acculturation rates. Settlement decisions may ultimately retard chances for economic and cultural survival in the United States, where language skills, job training, and networking outside the local neighborhood play such an important role.

Conversely, the cohesive spatial patterns of recent migrants in Pacific Rim cities could eventually accelerate their adjustment to American life. Gaining personal strength and extra help from religiously based social service agencies because of their church connections may assist many to develop the skills and strength to succeed in the larger world more rapidly than other immigrants living in more scattered locations in the city.

Do continued ethnoreligious connections impede or accelerate the immigrant acculturation process in contemporary urban America? This question forms the heart of the analysis of the Russian experience in the chapters that follow. Predictions about the survival of religion, language, and ethnic connections of Russian immigrants are overlaid on the acculturation process of earlier Russian groups still residing on the Pacific coast.

SIX

Great Expectations: Adapting to a New Life

The Adjustment Process

The difficulties of obtaining refugee status, the challenges of securing financial and legal support for settlement in the United States and Canada, and the sometimes overwhelming decisions about lifestyle and location after arrival here are only a few of the first steps in the often painful adjustment process of a typical immigrant.

There can be no doubt that the experience of leaving one's homeland and adjusting to a new place can be extremely stressful. Feelings of uprootedness and vulnerability, a sudden disconnection with homeland, friends, and family, and the difficulties of adjusting to a new place are only a few of the problems faced by refugees. In addition, immigrants from the former Soviet Union have had a special set of challenges to face, due to limitations imposed by the control and domination of all personal and public decision making by an extremely authoritarian political system.

This chapter investigates the adjustment process of Russians as they settle into their new life in North America. The experiences of Russian immigrants who have lived in the region for a longer period of time, such as the Orthodox, Doukhobor, and Molokan groups, are compared with more recent immigrants such as the Old Believers, Pentecostals, and Baptists. Rural and urban differences are also contrasted, and adjustment through time and space is explored. Following a discussion of the experiences of each religious group, a broad comparative overview of the Russian experience in North America is discussed. Finally, some predictions about the acculturation rates of glasnost-era Russians are postulated in an effort to shed further light on the role of religion and ethnicity in the adjustment process.

Despite an abhorrence of the former Soviet government, attachment to homeland remains strong in the new refugee. As do most cultural groups everywhere, Russians tend to view their homeland as the center of their world. Geographer Yi-fu Tuan found that this profound attachment to homeland appears to be a worldwide phenomenon and that it is

not limited to any particular culture or economy. It is known to literate and nonliterate peoples, hunter-gatherers, and sedentary farmers, as well as city dwellers. The city or land is viewed as mother, and it nourishes; place is an archive of fond memories and splendid achievements that inspire the present; place is permanent and hence reassuring to man, who sees frailty in himself and chance and flux everywhere. (1977, 154)

This profound attachment to home has not disappeared even in our rapidly urbanizing society. Loyalty to certain aspects of a culture group's homeland, socialized into the individual since childhood, remain important even when the group is transplanted to an entirely different place. This new place creates new social and spatial bonds based in part on former experiences and feelings.

Giving up one's homeland forever is a painful experience for all people no matter what the conditions. Even though recent Russian immigrants insist they will never want to return to "that terrible, terrible place," they remain attached to it at a deeper level. Later in the adjustment process, feelings of homesickness and a strong desire for "anything familiar" frequently rebound in many recent migrants.

New immigrants bring the connection to their Russian homeland with them and may transfer this earth attachment to their new environment. Despite a long distance and often complicated migration to North America, they (and, in many cases, their descendants) develop and maintain a symbolic and emotional attachment to their new place of settlement. This experience of local attachment is common among immigrant groups who have experienced long-range migrations and marked sociocultural and political shifts, because the struggle for group survival in a strange culture requires an intense reordering of past connections. The shared experience of survival often binds people tightly together. According to Oscar Handlin, chronicler of the immigrant experience in America,

The old folks knew then that they would not come to belong, not through their own experience, not through their offspring. The only adjustment they had been able to make to life in the United States had been one that involved the separateness of the group, one that increased their awareness of the differences between themselves and the rest of society. In the adjustment, they had always suffered from the consciousness that they were strangers. The demand that they assimilate, that they surrender their separateness, condemned them always to be outsiders. (1951, 285)

The language problem adds another layer of difficulty to the adjustment process. Since the vast majority of Russians never imagined gaining permission to leave their homeland, most never studied the English language in any depth. Some may have taken English courses in high school, but, since foreigners were not allowed in most Soviet cities at the time, their teachers were usually limited in experience with spoken English. The vast majority arrive with virtually no English skills, making their transition from old country to new country extremely stressful and confusing. According to one recent arrival, "I just do not think I will ever, ever learn to speak good English. I hear people talking all around me, so fast, so strange, and then they stop talking and wait for me to answer. Sometimes I just say 'yes' to every question because I don't know what else to say or do" (A. Borodaev interview, West Sacramento, 16 October 1990).

This communication problem, along with economic and cultural differences, makes the adjustment process even more challenging. In a free enterprise system, the seemingly simple act of securing food for one's family is almost impossible in the early days of resettlement. Locating and bartering (in English) for an apartment or house to rent also can be an overwhelming experience. Answering questions from the welfare "official" (or any perceived official) is frightening and confusing. Even the sight of local and state police patrolling streets and highways provokes almost unmanageable fear. After two months in California, a recent émigré exclaimed in fear and frustration:

I drive very slowly and very carefully, but they are always watching me. My children always wear their seatbelts and I always obey the traffic laws, but I am just certain they are going to arrest me and put me in jail because I am such a bad driver. I see so many different kinds of police in so many different uniforms, I never know who they really are or why they are watching me. (anonymous interview, 19 August 1990)

Subtle cultural differences also pose problems. To most Russian immigrants, everyone in America seems to be in such a hurry. The pace of day-to-day life is exhausting. The almost constant smiles and varied expressions on people's faces on the street, in offices, in passing cars often do not seem real. It seems Americans are always expressing their feelings in public, even when no one is really listening to them. To the newcomer, life in North America often feels superficial. New "friends" come and go quickly, many never to return again. Friendships in the Soviet Union were the lifeblood of individual survival. Friends stayed together no matter what happened, sharing problems at a deep level that made existence in a difficult place more bearable. In North America, new friendships seem fleeting and almost cold in comparison.

These stressful experiences both in North America and in their homeland have created distinct psychological and social characteristics in many Russian immigrants. After many years working as a social worker with immigrants from the Soviet Union, Irene Belozersky (1989) defined the following list of common characteristics of recent immigrants:

1. unrealistic expectations
2. sense of entitlement
3. loss of sense of security
4. loss of status
5. overdependency
6. perseverance
7. manipulative behavior
8. difficulty in establishing trusting relationships
9. strong reliance on family and friends

Although Belozersky has worked primarily with Jewish immigrants, her list rings true for Russians as a whole. Unrealistic expectations about life in America present the first shock to new arrivals. Citizens of the former Soviet Union tended to disregard the viewpoints of their government over the years, choosing to believe exactly the opposite of what they were told by officials. Thus, negative warnings about "evil, corrupt, and poor America" only intensified people's belief in this country as a wealthy, beautiful, indeed almost perfect, place. Instead, new immigrants often find crowded, crime-ridden neighborhoods, traffic congestion, expensive medical and dental care, and rampant social problems. Their disappointment is often expressed initially in depression and feelings of despair.

Special treatment by Jewish and Christian resettlement agencies made emigrants from the Soviet Union feel important and needed. Upon arrival in the United States, this sense of entitlement often becomes a problem. Disappointed at the realization that they are not going to receive long-term special treatment here, many become angry or resentful at the system or at resettlement agency workers. This results in a loss of their sense of security, and

often case workers witness dramatic emotional changes in their clients which occur between their first and second meetings with them. From being happy and even euphoric, immigrants become increasingly anxious, confused, and tense.

These changes occur when immigrants begin to deal with the tasks of daily living: looking for an apartment, enrolling children in school, learning the basics of job hunting, etc. These tasks are new and frightening to them and trigger emotional reactions. (Belozersky 1989, 3)

These feelings of confusion are accompanied by an abrupt loss of status. Immigrants are faced with a complete loss of employment, resulting in a loss of social, personal, and economic status. Many prefer welfare checks every month because it is so difficult to accept working in the lowest level of employment in minimum wage jobs. When asked about his occupation in Los Angeles, a Russian émigré replied: "Well, in Soviet Union, I was an engineer. You know, I designed parts in a factory. Here in America, they call that a nothing job. It just does not exist here. So neither do I really. I just tell everyone I am working for welfare company here in America. They are probably the only employers I will ever have" (anonymous interview, Los Angeles, 27 June 1990).

This confusion about employment and social status is also caused by the new immigrants' overdependency. American values of independence, individual motivation to succeed, and self-reliance have simply not been a part of the Soviet experience. In their homeland, people were forced to be subservient to the interests of the group rather than the individual. "Individual responsibility and the necessity to make choices are very threatening to some Soviet immigrants and this may trigger in them a childish, clinging behavior" (Belozersky 1989, 4). Coming from a system that told everyone what to do, where to live, and what to believe has left immigrants facing life in the "land of opportunity and self reliance" confused and angry. According to a Russian immigrant now living in Seattle,

I just do not know what to do. Should I go to school or should I work for low wages? Should I live in an apartment or should I look for a small house to rent? Should I drink this kind of milk or that kind, eat this kind of cereal or that kind. I am just completely exhausted from trying to make good decisions for myself and my family every minute of every day. I just want to give up sometimes. (anonymous interview, 9 May 1990)

Despite these difficulties, the vast majority of Russian immigrants exhibit remarkable perseverance. After the early months of adapting to life in North America, many begin to evaluate their choices and their possibilities for future success. Accustomed to surviving from day to day in the former Soviet Union, these hard-working survivors usually find a way to survive again. Toward this end, many resort to the use of manipulative behavior to achieve their goals. Using skills learned in the USSR, many push the system to the limit, straining for every advantage. Tired of dealing with this common characteristic, a caseworker at one Russian resettlement agency who prefers to remain anonymous recently complained: "They just push and push. It is too much to deal with sometimes. They want me to do everything for them, even get them more than the law allows, and they don't understand the limits. We have tried to find them employment, but they would rather just 'work the system.' It doesn't feel right to me."

The final characteristics, difficulty in establishing trust and reliance on family and friends, make life lonely and even more difficult for new arrivals. As mentioned earlier in this chapter, friendships meant more than anything else in the USSR. When Americans do not follow through with promises ("Let's do lunch," "I'll call you soon, OK?"), Russians are often disappointed. As Samuel L. put it, "I just don't understand. Last night at a party this woman asked me for my phone number and said, 'I will call you tomorrow and we'll go to lunch.' I have been sitting here by the phone waiting all day, and she hasn't called. Why did she want my phone number if she didn't really want to call me?" (interview, Chico, California, 14 October 1990).

While this list of refugee characteristics is a valuable summary of problems and behaviors of many Russian immigrants, it is important to keep in mind that individual differences exist within any group structure. The characteristics discussed here are broad descriptions of group behavior, and in no way describe the experience of every individual immigrant.

The following sections of this chapter detail the adjustment process of the six Russian religious groups discussed in previous chapters. Experiences of Orthodox Russians who have lived in the study area for the longest period of time are presented first, to lay a foundation for understanding the patterns and processes of more recent groups.

THE ORTHODOX EXPERIENCE

Louisa

Louisa Verasoff Vessell was born in San Francisco after her parents settled on Green Street in San Francisco in 1910. They left Russia several years earlier to work in the sugarcane fields in Hawaii, having been promised "enough rubles to be happy forever" by sugarcane plantation representatives who visited their neighborhood in Harbin. On arriving in Hawaii, the Verasoffs soon lost faith in their plan. After several weeks in quarantine on the beach near Honolulu, the Russian workers were transported in large groups to plantations far from the city. Not only were working conditions in the sugarcane fields difficult for the former urban dwellers, but "we were only paid half the rubles they were promised back in Russia" (P. Domasky interview, West Sacramento, 10 October 1984). Conditions soon became unbearable for the Verasoffs and most of the other Russian workers, and they began to plot their escape. Like so many others, the travelers eventually found their way to the emerging Russian neighborhood in San Francisco.

Louisa's life in San Francisco and later in West Sacramento was considerably easier than that of her parents. Born into a Russian-speaking Orthodox family and educated in American schools, she is fluent in two languages. Growing up within the culturally cohesive Russian neighborhood in San Francisco gave her a strong sense of her Russian heritage, her parent's sacrifices, and her potential for a better future in America.

After she met and married Raymon Vessell (Vesselleroff), a talented Russian musician, her sense of Russianness deepened. After spending the early years of their marriage in San Francisco, the Vessells moved to the tiny Russian neighborhood in West Sacramento where Raymon first worked as a piano player at Petrushka's Speakeasy on the banks of the Sacramento River. Life in this smaller city was slower and less expensive. Surrounded by other Russian Orthodox family and friends, the Vessells spent the rest of their lives living in this increasingly Russian enclave.

A second-generation Russian with deep connections to her parent's homeland, Louisa has taught her daughter, Louise, a great deal about Russian life and culture. Both cook a variety of Russian foods, especially at holiday time. They discuss current events in the former Soviet Union with concern and a sense of connection.

A widow now, Louisa remains involved in the activities of the West Sacramento Russian Orthodox church. At this stage in her life, she seems to be becoming more Russian as the years pass. She is pleased with her daughter's activism in church affairs and her interest in Russian history and art. In her eighties now, Louisa Verasoff Vessell is very much a Russian living comfortably within American culture.

Louisa is only one among many thousands of Russian Orthodox people who have adjusted to life in North America. Like so many others, her family left their country before the revolution, becoming a people without a country upon their arrival in the United States and Canada. At a deep level, most of these early migrants had ambivalent feelings about their homeland. This love/hate relationship with all things Russian often led to confusion about cultural values in their new environment. Throughout the adjustment process, first-generation Orthodox immigrants clung to their religious beliefs as the only sure thing in a strange and often confusing place.

However, the identity of the Orthodox church itself was also in a state of confusion after the Russian Revolution. As was discussed in chapter 4, Eastern Orthodox immigrants had to choose between an Orthodox church governed from outside the Soviet Union or a Soviet-dominated institution. This division tore apart the Orthodox émigré community in North America, which has not healed even in the last decade of the century.

Day's analysis of early Russian Orthodox immigrants in Hollywood captured many fascinating insights into the important role of the church as a cultural institution. According to one of Day's informants, "I go to the Russian church for worship because I can come into closer communion with God in our own church than in American churches. I love also our music and our Russian traditions" (Day 1934, 54).

Another early Orthodox settler in Los Angeles expressed her concern that the church would not survive in America:

The future of the Russian church will not be successful on account of the church here being a connecting link between Russia and this country. We are fond of it because we are just from Russia. The children are indifferent, slowly they will go away. Old people will die, the connecting link between Russian culture will die. But, if the church will modify and make possible American and other nations' attendance, it will live. Even now we have America, Polish, and Serbian people attending the church. Now the church is purely Russian, it can't live in the pure way it is now. (Day 1934, 55)

This woman's fears about second-generation withdrawal from Russian church activities were well founded. As is typical of other second-generation immigrants, many of the children of these early-twentieth-century Russians left the Orthodox church and tried hard to leave their Russian heritage behind as well. As the attitude of fear and hatred toward the Soviet Union intensified in the United States and Canada during the Stalin years, many people denied their Russian heritage altogether. Day collected the following comments from two second-generation Russians in Los Angeles in the 1920s that speak to other reasons for the gradual decline of church membership:

I hardly ever go to the Russian church. I did when I was in Seattle. Here I am busy with the girl friend on Sunday. I respect it, am conscious of its presence, believe in it; but I have gotten away from going.

I haven't any church. At least none for the last two years. The Russian church is all right, I guess. It entertains the people—it's like a little hobby for them. (Day 1934, 63)

The vast majority of second-generation Orthodox Russians also lost much of their background in the Russian language. Despite efforts by their parents to teach them Russian language and culture at home and in private Russian schools, many resisted these attempts to preserve culture after they reached adolescence, seeing little use for it in an English-speaking country. In a pattern shared by other immigrants, many second-generation Russian-Americans maintain a loose connection with the Russian church and speak Russian with their parents and older relatives, but function as fully American in the outside world. As with their parents' generation, they are a part of two worlds, but unlike their parents they are more comfortable in the North American world.

Church membership and language retention as indicators of Russians' adaptation to their new life have been accompanied by changes in their spatial patterns. While many first-generation Russian Orthodox immigrants have remained in original settlement nodes in Los Angeles, West Sacramento, San Francisco, Seattle, and Vancouver, most of their children have moved away from the older neighborhoods. According to numerous interviews with second-generation suburban and small-town Russians, their flight from these older ethnic enclaves followed much the same pattern as other upwardly mobile residents of North American urban areas. Life in the nonethnic suburbs was viewed as safer, more attractive, and proof of acceptance as a 100 percent American. As one fifty-year-old second-generation Russian engineer who now lives on the peninsula south of San Francisco phrased it: "People always think we Russians are all peasants. Well, I showed them, didn't I? I wish my parents would move away from that old and dangerous neighborhood in San Francisco they still live in, but they say they want to be with other good Russians until the day they die" (anonymous interview, San Mateo, California, 15 July 1984).

Because very few Orthodox Russians have come to the United States and Canada in recent years, these older neighborhoods and their Orthodox churches remain the domain of mostly older members. It is interesting to note, however, an upsurge in membership of Russian Orthodox churches outside of large cities in the United States and Canada in the late 1980s, continuing in the 1990s. This increase in the membership lists of suburban and small-town Orthodox churches is partly a result of the inevitable return of many third-generation Russian-Americans to their heritage. But numerous non-Russians are also increasingly drawn to Orthodoxy as their religion of choice. One especially active Orthodox group, the Valaam Society, now sponsors evangelistic outreach activities and operates Orthodox bookstores in cities and towns from Alaska to California. The society is named for the Valaam Monastery on Lake Ladoga near St. Petersburg, the home of Father Herman, Alaska's first

Russian Orthodox missionary. Most of the Orthodox members of the Valaam Society have virtually no ancestral connections to Russia or the Soviet Union.

The return to Orthodoxy by third-generation Russian-Americans is not surprising, since many ethnics of later generations embrace their heritage more enthusiastically than did their parents. But the large increase of non-Russians in Orthodox church membership is more difficult to explain. The Valaam Society, for example, largely attracts middle-aged, counterculture baby boomers—a slice of American demographics that typically has searched for some type of spirituality. One might speculate that Orthodoxy is close to the Christian belief system of their childhood, but seems more exciting than standard Protestantism or Catholicism because of its connections with the mystical East and its ritual use of candles and incense.

The Old Believer Experience

Another group of Russian Orthodox immigrants, the Old Believers, have different temporal and spatial patterns of settlement than did these early-twentieth-century migrants. Arriving in rural Oregon only thirty-five years ago, they found a different environmental and cultural setting awaiting them than did Orthodox Russians who arrived before and immediately after the Russian Revolution.

Ilia

Ilia Kuzmin was born in the Russian Old Believer village of Nikolaevsk, Alaska, fourteen years ago. His parents were born in China, lived in Brazil, and met and married in Woodburn, Oregon. Ilia's lifestyle and beliefs represent the amazing perseverance of Old Believer culture and religion in North America, even though he functions comfortably in both American and Russian worlds.

Ilia's mother died in an automobile accident just two years ago. Since that time, he and his father and his eleven brothers and sisters have worked hard to hold the family together. After the accident, Ilia was sent to remote Raspberry Island near Kodiak to fish with his uncle, who is a resident of the tiny Old Believer village there. Although Ilia finished eighth grade ("I got my certificate right before my mother died, and she was so happy" [interview, Kodiak, Alaska, 11 July 1990]), he passed up the opportunity to attend high school ("I wanted to get my welding certificate there, you know, but my father needed me"), to add to his father's labor force.

Ilia is comfortable speaking both Russian and English because of his education in an American school, but, as in all Old Believer families in Alaska, he speaks only Russian at home. When asked about his bilingual communication with non-Russian residents in the area, he replied: "We speak in our language and they speak in theirs. That is the way it should be." Life in two worlds seems normal and easy to him. In a recent letter (1991) from Alaska, Ilia writes: "No, I'm not going to high school because I have a lot of work to do. Right now we are digging potatoes and getting all the vegetables out of the garden for the winter. Our weather out here is cold and rain almost every day, so all I can do is work."

Despite the daily hard work, as a typical Russian-American teenager, Ilia's favorite topic of conversation is his brother's new truck. Sounding like any other modern adolescent, he explains:

All the guys in my Russian town have brand new pickups. My brother just bought a hot new 250 Chevy. It is all black with a stripe. But last month, someone in our village broke into the truck by smashing a window with a rock, and they stole his radar detector. He found it at one of our neighbor's houses, and they gave it back. A lot of the people in Homer don't like us because they think we all have new trucks. They should work harder and make lots of money like we all do. (interview, Kodiak, Alaska, 11 July 1990)

Ilia Kuzmin's attitudes about money, hard work, and material possessions are evidence of his unconscious acceptance of American values. As a second-generation North American Old Believer, he has found a way to exist relatively comfortably and without question in two worlds. This coexistence does not always please older members of the group, whether in Alaska or in Oregon. The majority of first-generation Russian residents in these two places, especially those over the age of fifty, favor a more exclusively Russian existence. They attend church regularly, keep all religious holidays in the traditional way, wear strictly Old Believer clothing and hairstyles, and live as uncontaminated a life as possible.

But not all members of the group are finding it easy to abide by the old ways within the context of American society. According to forty-six-year-old Woodburn resident Isaak Basargin,

Everybody losing tradition. Things are changing fast. The religion can't stop it. The young generation changes itself, no matter what you do. You can't stop them. The elders, they worry. A lot of families have left. They've gone to Alaska and Alberta and places like that. They think they can raise their children in the old ways there. They think they are going to run away from the world . . . I realize if I had stayed in South America, I would probably still be in the church and still be traditional Old Believer. But is different here. You are free. There is money. Your family does not control you. America changes you. (*Eugene Register Guard,* 10 February 1991, A4)

One of the growing number of younger first-generation Oregon Old Believers, Isaak Basargin has all but left the Old Believer church and ethnic community. Although he still speaks with a heavy Russian accent, he no longer lets his beard grow untrimmed, and he eats meat and works on religious holidays. Yet the old ways (and his wife, Irina) tug at him almost every day as he works hard to find his niche within American society. Now an owner of four small factories that produce consumer goods such as Jacuzzis and speedboats, Isaak began his life in Woodburn working side by side with his wife in the fields. He remembers those first years in America vividly: "I got off the plane one day and went to work in the hop fields at Woodburn the next day. After the hops it was strawberries. My wife and me, we worked dark to dark every day. And I was happy" (*Eugene Register Guard,* 10 February 1991, A4).

After almost thirty years in North America, many of the Old Believers are beginning to question their dual existences. Most remain heavily traditional, but change is beginning to trickle into their communities. Several potent agents of change have contributed to this almost inevitable process. These include changes in residential patterns, employment in the outside world, enrollment in public education, and changes in their surrounding environment.

Old Believers in Oregon and Alaska live in very different worlds. Most families in the Willamette Valley have purchased a home in a semirural environment, near a small town, with open land around it. While they may live near others of their group, there is no ethnic village atmosphere among the Oregon Old Believers. Some live in town or on suburban culs-de-sac, among Euramerican and Mexican neighbors. Their children play on the street or in the field with friends of other cultures. First-generation Oregon Old Believers repeatedly say they miss the camaraderie of the village life they had in Brazil and China. Many express concern that they must drive their cars to church or to visit another Russian family. However, the majority of younger members of the group seem to strongly prefer living in an ethnically mixed setting where "I can make choices about what kind of people I want to spend time with" (*Eugene Register Guard,* 4 August 1991, B6).

Old Believers living in Alaskan settlements continue to maintain their isolation from outsiders. Russian residential patterns in Alaska are much like those of their former Siberian villages—narrow dirt streets with houses in close proximity along both sides. In the village of Nikolaevsk, churches are centrally located near residences, allowing families to walk from house to house to greet each other on holy days much as they have done for centuries.

But even in these remote Alaskan Old Believer settlements, contact with the outside world is increasing. Outsiders come to places like Nikolaevsk, not to live, but to work at the school or to buy things at the Russian store. Old Believers also travel out of their villages regularly, to make purchases in Homer or Anchor Point or to travel to work at nearby harbors. Employment in canneries in Alaska and in woodworking and other small businesses in Oregon is just one of many ways Old Believers are making regular connections with non-Russians.

After generations of poverty and hard physical labor, most Old Believers in Oregon and Alaska have at last found economic stability. Employed initially in the woodworking business and in agricultural labor in the Willamette Valley, most of Oregon's Old Believers now own their homes, have large savings accounts, and are proud of their success as upwardly mobile Americans. According to anthropologist Richard Morris, discussing Old Believers in the town of Woodburn, "The Russians have economically integrated here and things have gone well. If it weren't for seeing the changes in their kids, they'd be perfectly happy" (*Eugene Register Guard*, 4 August 1991, B6).

Old Believers in Alaskan communities were originally those who were most concerned about the infiltration of American values into their children's lives. Initially settling in a remote location on the Kenai Peninsula, these particularly rigid members of the group soon found themselves working in the outside world among other residents of the area. Women and older children were in contact with other Americans at their seasonal work in the fish canneries. And despite their work in deep-sea fishing boats, owned and operated strictly by members of their own group, Old Believer men are also exposed to the outside world since they must secure licenses, register their boats with the state, and make harbor arrangements.

The cultural adjustment to working in the outside world is made easier for younger members of the group by daily exposure to other Americans in school. As with other immigrant groups in other places in North America, attending classes in the English language and learning about American culture firsthand is one of the most potent agents of cultural change operating in the lives of Old Believers.

The completion of sixth grade has been the norm for several generations of Old Believer children. However, increasing numbers of Russian parents have begun to support the idea of high school and college education for their children. Constant exposure to classes taught in English has resulted in fewer and fewer children who are able to speak or read

Russian as well as their parents. In school, they also meet and become friends with outsiders, wear modern clothing (often on top of their traditional required ethnic clothing), and sometimes establish relationships with the opposite sex that lead to marriages outside the church. According to recent high school graduate Mike Frolov, "I think the church might go right past our generation. A lot of the young people are going to make their own choice. Why shouldn't I be an average American Joe, instead of Ivan the Churchgoer?" (*Eugene Register Guard,* 4 August 1991, B6).

Mike's father, Fred Frolov, born in China, has encouraged his children to pursue their education. His daughter was one of the first to complete her college degree. Frolov believes that "every family should push for education . . . Pulling children out of school after sixth grade is Old Believer tradition, not dogma. Some of the people in my kids' generation will become more involved" (*Eugene Register Guard,* 4 August 1991, B6).

In Alaska, educational facilities pose a much smaller risk to loss of Russian culture, because the school is located within the Russian village of Nikolaevsk and has primarily Russian students. The new, modern school enrolls children from kindergarten to twelfth grade. Non-Russian classroom teachers and counselors do not openly contest the religious ideas of Old Believer children, but exposure to new ideologies and "foreign" concepts, as well as daily training in the English language, can reasonably be expected to have a long-term effect on cultural and religious retention among Old Believer families. Interviews with the principal and staff at Nikolaevsk School in 1990 revealed that two graduates of their school were attending the University of Oregon, a first for Alaskan Old Believers.

Despite these successes, some parents in Nikolaevsk remain skeptical about the value of higher education. One father expressed his concerns to the principal of the school when it first opened: "Educate them, it is okay, but please don't make them smarter than us. We need our children to believe we know more than they do for life to go on in this same good way" (B. Moore interview, Homer, Alaska, 6 July 1990).

Even though the staff and administration at Nikolaevsk School is non-Russian, until recently all students enrolled in the school were from the Russian village. In the past two years, however, because of its academic success, small classes, and perceived advantages of bilingual classrooms, non-Russian parents from nearby towns have insisted that their children have the right to be bused into the village to attend the state-funded school. This has resulted in a more mixed school enrollment and more potential for the cultural amalgamation of students. Fears of loss of

Russian culture were expressed recently by Natalia and Paul Fefelov, typical Old Believer parents in Nikolaevsk: "The kids are losing their Russian. Everything around them is in English. If we do have a lot of Anglo kids come in, I would like to see more stress on bi-lingual education. From the village point of view, if the school board wants to send in more outside students, that's fine. As long as they don't start creating assimilation with other schools" (*Anchorage Daily News,* 17 July 1990, A7).

Internal issues such as employment and education are not the only active forces bringing change to many Old Believers. Numerous external forces have also been at work. Much of the overall physical and human environment of settlement sites in Oregon and Alaska has changed significantly since Russians first arrived. Woodburn and the surrounding area has mushroomed into a more densely populated, more multicultural region since the 1960s. It also serves as one of Oregon's most popular retirement destinations. Increasing land prices, competition for employment, overcrowded schools, and other urban maladies have changed this part of Oregon from a region of slow-paced farm villages to a rapidly urbanizing subregion of the Pacific Northwest. Russian residences, once separated from neighboring houses by vacant lots and other open space, are now surrounded by houses and apartments, often owned or rented by retirees from California or by Mexican-American families.

Land and people around the more remote Russian settlements on the Kenai Peninsula of Alaska have also changed. When Nikolaevsk was founded in 1968, the nearest towns of Anchor Point and Homer were tiny fishing villages of less than one thousand people each. The tsunami triggered by the Alaska earthquake of 1964 caused significant damage to the Homer spit and retarded overall coastal development in the region. In the twenty-five years since the earthquake, however, the area has witnessed increased development of the tourist economy, expansion of its sport and commercial fishing industries, and a significant increase in its total population. In addition, Old Believers began to subdivide their land in the 1970s as the petroleum industry greatly improved the Alaskan economy. As a result, modern non–Old Believer homes now line both sides of Nikolaevsk Road on the way into the Russian village. Old Believers may soon find themselves surrounded by the very people they came to Alaska to avoid.

Because of these internal and external factors, it is difficult to predict the future adaptation of Old Believers to American life. Untiedt's dissertation on Old Believer acculturation in Oregon concluded with the following summary statements:

The process of acculturation continues in a soft, insidious manner as it operates on Old Believers. Concessions are made, facilitative individuals attempt to ease the process by acting as interpreters or explainers of the host society's culture, and new entities are created to deal with the problem. The direction of thrust is always toward acculturation, however. There are no backward steps in the process. Group boundaries and belief systems have been penetrated with no advances or counter attacks evidenced by the Old Believers.

The homogenizing of the alien subgroup continues through the operation of the bureaucracy of the larger society. The "mosaic" conceptualization of cultural pluralism is given lip service, but the reality is that the Old Believers are treated as an oddity. (1977, 132)

Fifteen years later, Untiedt's final analysis remains questionable. Despite cultural and economic changes from within and without, Russian Old Believers remain a viable ethnic group on the North American Pacific Rim. These persevering people have survived over five hundred years of migration, harassment, and persecution for their beliefs and fought for their very existence. Even though challenges from the ever-encroaching dominant culture will continue to pose problems for survival of the group, especially for the younger generation, it is difficult to imagine the disappearance of this ethnoreligious group from the American cultural landscape in the near future.

THE DOUKHOBOR EXPERIENCE

Nastasia (Nell)

One would never expect retiree Nell Chursenoff Coger to have any connection with Russia or the Soviet Union. She speaks English without a trace of accent and, since the death of her husband several years ago, has lived alone comfortably in her suburban ranch house in north Sacramento. But Nell was born into a Russian Doukhobor family in Saskatchewan in 1915. Her grandfather Gregory Daniel Chursenoff was one of the first of the Doukhobors to enter Canada in 1899, and, after many years working on the Canadian railroad to help earn money to purchase communal Doukhobor farmland, he had become a successful farmer in the Doukhobor prairie settlement there. Nell's maternal grandfather was exiled to a Siberian prison camp in the late 1800s for his religious beliefs. Strangely enough, it was this Siberian exile that ultimately brought Nell to California. Her grandfather never expected to be released from prison (and thus never expected to see his daughter again). His wife died shortly after the migration, so he married a local Molokan woman in Siberia. They later migrated to California with a group of Molokans, eventually settling in the town of Shafter in the San Joaquin Valley. Nell's father, an Independent Doukhobor, later decided to move his family from Saskatchewan to a neighboring farm in Shafter so that his wife would have the opportunity to know her father at long last. Nell's parents and her brother Alex Alexevitch Chursenoff lived in their Shafter farmhouse until it burned down in 1923.

Nell thus grew up in a California Molokan community after 1920. Her Doukhobor parents continued to practice their vegetarian dietary laws, worshiped as a family apart from the Molokans, and despite their later move to San Pedro, maintained their unique Doukhobor belief system as long as they lived.

Despite outward appearances, Nell, now active in the Baptist church in Sacramento, still feels deeply connected to her Russian Doukhobor heritage. She recently traveled to British Columbia with her daughter to attend a Doukhobor family reunion. She was amazed at her lingering Russian-language skills and her sense of belonging while she was in Canada. It was the first time she had been with her Canadian family in over twenty years, yet she still felt a part of it all. As a child growing up away from the center of Doukhobor life and culture, Nell's assimilation into American life was more rapid and more complete than that of her relatives who stayed in Canada. When asked to define her ethnic and religious connections to Doukhobors today, her nephew helped her explain that "I look at being a Doukhobor today like a Jew looks at being a Jew. Whether or not you believe in the faith, you still have the cultural identity of being a Doukhobor" (N. Coger and M. Chursenoff interview, Orangevale, California, 8 July 1991).

Nell Coger's adjustment to American life was influenced by the residential decision making of her family during her formative years. Other Doukhobors who stayed in Doukhobor villages in Saskatchewan and later in British Columbia maintained their Russian ethnic and religious ties well into the twentieth century. But Hawthorn's comprehensive study of the Doukhobors in Canada observed that "a three-way conflict between Russian peasant tradition, Doukhobor religion, and forces emanating from the Canadian environment" had divided Doukhobor groups into various factions by the early 1950s (Hawthorn 1955, 48). Hawthorn also noted that the Doukhobors' economic self-sufficiency had been destroyed by opportunities offered by the "more advanced" Canadian society, and the strength of the culture and traditional lifestyle had been undermined by this economic conflict. The decision by the British Columbia attorney general and the president of the University of British Columbia in early 1950 to conduct a comprehensive study of the "Doukhobor problem" and suggest ways it might be improved resulted in this Hawthorn report and marks the end of an era. From the publication of this study's recommendations in 1952 to the early 1990s, traditional Doukhobor life in Canada has been different from preceding centuries. By the early 1950s, in fact, all Doukhobors had abandoned the communal system of farming, with the exception of one small village on Vancouver Island.

Doukhobor residential patterns also reflect an increasing assimilation into Canadian life. Today, with few exceptions, Doukhobors in the West Kootenay and boundary areas of British Columbia live in single-family homes, not in traditional community houses. Homes are generally dispersed, and settlement patterns are difficult to distinguish from those of other residents in the area, although relict orchards surround some of the former Doukhobor properties. A large Community Hall has been built at Brilliant, where regular Doukhobor gatherings are held, and a Doukhobor Museum has been organized in Grand Forks. These evidences of the lingering identity of Doukhobors on the cultural landscape are complemented by Doukhobor retirement and care centers, such as the one at Castleview, and Russian cemeteries.

It is difficult to predict with any degree of certainty how long a distinct Doukhobor identity will endure in British Columbia. Family reunions center on members of the older generation. Young people have largely moved away from the older Doukhobor communities in the Kootenays. They have settled in Vancouver and other large cities where employment opportunities are better. Most second- and third-generation Canadian Doukhobors cannot speak the Russian language and do not feel a part of Doukhobor life. Unlike other more obviously persistent ethnoreligious groups such as the Amish or Hutterites, it would seem on the surface that the Doukhobors are destined to disappear from the North American landscape.

However, once again the role of religion in maintaining ethnic identity is evidenced. A large organizing religious body, the Union of Spiritual Communities of Christ, is becoming increasingly active in Doukhobor affairs. This group organizes annual reunions, picnics, and retreats; publishes a monthly magazine (in Russian and English); and generally speaks for the continuation of Doukhobor consciousness. With the opening up of the Soviet Union after 1987, communication has developed between Doukhobors still living in Russia and those in Canada. Several trips to Russia occurred in 1992, with the objective of bringing these two groups together.

One of the most fascinating activities of this religious group is the recent recommendation that Doukhobors need to once again form a communal village in Canada. Two steering committees have been organized to date, one to plan for a return to the Doukhobor homeland in Russia and the other to investigate the possibility of "establishing an alternative lifestyle within the Canadian context" (*Iskra Magazine*, 1991, 13–14). These exciting possibilities suggest that a renewed and invigorated Doukhobor identity may yet blossom in western Canada.

In an interesting sidelight, numerous members of the younger generation, as staunch pacifists, organized antiwar protests during the American war in Kuwait in early 1991. This activism is a vivid reminder of Doukhobor protests in their nineteenth-century Caucasus villages against involvement in Russian wars.

Doukhobor adjustment to life in North America is different from that of their sister sect, the Molokans. The isolation of Doukhobor families in rural communal villages of Saskatchewan and British Columbia contrasts drastically with the Molokans' decision to settle in the heart of an urban neighborhood in Los Angeles. Their similar backgrounds in Russia and their related religious beliefs notwithstanding, these two groups have had very different experiences adjusting to their new environment.

THE MOLOKAN EXPERIENCE

Tanya

Tanya Desatoff, now deceased, was born in a Molokan village near Kars in the Caucasus Mountains of Russia. In 1905, when Tanya was eleven years old, her father, Phillip Mikhail Shubin, led one of the earliest group of Molokans from Russia to Los Angeles. On a tape made by one of her daughters, Tanya vividly described how a group of about 150 Molokans left their village and traveled by train and freighter from Kars to Marseilles and then to California via the isthmus of Panama. She would never forget that long trip and the June day she finally set foot on American soil.

Tanya met her husband in their Molokan neighborhood in East Los Angeles several years later. He had grown up in a Russian village about seven miles from hers, but they first met in California. Married at age fifteen, Tanya eventually had twelve children. Over the years, she worked in a laundry and in a garment factory, but is best remembered in her role as head cook at the Molokan church in Los Angeles, where she worked for over forty years. She taught herself to read, write, and speak English within the first years of life in California and despite a very "modern" attitude, remained devoutly attached to Molokan beliefs all of her life.

Tanya's life was typical of many thousands of other Molokan women struggling to find their identity in a new environment. After her marriage, she agreed to move with her new husband and his parents to the Molokan village of Guadalupe in Mexico. But her husband soon grew tired of life in Mexico and insisted they move back to California. On the overheated train to Bakersfield, her infant died in her arms, but she determinedly followed her husband to his dream of owning a farm in the San Joaquin Valley. He soon tired of the labor involved in agricultural work and moved his family back to their original life in Los Angeles, where he became a taxi and truck driver in the midst of a rapidly expanding urban area.

Despite Tanya's role of wife and mother within a traditional society, Tanya's daughter remembers her mother as a "very independent and strong woman." In her later years, she encouraged her children to pursue their education. Like so many other first-generation Molokans in California, Tanya seems to have found a way to live comfortably within two worlds but strongly preferred the Molokan world. After living in two cultures for over eighty years, she handled her dual existences with apparent ease, clinging to her Molokan beliefs while living successfully within rapidly changing California culture until the end of her life.

Tanya's experiences represent the experiences of thousands of Molokans who came to the United States to find a new life. Although she married a Molokan, raised her children to believe in the church's teachings, and spoke fluent Russian all her life, she lived like a typical California woman. She traveled frequently, worked outside the home, and, according to her children, had an independent spirit and mind. She spoke English as well as she spoke Russian. To an outsider, it would be easy to assume that Tanya Desatoff was much more American than Russian.

Yet Tanya's attachment to her Russianness remained strong throughout her ninety years. As with other first-generation immigrants, she served Russian foods, spoke Russian at home, and much preferred the company of other Russian Molokans. And Tanya's strong desire to leave the city and return to the land was typical of the vast majority of first-generation Molokan immigrants in California.

As discussed in chapter 4, Molokans often viewed resettlement in isolated rural areas as the solution to problems of urban life. This attachment to the land remains strong even in many second-generation Molokans. Dispersal to agricultural nodes in the Central Valley of California and the Willamette Valley in Oregon are locational evidences of this yearning. As discussed earlier, numerous and varied attempts to return to the land took the Molokans not only to Oregon and rural California but also to Mexico, Arizona, Utah, and Washington.

As we have seen, the group in rural America often failed to let go of their former agriculturally based lives in Russia. The problems faced by early Molokan efforts to buy land were summarized by Peter Speek, who made a comprehensive study of the Molokan experience:

First, they have not enough money to buy immediately a large tract of land, irrigate and improve it, and give the families a good start. Second, they do not know the country and conditions well enough, especially the agricultural possibilities. Third, the private land dealers are mostly crooks who cheat them, either by misrepresenting the quality of the land, or by not fulfilling their contract promises, or by making contracts so complicated and so filled with catches that they afterward prove the ruin of the settler. (1932, 258)

Today's Molokan settlements in the San Joaquin and Willamette valleys remain contemporary evidence of this continuing search for a more rural lifestyle. Many second- and third-generation Molokans continue this rural tradition as successful grape, vegetable, and flower farmers supplying products for California cities.

But numerous Molokans have also clung to their traditions in urban areas. Sociologist Pauline Young conducted an intensive study of early Molokans in Los Angeles (Young 1932). She was especially concerned with the adjustment process of younger members of the group. Her analysis suggested the following list of ways in which Molokans struggled to perpetuate their religion and culture among future generations in California:

1. Emphasis on the "glorious past": Elders traditionally won respect from younger members by constantly discussing traditions and customs from their homeland. The sufferings of religious martyrs, heroes and leaders of the early years of the movement, and stories of the wisdom of their prophets were important topics of discussion in family and social gatherings. Young people often rejected these stories as "too gruesome to be reviewed" and too unpleasant in the context of their new life in southern California.

2. Role of ritual and ceremonies: Younger members of the group were much more affected by ceremonies such as weddings, funerals, christenings, and memorial days than they were by oral tradition. Molokan ceremonies are dramatic and emotional, and young people are often attracted to the faith during these special days.

3. Appearance of written tradition: Early Molokans in California realized the importance of writing down their Old World oral tradition in

self-published early histories of the experiences and beliefs of the group. As with oral tradition, older members of the group initially showed more interest in these writings than did the young.[1]

4. Repelling invaders: As with other religious and ethnic groups, Molokans tried hard to limit the associations of their children. Children were often rebuked in public for their association with people of other cultures.

I frequently saw a Molokan man who knew his son had entered a local restaurant or pool hall call him out on the street. When the latter made his appearance, the father beat him in the presence of his associates. The most astonishing thing to me was that the son took it from him and never snapped back. You could hardly expect that much from the average American boy. The son rarely approached the same place again, being ashamed to face his associates, but he visited halls outside of this district. (Young 1932, 244)

5. Discussion of personal conduct: Public and private "talk" was also used as a device to control young people's wanderings. But many refused to be influenced by the attitudes of the group. According to one young woman,

When the women started to talk and gossip about me because I refused to live with my mother-in-law after marrying her son, I was determined not to give in. If the old folks are so selfish and 'talk' when their children don't care to follow the old ways, then the children have a right to look out for themselves . . . Oh, I can't be bothered with custom. All I know is that it does not suit me and that's enough. Nowadays, everybody must look out for himself. It doesn't matter much what these Russians say. We couldn't please them any how. We are just different and why should we go back to their stage of life when we live in America? We must get someplace. (Young 1932, 246)

One of the many differences between younger and older members of the early settlers in California was their emphasis on the importance of the individual and the importance of the group. Molokans originally thought of themselves as a brotherhood (*bratstvo*) rather than a community (*obshchestvo*). Decisions were reached by the elected leaders of the group through consensus, and communication was face to face. First-generation Molokans had no interest in individual decision making or respect for individual rights within the group. This was acutely different from values inherently important to life in the American West, where individual freedom was valued almost beyond all else. Young expressed this conflict:

Village life in Russia had been personal and intimate and characterized by economic self-sufficiency and primary group organization and control. In America, they faced a social-economic organization characterized by impersonal, anonymous, secondary relationships with an endless variety of strange activities, customs, and beliefs. Industry, school attendance, real estate agents, clever salesmen, public officials, social reformers, slowly and subtly penetrated the colony, lured their children into the outer world and gradually broke down the social isolation and cultural integrity of the group. (1929, 398)

Indeed, the culture shock and extreme polarity between first- and second-generation Molokans described in Young's pioneering work in southern California would seem to point to an eventual disappearance of Molokan values, beliefs, and identity in North America. Recent interviews with numerous Molokans in California and Oregon, however, point to an increasingly strong identity within the group, especially among second- and third-generation Russian-Americans seeking a link to their past.

Young's analysis of the acculturation experience of these early Molokans in Los Angeles lays a firm foundation for the observation of this group during the remainder of the twentieth century. As Molokans intermarried and raised their families in increasingly multicultural neighborhoods, change was bound to occur. Today's Molokans appear to be more connected to the group's religious beliefs than to any other part of their identity. Clinging to the importance of the church's values for the safety and spiritual well-being of themselves and their children in an increasingly challenging world, Molokans may wear traditional clothing to church services, celebrate Molokan religious holidays, and cook Russian foods on special occasions, but otherwise they are fully assimilated into the economic and social fabric of their communities. Most of today's Molokans do not speak or read the Russian language, and many participate in English-language worship services.

Yet despite social and spatial dispersal over the past ninety years, more than four thousand people in over three hundred towns and cities in the American West continue to identify themselves as Molokan in the 1990 *Molokan Directory*. And Molokan John Berokoff (1969) estimated that there were at least fifteen to twenty thousand Molokans in the region in the 1960s. Many thousands attend Molokan religious services regularly in Oregon, California, and Arizona and are raising their children firmly in the faith. Russian-language and -culture classes to further indoctrinate the younger generation in Molokan teachings are held regularly in Los Angeles, Kerman, and Woodburn, as numerous second- and third-generation Molokans are taking the lead in organizing new and renewed social and religious networks in the region via newsletters such as the *Christian Molokan Besednyik*, published by the Reformed Molokan church, membership directories, and other publications.

It appears that Molokans living in more rural parts of the study area are maintaining this ethnoreligious identity more devoutly than those living in metropolitan areas. An examination of addresses listed in successive issues of the *Molokan Directory* reveals that many third-generation urban Molokans are beginning to move away from older Russian neighborhoods to more suburban districts of the city. Despite a new influx of Molokans from Iran between 1947 and 1953, many of those who grew up in the ethnically diverse Potrero Hill neighborhood of San Francisco, for example, are moving to more suburban communities. This dispersal reflects not only the desire of younger urban Molokans to live in more upwardly mobile communities, but also their move into professional-level employment.

In Los Angeles, the same type of suburban dispersal is occurring. The urge to "get ahead" financially and socially is tempting many younger Molokans away from older neighborhoods. According to Moore,

The most real threat from the American world of Los Angeles is the temptation of materialism and "getting ahead." Molokan parents live in constant fear that their sons and daughters will fall into a pattern of unacceptable and perhaps destructive behavior through contact with the non-Molokan world in public schools, colleges, and in jobs. Unacceptable behavior is poor attendance at church or Bible classes, refusing to wear a Russian shirt, absence from family prayers, and attending the movies. Destructive behavior includes associating with "ne nasi" (non-Molokans), thus opening oneself up to outside influences, compromises, and pollution. Naturally drinking, drug usage, sexual promiscuity, and "marrying out" receive the most severe rebukes. (1973, 16)

The Baptist and Pentecostal Experience
Elizabeth

For the past twenty years, Elizabeth Loscutoff has lived in Woodburn, Oregon. Now a Russian Pentecostal, Elizabeth was born into an Orthodox and Molokan family in a Molokan village in Russia. In 1933, at the age of five, she, her family, and five other families escaped from Russia and resettled in Persia (Iran), where they were associated with the Baptist faith. Elizabeth recalls that Molokans, Baptists, and Seventh-day Adventists worked together closely there and that they attended each other's religious services.

At first, "life was really bad in Persia . . . we lived only on buttermilk and dark bread" (E. Loscutoff, Woodburn, Oregon, 10 March 1991). They were sent to places where there was no work and very little food. Political pressures from the shah and ethnic tensions among the Muslims forced them to prepare for another migration after World War II. In

1949, Elizabeth and a small group of other Russians from Tehran settled in San Francisco.

Elizabeth met and married her Russian husband in San Francisco, and they were both converted to the Pentecostal religion. They had four children and were later divorced. It was then that Elizabeth began to consider moving her family to a smaller, more rural place. Because her aunt had moved to Gervais, Oregon, several years before, Elizabeth decided to move her children north to the Willamette Valley, where "life would be safer and cleaner." Elizabeth's aunt had been the first Russian Molokan to settle in Gervais, and the Loscutoffs arrived fifteen years later. When asked about her life in Oregon, Elizabeth replied enthusiastically: "Russian people love nature so much. That is why there are so many of us here now. Nature is gift from God. Many moved here from big cities like Los Angeles and San Francisco to be close to nature and close to other Russians. They love the quiet here" (interview, 10 March 1991).

After her years in Russia, Persia, and the San Francisco Bay area, Elizabeth seems content living a quiet Woodburn lifestyle. She owns her modest home located on the edge of town and is involved in Russian Pentecostal and Baptist church work with new Russian refugees. She speaks both English and Russian comfortably and feels a part of both worlds. In Woodburn, she has had many opportunities to mix with other Russians as well as other Americans.

Elizabeth Loscutoff's decision to move to a rural area to raise her children in the 1960s was not unusual for many Americans. But her choice of a distinctly Russian town is significant. She may appear fully American and speak flawless English, but, like so many other first-generation immigrants, she still has strong ties to the "old country."

The adjustment of Russian Baptists and Pentecostals to life in North America is more difficult to assess than that of earlier groups such as the Molokans or Doukhobors. Most arrived much more recently than the other groups investigated in this book. With the notable exception of the West Sacramento enclave, no other significant residential clustering of Baptists or Pentecostals existed in the study area before World War II, although dispersed Russian Baptist families had settled in Los Angeles, San Diego, San Francisco, Portland, Seattle, and Vancouver. After the war, new groups of Russian evangelicals settled in these cities and in Monterey Park and Vernon, British Columbia.

Like Molokans, Doukhobors, and Old Believers, Russian Baptists and Pentecostals have rigid rules about everyday life that must be observed to remain active in the faith. These requirements include strict observance of Sunday as the sabbath day, avoidance of cosmetics and fancy clothing, and maintenance of close family relationships. These Russian evangelicals find themselves in a different cultural and socioeconomic context than that of immigrants who arrived in earlier decades. Cities are larger, life is faster paced, and neighborhoods are more multicultural. Refugees arriving in the early 1990s also find themselves in a tight economic situation as the recession permeates all regions of the United States. Employment opportunities during this difficult time of economic cutbacks are limited, especially for people with poor English-language skills. Today's refugees find themselves faced with dwindling economic resources. This often results in depression and a feeling of hopelessness as month after month passes without employment.

Russian Baptists and Pentecostals cling to their religious beliefs and to each other ever more tightly during these uncertain times. This has resulted in distinct spatial patterns of settlement. Even though new immigrants may live in many parts of cities in California, Oregon, and Washington, they often rent apartments in the same building or rent houses near each other. Neighborhoods near older Baptist churches, meanwhile, have acted as magnets for the settlement of new refugees. Numerous new church congregations have been established in other parts of cities, away from older districts, to accommodate more dispersed residential patterns.

Despite residential dispersal, religious groups have formed tight social networks to help solve their members' problems of adjustment to life in North America. Clinging to tightly structured social and religious networks thus offers economic and emotional support during the stressful adjustment to a new life. But this ethnoreligious cohesion may also retard eventual assimilation. There is no need to learn to speak English when most contacts are in Russian. There is likewise less motivation to replace welfare checks with full-time employment when all one's friends are also supported by the government. Interviews with Russian families who live in an all-Russian apartment complex or neighborhood reveal that they are learning English much less quickly and moving into the economic mainstream at a much slower pace than those living on their own in more ethnically mixed neighborhoods.

Despite the obvious limitations of residential clustering for adjustment to American life, education is a strong counterforce in the assimilation process. Since everyone over the age of eighteen must take English classes to receive welfare support, they are at least laying a foundation in the language. In addition, Pentecostals and Baptists frequently have large families, so they have a great deal of contact with public schools. Children learn English quickly at school and bring it home to their parents. This process, along with exposure to television and radio, force parents to hear English much of the day.

Even though religious services are held in the Russian language, Baptist and Pentecostal immigrants are more closely connected to North America in their religious background than are other groups discussed in this chapter. The Baptist and Pentecostal religions diffused into Russia and the Soviet Union primarily because of support from the United States and Canada. Despite the use of the Russian language, all other aspects of these two religions are distinctly mainstream fundamentalist American-style Christianity. Religious songs, teachings, and prayer customs are almost exactly like those in North American counterpart churches. This close connection between the immigrants' early religious training and their new environment makes life in North America seem less foreign. In the words of a recent Baptist immigrant now living in Sacramento, "I was already an American when I was a boy. You see, everything about my life has always been American. My church came from here, and it is the most important thing in my life. So when I first came to California, everything felt normal to me. It was no big adjustment" (V. Morgunov interview, West Sacramento, 23 October 1990).

The man quoted above, incidentally, has overcome the economic recession by starting his own Russian-American Amway Company. Selling cleaning products to Russian customers within his social and religious network, Morgunov has thus far laid the foundation for a successful business. Many new Russian immigrants find themselves at his introductory sessions eagerly supporting his "cleanliness is next to godliness" presentation.

Educational and employment opportunities for Russian Baptists and Pentecostals in North America are paving the way for their future adjustment to an often stressful new environment. Also useful in nudging the process along more quickly is the anti-Soviet attitude almost all have about their homeland. As discussed in earlier chapters, many Russian Baptists and Pentecostals were severely persecuted by the Soviet government for their religious beliefs. As emigrants who left their country during the final years of Soviet domination, these two groups are experiencing a particularly confused set of feelings about their homeland. While they remain ethnically Russian and thus culturally and ethnically connected to their former home, they are distrustful about anything that is in any way connected with Russia or the former Soviet Union. In the confusion of Gorbachev's resignation and Boris Yeltsin's rapid ascendence to power, along with the rapid reorganization and renaming of their country in early 1992, many now feel as if they do not have a country. According to a thirty-three-year-old Russian Pentecostal woman in Seattle, "I really don't know what country I come from any more. Really, it is hard to know. People ask me where I am from when they hear my accent, and I have no answer. I only know where I *used* to be from. That country does not exist any longer" (anonymous interview, 15 November 1991).

Russian Baptists and Pentecostals, much like other religious groups analyzed here, are continuing their adjustment process in the early 1990s. The process of remaining attached to their Russianness while establishing themselves in a new and drastically different environment is a delicate balancing act.

Adaptation in a Comparative Perspective

Russian immigrants who migrated to the shores of the North American Pacific Rim came from a place that severely restricted their religious freedom and everyday decision making. Sects such as Old Believers, Molokans, and Doukhobors had clustered in rural Russian villages to protect not only their religious beliefs but their lives. In this cloistered environment, they learned not to venture out into the wider world. Ridicule and persecution often awaited them outside of their own village. More recently, Russian Baptists and Pentecostals in the Soviet Union experienced many of the same threats. While earlier groups were persecuted by the authoritarian Orthodox church, evangelical Christians feared the Communist authorities. In all cases, these groups preferred staying close to home, where they felt safer from persecution by outsiders.

The decision of Russian Christians to migrate en masse to a distant place is in itself remarkable. Their tendency to stay close to home must have made the idea of long-distance travel to an unknown country seem inconceivable to many, impossible to most. Without the support of strong leadership from within and foreign sponsorship from without, these groups would have found the decision to leave Russia impossible.

In almost all cases, Russian immigrants arrived in North America in a desperate state. Most were financially and emotionally destitute from years of surviving within a system of economic and political persecution. Their experiences in Russia and the Soviet Union also made them extremely hesitant to trust the outside world. Authority figures of any kind intimidated them, and even simple day-to-day decisions overwhelmed them.

This challenging migration experience has made the adjustment process even more stressful for Russian immigrants than for many other groups who have resettled in North America. Recent arrivals almost always pass through a series of emotional stages as they experience this difficult process.

The adjustment experiences of recent Russians are undoubtedly similar to earlier groups who settled in the study area. The first emotions upon arrival are often relief and euphoria. They are free. They are here at long last. It is a time, albeit a short time, of great joy. These feelings are often quickly followed by an almost overwhelming feeling of confusion and indecision. The sound of rapid English everywhere, the fast-paced lifestyle of almost everyone they meet, and the inability to make decisions haunts many Russians in this second stage. These emotions often lead to rage at the system and at life in general, but most often at their Russian homeland for making all this necessary. In this stage of the adjustment process, most immigrants blame their old country, not their new country, for their problems. This anger is often followed by resignation that life is still going to be difficult in the new environment and a sense that life will never be easy. This resignation stage often lasts many months or even several years. It is sometimes followed by a feeling of acceptance, as language skills and economic conditions improve and life in their new environment begins to seem almost "normal" at last. Immigrants begin to accept certain aspects of their new life that they once resisted. Watching television, eating in fast-food restaurants, and even playing video games soon become acceptable behavior. Except for their Russian accents, these Russians blend easily into the mainstream culture. It may seem to many outsiders almost as if the immigrants have given up their Russian connections altogether. However, religious beliefs brought with them from their homeland preserve their Russian identity even as they learn to survive almost invisibly within mainstream culture.

Religion: Clinging to the Old Ways

While these cultural, economic, and social forces act against preservation of Russian culture in Russian enclaves in North America, religion continues to act as an integrating counterforce. Throughout the often complicated and difficult migration and resettlement process, spiritual beliefs have helped hold immigrant groups together. Church membership implies both behavioral and social consensus of its members, with conscious and unconscious suppression of individual traits. Repeated interaction with others of similar religious backgrounds helps define a distinctive subculture. Because a great amount of conformity of attitudes and beliefs is required for religious groups to function effectively, they play a potent maintenance and integrative role in Russian communities.

This link between religious expression and identity was explored by Gans in his study of Italians in Boston (1962). Gans found that even religious divisions within ethnic communities intensify group solidarity. Just as Italian Catholics in Boston scorned a small Protestant group of "holy jumpers," so too do Russian Orthodox believers ridicule Russian Pentecostals and Baptists in communities in California, Oregon, and Washington. As in the American West, this religious differentiation defined ethnic identity in Boston even more strongly than if the group had all been members of one faith. Differences in religious ideology lend further social definition to residents. As Russian Baptists disapprove of their Orthodox neighbors' "Vodka lifestyle," so too do Russian Orthodox members react negatively to the expressive nature "of those Bible-thumping Baptists."

Even the schism that exists between the Alaskan Popovtsy and Bezpopovtsy Old Believers acts as a binding force for each of these religious subgroups. The insistence on one's identity with one group or the other intensifies ethnic and religious commitment and helps maintain the Russianness of each group.

A unique, self-described characteristic of the Russian-American community is the almost necessary requirement for a difference of opinion concerning major internal and external issues. "If you have two Russians, you have at least five opinions" is a common comment among many Russians in North America. An often-told joke is that a lone Russian stranded on a tropical island told his rescuers that he had built two churches on the island—one for him to attend and one for him *not* to attend (V. Alexseov interview, Berkeley, 27 February 1985).

Despite the common religious differentiation between Russian groups, best expressed in Woodburn, Oregon, where Old Believers, Molokans, and Pentecostals live in relative harmony, Russian churches remain one of the most important ethnic mediating structures in the community (Berger and Neuhaus 1977). According to Peter Berger, "These institutions which stand between the individual in his private sphere and the large institutions of the public sphere" provide stability in the private life of the individual (Berger and Neuhaus 1977, 17).

There can be no doubt that religious structures and religious beliefs play a pivotal role in cultural maintenance in the everyday life of the community, not only in the physical sense but also in a symbolic sense. In over two hundred interviews conducted for this study, an individual's identity as a Russian was important, but one's identity as a Baptist or Molokan was even more significant.

Rural and Urban Differences

Culture groups everywhere are held together and pulled apart by both centripetal and centrifugal forces. Russian groups, such as the Old Believers and Doukhobors who settled in isolated rural areas through their "flight into refuge," have maintained their separateness from the majority culture more effectively than groups, such as Orthodox, Molokan, Baptist, and Pentecostal Russians, who migrated to more urban areas. In a similar way, urban groups who settled in distinct ethnic neighborhoods have remained more "Russian" than groups settling in integrated neighborhoods. Decision making about initial residential patterns shapes social processes in a very real way.

Whether clustered or dispersed in their settlement patterns, Russian immigrant groups on the Pacific Rim of North America have maintained their isolation from mainstream culture into the 1990s effectively enough so that a distinct Russian identity remains in many diverse parts of the region. As long as members of each Russian ethnoreligious sect can identify with a common social and religious structure, their identification as a distinct group lingers on the maps and the cultural landscape of the North American Pacific Rim.

SEVEN
Conclusions

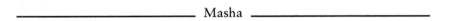

———————————— Masha ————————————

Six-year-old Masha was born in Russia and now lives in Woodburn, Oregon (fig. 13). She moved to this small agricultural town with her parents in 1990. Masha has just found a new friend in the neighborhood, a Russian Old Believer girl, Irina, who is standing on her right in the photograph. Masha used to live in a crowded apartment in downtown Moscow; she enjoys playing outside in the yard with other Russian and American children in her neighborhood. Masha already knows many English words. She speaks and sings in Russian and English with equal skill. Masha and her friend Irina are starting public school in the fall, where they will have to speak and understand English all day. By the time she graduates from high school, Masha will be like most other American girls her age. Despite her Russian heritage, she will have become a part of the mainstream North American culture.

Recent Russian immigrants, like Masha, who are now living in the United States and Canada are a people without a country. Their homeland has a new name, it is governed by a new power, and it operates within a new political and economic system. Their group identity as "Russians opposed to communism" has become less clear as conditions change almost daily in the newly formed Commonwealth of Independent States.

Russian immigrants who arrived in North America during earlier waves of settlement faced similar identity problems. Cut off from their

187

Figure 13. Masha (*left*) and her Old Believer friend play together in the yard of Masha's home in Woodburn, Oregon. Photo by author.

homeland by political and religious differences, they too were a people without a country. They were a group in exile, alienated from Russia by political schisms and deeply felt emotions of hostility and hatred toward the government that had "driven them out." In a sense, despite the date of their arrival, all Russians in North America find themselves in the often painful, often confusing position of not belonging to any particular nation or culture. They no longer feel a part of their Russian heritage, but neither do they feel completely American or Canadian. Cut off from their homeland, confused by their dual identities, the Russian immigrants' story is much like the story of thousands of other immigrants in North America.

Russian migration, settlement, and adaptation incorporates some of the same processes and problems of all migrations of all people in all places. General processes that shape relocation experiences include, but are not limited to, the following:

1. Long-distance travel and lack of communication with their homeland increases the groups' sense of isolation in their new environment.
2. Larger immigrant groups tend to need outsiders less; thus the size of the incoming group affects the acculturation process.
3. Groups that settle in tightly focused ethnic enclaves remain more attached to their original culture than do groups that settle in a more dispersed pattern.
4. Groups that cling to antecedent religious affiliations adjust more slowly to life within mainstream culture than do groups that abandon original spiritual connections.

The long migration, large size, clustered settlement pattern, and tight religious networks of certain groups of Russian immigrants thus suggest continued isolation from mainstream culture and a relatively slow adjustment process.

But the Russian experience is also unique among immigrant experiences. Each incoming group of Russians arrived in North America in distinct waves of settlement. Each of these intense, short waves was followed by long periods of isolation when very few newcomers arrived to bring renewed cultural connections and vitality to ethnic settlement nodes. These periods of limited Russian immigration into North America were the result of restrictive political conditions in Russia and the Soviet Union along with changing immigration policies in Canada and the United States.

Russian Doukhobors and Molokans, for example, arrived in North America from the 1890s to the 1910s, with no significant number of arrivals in later years. Old Believers arrived in Oregon in the 1960s, and, except for their secondary migration to Alberta and Alaska, no new groups of Old Believers have relocated in the region since that time. Even Orthodox Russians arrived in three different bursts, followed by periods of relative stagnation.

Despite new freedoms to emigrate from their homeland, Russians settling in North America since 1988 find themselves in a situation similar to that of earlier groups. Because their country of origin is no longer viewed as a place of religious and political persecution, Russians are no longer considered refugees by the United States government. This denial of refugee status means (1) Russians no longer have permission to enter the United States and Canada in such large numbers; (2) their airfare is no longer paid for through loans from the American government; and (3) they no longer have sponsors to arrange for housing and employment. Deteriorating economic conditions in the Commonwealth of Independent States has also severely limited the number of Russians who can afford to emigrate. Both push and pull factors will be weakened significantly for Russians, therefore, in the coming years. In a sense, then, every Russian immigrant group has faced this same isolation from new arrivals from their homeland once they have settled in North America, including the most recent group.

The question that immediately arises from an analysis of the Russian immigration experience is, What is the probability of cultural retention among recent Russian immigrants as compared to groups that arrived during earlier periods of settlement? Chapter 6 discussed factors that encouraged cultural retention among earlier groups. The two primary factors are location patterns and religious affiliations. As was shown, those who stayed in cohesive Russian neighborhoods or rural settlements and who maintained their close ties with the Russian church have retained more of their Russian identity than those who dispersed to other residential areas and/or drifted away from Russian religious networks.

The vast majority of recent Russian immigrants have settled in densely populated urban areas on the Pacific Rim of North America. This environment presents a special set of problems for newcomers. According to David Ley,

The existence of large cities has permitted the emergence of plural life styles because, unlike rural and small town society, population thresholds are sufficient to maintain diverse subcultures and their institutional supports. It is therefore probable that urbanization encourages divisiveness among people as each seeks the solace of his or her own cluster of like-minded peers. (1983, 202)

This urban-induced divisiveness has encouraged Russians who are dispersing out of older ethnic neighborhoods in West Coast cities to settle near one another in new settlement nodes. Families leaving older West Sacramento Russian neighborhoods, for example, have relocated to newer apartments and subdivisions in places such as Rancho Cordova and Carmichael. It is anticipated that those who stay together spatially will maintain their connections with Russian culture for the longest time. Encouraged by neighbors with similar religious beliefs, they also maintain Russian church connections longer.

It is also significant to note that the first arrivals in any wave of immigration have different characteristics than later arrivals. Those who come first are usually the greatest risk takers. They are often more ambitious and adventurous and are willing to make new decisions as conditions change. They have also had the longest period of adjustment in their new environment. The earliest glasnost-era arrivals in the study area, therefore, have been the first to move away from older neighborhoods, seeking better conditions for themselves and their families. As more recent immigrants become better acquainted with the system and gain confidence in their new environment, it is anticipated that they, too, will disperse to other parts of the city. This residential dispersal will no doubt encourage more rapid adjustment to life within the majority culture.

Strong centripetal and centrifugal forces are acting on recent Russian settlement nodes. These forces will shape spatial patterns as well. Changes in food habits (traditional family dinners versus "eating on the run"), language retention (Russian-language classes sponsored by churches versus public education taught in English), religious affiliations (membership in a Russian church versus membership in an American church), and employment (exposure to a Russian community versus daily contact with the outside world) are influencing residential decision making as new immigrants become adjusted to the North American way of life.

As mentioned in chapter 6, recent Russian immigrants have come face to face with sociocultural and economic conditions very different from the environmental conditions that greeted earlier waves of immigrants. New arrivals are faced with high unemployment rates, crowded low-income neighborhoods, ethnic conflict, and negative attitudes of the majority culture toward immigrants in general. These challenges are partially offset by the new and extremely positive feelings of Americans and Canadians toward anything "Russian" in the 1990s. National feelings of concern for the welfare of people in the former Soviet Union (including food, medical aid, and other social programs) have spread to feelings of support for Russian immigrants as well. In addition, Russians have not faced problems of racial discrimination and negative stereotyping because of their skin color or ethnic background, as have so many other immigrant groups in the United States and Canada. This will also speed their acceptance by the mainstream culture.

Both the characteristics of individuals of the incoming group and the conditions and attitudes of residents of the receiving area, then, influence the adjustment process. Throughout human history, people have traveled to new places. Because people carry their cultures with them, the process of migration has most often been the mechanism for the spread of culture around the globe.

The Russian migration experience is particularly dramatic and immediate. Because of the difficulty of securing archival data, the challenges of interviewing often distrustful Russian immigrants, and the complexi-

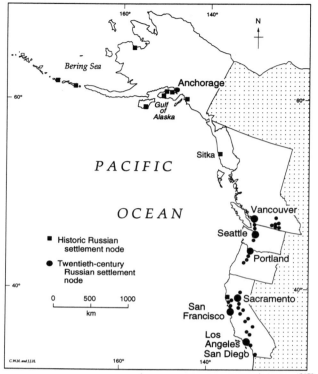

Map 23. Russian settlements on the North American Pacific Rim

ties of conducting research on so many diverse groups, this book is the first to provide a comparative overview of the Russian experience in a large regional setting. Much future work remains, however, to document the adjustment process and regional dispersal of Russian immigrant groups in the coming decades. Analyses of religious and ethnic bonds among second- and third-generation Russians are also needed, especially as these bonds become visible or invisible in household residential choice. A well-known tendency of second-generation immigrants is a rejection of their parents' values and culture, while third-generation ethnics are often more willing to explore and celebrate their grandparents' heritage. Another line of research growing out of this study, therefore, might examine the adjustment of second- and third-generation Russians.

A final cartographic summary of data locates Russian nodes on the Pacific Rim of North America (map 23). A strong north-south linear settlement pattern, broken only by Doukhobor settlements in southeastern British Columbia, suggests close connections to the physical environment as well as to transportation corridors. During the 1990s, this map will undoubtedly become more "Russian," as new immigrants find their way to the region via secondary migration streams from eastern and midwestern cities. What lies ahead for these newest Americans and Canadians is, as yet, uncharted.

NOTES

Chapter 1

1. Scholarly studies on Russian settlement in North America are widely scattered and limited in number. Most of the work accomplished to date has focused on the eastern and midwestern experience (see, for example, Davis 1922a; Glazer and Moynihan 1963; Lieberson 1961, 1963; Simerenko 1964; Wertsman 1977; Johnston 1981). Previous work has emphasized economic mobility, suburban versus central city residential patterns, and Russian assimilation and acculturation rates.

Most notable of previous work on Russian settlement along the North American Pacific Rim are the numerous publications of James Gibson on Alaska and California (1971, 1972, 1976, 1978, 1980, 1986). Other work by geographers documenting the Russian experience in California is contained in one thesis (Tripp 1980) and one dissertation (Hardwick 1986).

2. Geographic studies of ethnic settlement have investigated themes such as landscape change through time, diffusion of culture traits and belief systems, adaptation to the host society, and settlement patterns of selected groups. Other social scientists have traditionally been more interested in issues such as interethnic conflict (see, for example, Alba 1990; Waters 1990; Portes and Rumbaut 1990; Sowell 1978, 1981; Light 1972; Isaacs 1975; Gans 1962; Suttles 1968; Gordon 1964). Cultural and historical geographers, such as Jordan (1966), Meinig (1971), Mannion (1974), and Ostergren (1979, 1981a, 1981b, 1988), have emphasized topics involving a more spatial dimension.

Allen's and Turner's comprehensive atlas *We the People* (1987) reinspired a new generation of geographers interested in ethnic settlement patterns. This award-winning atlas applies ethnic census data in cartographic representations. Detailed ancestry counts from the 1980 census remain particularly useful in settlement studies. Computer cartography and Geographic Information System mapping techniques have made the merging of census data and boundary files of states and metropolitan areas possible. Allen and Turner's atlas on American ethnicity is the most comprehensive example to date of the strengths of this method of analysis.

3. A few geographers have used interviews and participant observation as their primary method of analysis. Symanski's work with Salvadoran refugees in Texas and Mexico (1986) and Desbarats's analysis of Thai migration to Los Angeles (1979) are two examples that illustrate the value of fieldwork and interviewing in geographic analysis.

4. Much debate has divided scholars who study "religious geography" (the study of the role of religion in understanding humanity's place in the universe) and those who examine the "geography of religion" (Sopher 1981; Isaac 1965). The second approach "views religion as a human institution, and explores its relationships with various elements of its human and physical settings" (Stump 1986, 1).

The relationship between the natural environment and religious beliefs has been of particular concern to geographers. Huntington (1945) and Semple (1903) both emphasized the natural environment as the primary reason for the emergence of religious symbols and images. These environmentally deterministic explanations were replaced by a more economic and political approach after the publication of sociologist Max Weber's arguments linking Protestantism and capitalism (Weber 1976).

Recent decades have witnessed a return to the geographic study of environment and religion with an increasing awareness of the world's vast environmental problems. These recent publications argue that religious beliefs have been the primary cause of the earth's environmental crisis (see, for example, Doughty 1981).

Geographers have also been interested in religion as a basis for defining culture regions and explaining cultural landscapes. Traditional cultural geographers, influenced strongly by the Berkeley tradition, examined religious features on the cultural landscape (see, for example, Jackson 1980; Manzo 1983; Biswas 1984; Laatsch and Calkins 1986). The spatial distribution of religious groups on earth has also been of importance in these traditional cultural studies (Stump 1984a, 1984b; Zelinsky 1961; Shortridge 1976).

Chapter 2

1. Sources on the origin and diffusion of eastern Orthodoxy abound. Three of the most useful overviews include Ware 1964, Ellis 1986, and Meyendorf 1962. Also useful for general background information on the topic is Zernov 1961. Information on church ritual and beliefs is contained in Dabovich 1898. A fascinating look at Orthodoxy from an outsider's viewpoint is contained in Forest 1988.

2. The relationship between Russian religion and Russian culture is explored in detail in two volumes by G. P. Fedotov (1946–66). P. Miliukov (1943) also explores this connection.

3. In addition to sources on Old Believers cited in this chapter, other useful

references are Billington 1966 and Scheffel 1991. Doctoral dissertations containing background on Old Believer migration and settlement include Morris 1981, Colfer 1985, and Smithson 1976.

4. These three changes were only a few of the radical recommendations of Patriarch Nikon. He also suggested consecrating five loaves of bread instead of seven at the offertory; having one loaf of bread on the church altar instead of many; changing the procession around the church and around graves to a movement against the direction of the sun (counterclockwise) as opposed to with the direction of the sun (clockwise); saying "our God" instead of "our Father"; and other changes in church architecture and rituals.

5. A particularly compelling discussion of the Old Believer "death by fire" that occurred during these dark days of the schism is in Crummey 1970, chapter 3.

6. Members of Khlysty, Skoptsy, and other sects that emerged in this postschism era participated in some extremely unusual forms of worship. Khlysty, for example, believed in mortification of the flesh and reception of the Holy Spirit through trances, dancing, convulsions, and wild contortions. Other groups required celibacy of their followers, believing that a physical union between husband and wife disobeyed the laws of God. Others believed in the practice of polygamy. Khlysty beliefs seem to have grown out of Skoptsy, as they practice the same form of ecstatic worship. In addition, this sect is best known for its requirement of the castration of all males as the supreme act of obedience to God. Further details on these two sects and others that evolved during the early years of the schism offer fascinating topics for future research.

7. A detailed discussion of the worship services of the various religious groups is beyond the scope of this book, but it is worth mentioning here that Doukhobors did not construct official church buildings. A plain white table in the middle of the meeting room always contained a loaf of bread, a cellar of salt, and a jug of water, symbolizing the basic elements of their existence.

8. Economic prosperity brought on by Doukhobor assistance to the Russian military during the Crimean War was not without its negative aspects. Luker'ia Vasil'evna Gubanova, wife of deceased Doukhobor ruler Peter Kalmykov, was in power during this war, and she faced many difficult moral decisions concerning Doukhobor involvement in assisting the czar's army. Finally convinced to help in the war effort by the czar's brother, governor-general of the Caucasus in the 1870s, Luker'ia agreed to allow Doukhobor wagons and horses to transport ammunition to the soldiers. In the end, no pacifist Doukhobor was ever forced to bear arms, but Luker'ia's guilt and confusion over the incident haunted her for the remainder of her rule.

9. The word *Molokan* most certainly originated with this "milk drinker" connection. However, according to the Molokan minister of the Sheridan, California, Molokan church, V. Luscatoff, many have also speculated that the name of this religious group came from their exile in the fertile land of the valley of the Molochnaya River, known in English as Milky Waters. Luscatoff and most other California Molokans view the latter explanation for their name as ridiculous.

10. Subbotniki (Sabbatarians) were only one of many different Russian sectarian groups that evolved in response to the domination of the Orthodox church. Other groups included Don Molokans, the Kristovshchina, the Postniki, and the Katasonovites. Although related in their resistance to Orthodox teachings, each had their unique belief system. A discussion of the origin, diffusion, and beliefs of these sectarian groups, however, is beyond the scope of this book since none migrated to North America.

11. In October 1990, just three weeks after the Soviet parliament passed the new law on religious freedom, over one thousand Soviet evangelical church leaders gathered for the Soviet Congress on Evangelism in Moscow. Participants in this huge conference came from all fifteen Soviet republics and every evangelical denomination (*Slavic Gospel Association Newsletter*, April 1990–91).

Chapter 3

1. Scholarly and popular sources on Russian exploration and settlement in frontier North America abound. Much of the information published to date originated in records kept by the Russian-American Company, church archives, accounts kept by government officials, and the diaries and letters of visitors to the area. This chapter depends on a variety of sources, including Russian Orthodox church records and diaries and letters housed at Bancroft Library in Berkeley, the Golder papers at the Hoover Library at Stanford, Orthodox church archives at the Library of Congress, documents held at Rasmuson Library at the University of Alaska, Fairbanks, and original source material on the era in the Oregon Historical Society collections in Portland. I am especially indebted to the work of Canadian geographer J. R. Gibson, who has published numerous geographical interpretations of Russian settlement and expansion in North America; B. Dmytryshyn, E. A. P Crownhart-Vaughan, and T. Vaughan for their voluminous work on the continuing series on the North Pacific region for the Oregon Historical Society; S. Watrous for his translations of Russian perceptions of early California; and the numerous translations and publications of R. A. Pierce. Finally, the work of Soviet scholar S. G. Fedorova, who has written extensively on the subject of Russian America, was extremely useful. The exact sources used to compile this chapter are listed in the narrative and bibliography.

2. Notable exceptions have been published in recent years. In the last decade, a renewed surge of interest in Orthodox church history in Alaska grew out of the comprehensive bibliographic work accomplished by B. S. Smith in 1980. Her organization and analysis of the archives of the Alaska diocese of the Russian Orthodox church provided invaluable source materials for the discussion in this chapter of the role of Orthodoxy in the settlement of Alaska. In particular, details for this analysis were provided by Smith's work, along with the *Russian Orthodox American Messenger,* a periodical covering the activities of the Orthodox community from the late nineteenth century up to the present, publications of St. Herman's Theological Seminary at Kodiak, and the work of L. Black and R. A. Pierce.

3. Ivan Glotov was actually the first Russian to carry the Orthodox faith to North America. During his stay on the island of Umnak in the Aleutians, Glotov,

the commander of an exploration mission, is reported to have Christianized many residents of the island, including the nephew of the chief. The Russian explorer later took this young man to Kamchatka for instruction in the Orthodox religion and the Russian language. This Russified native American was renamed Ivan Glotov and taken back to Umnak for missionary work among his people (Veniaminov 1836, 233).

4. Three Saints Harbor at Kodiak was named for the largest of Shelikov's ships. This Orthodox name is short for saints Basil the Great, Gregory the Divine, and John the Golden-Mouthed (Chevigny 1965, 53).

5. Veniaminov's records list the personnel of this spiritual mission. Archmandrite Ioasaf left Alaska for Irkutsk for consecration to a higher rank in 1797; he drowned when returning to Kodiak on the ship *Phoenix*. Hiermonk Iuvenalii was killed by native Americans in 1796 near Lake Iliamna. Hiermonk Makarii, the "Baptist of the Aleuts," left for Irkutsk in 1796. He drowned with Ioasaf off the ship *Phoenix*. Hiermonk Afanasii left for Irkutsk in 1825. Hierdeacon Stefan drowned off the ship *Phoenix* when he was accompanying Ioasaf back to America from Irkutsk. Hierdeacon Nektarii returned to Irkutsk in 1806 and died in 1814 in the Kirenskii Monastery. Monk Ioasaf died at Kodiak at 1823. Monk German (Herman) stayed at Kodiak, eventually settling on nearby Spruce Island, where he died in 1837.

6. It is beyond the scope of this chapter to detail the role of the Russian-American Company in the development of Alaska. Among the numerous sources available on this tightly controlled organization, the most useful include Pierce 1976, Pierce and Connelly 1979, and Dmytryshyn, Crownhart-Vaughan, and Vaughan 1989.

7. Cooper was an American trader and smuggler who acted as a broker among Mexican, Russian, and American outposts all along the west coast of North America. He was issued this strategically placed land grant to effectively block Russian settlement in the Sacramento Valley, hinting at other, as yet undocumented, visits by Russians to the area during this frontier era.

Chapter 4

1. An interesting sidelight to the Doukhobors' refusal to take an oath still exists in courts of law in British Columbia. According to Doukhobor M. Chursenoff, when a person is asked to take an oath, he or she may choose either to lay a hand on the Bible or place it on a bowl of salt. This reverence for salt as one of the three spiritual symbols of the Doukhobor religion is a viable reminder of historical problems between the courts and the Russian sectarians in British Columbia in earlier decades.

2. According to P. Avrich (1962), in a rare migration reversal the Sons of Freedom asked the Soviet government for permission to return to their homeland. Although the Soviets eventually turned them down, the desire of a devoutly Christian group to live in an atheistic society illustrates the seriousness of their concerns about life and freedom in Canada. It also represents the belief by many sectarians in both Canada and California that conditions in the Soviet Union had improved significantly after the Revolution. In 1923–24, Canadian Douk-

hobors were given land in Ukraine. Other communal Soviet farms were offered to North American Russian sectarians as well (see Dunn 1970). Interestingly, several groups of Canadian Doukhobors have again discussed returning to Russia in the 1990s.

3. According to Moore (1973, 48), these prophecies did not stop after migration to the United States, and occasionally the prophecies had interesting geographical connections. In 1912, for example, the most respected Molokan prophet in California, Afonasaj T. Bezaev, predicted an earthquake several days before it occurred.

4. It is interesting to note here that, according to interviews conducted by M. Smithson (1976, 162) and M. Colfer (1985, 9), not all Old Believers left Brazil in the 1960s. Some remained there and purchased a large tract of land in Mato Grosso, near Maracaju. Since then, several families from Oregon have returned to Brazil to assume ownership of this land. A comparison of the cultural landscape and adaptation to majority cultures in Brazil and North America offers yet another fascinating topic for future research.

Chapter 6

1. One such collection, *Duch i Jizn* (Spirit and life), published in 1915, supplements, explains, and interprets the Bible. This book continues to be a subject of discourse among Molokans, and agreement or disagreement with its teachings has divided the sect into several dissenting groups.

SELECT BIBLIOGRAPHY

Adams, G. R. 1865–67. *A Story of the First American Exploring Expedition to Russian-America.* Microfilm P-K, 2. Bancroft Library, Berkeley.

———. N.d. *Pioneer Fur Sealing in Alaska.* Microfilm P-K, 2. Bancroft Library, Berkeley.

Alba, R. 1990. *Ethnic Identity.* New Haven: Yale University Press.

Alexeyeva, L. 1987. *Soviet Dissent.* Middletown, CT: Wesleyan University Press.

Allen, J. P. 1977. "Recent Immigration from the Philippines: Filipino Communities in the United States." *Geographical Review* 67:195–208.

Allen, J. P., and E. Turner. 1987. *We the People: An Atlas of America's Ethnic Diversity.* New York: Macmillan.

Altizer, T. J. J. 1975. *Mercea Eliade and the Dialectic of the Sacred.* Westport, CT: Greenwood Press.

Anderson, K. J. 1987. "The Idea of Chinatown: The Power of Place and Institutional Practice in the Making of a Racial Category." *Annals of the Association of American Geographers* 77:580–98.

Arreola, D. D. 1984. "Mexican American Housescapes." *Geographical Review* 78:299–315.

Atherton, G. 1893. "Romance of Fort Ross, California." *California Illustrated Magazine* 5:57–62.

Avakumovic, I. 1979. "Dukhobory." In *The Modern Encyclopedia of Russian and Soviet History,* ed. J. L. Wieczynski. Gulf Breeze, FL: Academic International Press.

Avrich, P. 1962. "The Sons of Freedom and the Promised Land." *Russian Review* 21:264–76.

———. 1978. *The Russian Anarchists.* Princeton, NJ: Princeton University Press.

Aylmer, M. 1904. *A Peculiar People: The Doukhobors.* London: Grant Richards.

Bach, M. 1961. *Strange Sects and Curious Cults.* New York: Dodd.

Bailey, J. M. 1987. *One Thousand Years: Stories from the History of Christianity in the USSR.* New York: Friendship Press.

Bancroft, H. H. 1886. *History of Alaska.* San Francisco: A. L. Bancroft and Company.

Barron, J. B., and H. M. Waddams. 1950. *Communism and the Churches: A Documentation.* New York: Morehouse-Gorham.

Bean, F. D. 1989. *Opening and Closing the Doors: Evaluating Immigration Reform and Control.* Washington, DC: Urban Land Institute.

Belozersky, I. 1989. "Psychocultural Frames of Reference of Refugee Groups." Paper presented at the Making It in America Conference, 14 Sept., New York. Photocopy.

Bennett, J. C. 1970. *Christianity and Communism Today.* New York: Association Press.

Bensin, B. M. 1967. *Russian Orthodox Church in Alaska, 1794–1967.* Sitka: Russian Orthodox Greek Catholic Church of North America, Diocese of Alaska.

Berger, P., and R. Neuhaus. 1977. *To Empower People: The Role of Mediating Structures in Public Policy.* Washington, DC: American Enterprise Institute for Public Policy Research.

Berokoff, J. K. 1969. *Molokans in America.* Whittier, CA: n.p.

Berreman, G. 1955. "Inquiry into Community Integration in an Aleutian Village." *American Anthropologist* 57:51–58.

Berry, W. G. 1950. "Doukhobor Sect Poses Problem." *Christian Century* 67:737–38.

Bigelow, B. 1986. "The Disciples of Christ in Antebellum Indiana: Geographic Indicator of the Border South." *Journal of Cultural Geography* 7:49–58.

Billington, J. H. 1966. *The Icon and the Axe: An Interpretive History of Russian Culture.* New York: Alfred A. Knopf.

Biswas, L. 1984. "Evolution of Hindu Temples in Calcutta." *Journal of Cultural Geography* 4:73–85.

Bjorklund, E. M. 1964. "Ideology and Culture Exemplified in Southwestern Michigan." *Annals of the Association of American Geographers* 54:227–41.

Black, L. 1989. "Russia's American Adventure." *Natural History* 12:46–56.

Blane, A. 1964. "The Relations between the Russian Protestant Sects and the State." Ph.D. diss., Duke University.

Bloch-Hoell, N. 1964. *The Pentecostal Movement: Its Origins, Development, and Distinctive Character.* Oslo: Scandinavian University Books.

Blok, T. 1850. *Brief Geographical-Statistical Description of California.* St. Petersburg: Imperial Navy Printing Office.

———. 1933. "The Russian Colonies in California: A Russian Version." *California Historical Society Quarterly* 12:189–90.

Bloodgood, C. 1869. "My Eight Months at Sitka." *Overland* 2:175–86.

Blouet, B., and M. P. Lawson, eds. 1975. *Images of the Plains: The Role of Human Nature in Settlement.* Lincoln: University of Nebraska Press.

Bockemuehl, H. W. 1968. "Doukhobor Impact on the British Columbia Landscape." M.A. thesis, Western Washington State University.

Bolshakoff, S. 1950. *Russian Nonconformity*. New York: AMS Press.

Bonch-Bruevich, V. D. 1959. *Izbrannye Sochineniia*. Moscow: n.p.

Boswell, T. D., and T. C. Jones. 1980. "A Regionalization of Mexican Americans in the United States." *Geographical Review* 70:88–98.

Bourdeaux, L., and M. Bourdeaux. 1987. *Ten Growing Soviet Churches*. Bungay, Suffolk, UK: Richard Clay.

Bourdeaux, M. 1966. *Opium of the People*. Indianapolis: Bobbs-Merrill.

———. 1968. *Religious Ferment in Russia: Protestant Opposition to Soviet Religious Policy*. London: Macmillan.

———. 1970. *Religious Minorities in the Soviet Union*. London: Minority Rights Group.

———. 1983. *Risen Indeed: Lessons in Faith from the USSR*. Crestwood, NY: Seminary Press.

———. 1990. *Gorbachev, Glasnost, and the Gospel*. London: Hodder and Stoughton.

Bouvier, L. F., H. S. Shryock, and H. W. Henderson. 1977. "International Migration Yesterday, Today, and Tomorrow." *Population Bulletin* 32:1–42.

Bowman, I. 1931. *The Pioneer Fringe*. New York: American Geographical Society.

Bradley, A. G. 1903. *Canada in the Twentieth Century*. Westminster, Ontario: Constable.

Bratskii Vestnik. 1945, 3; 1947, 5; 1954, 3–4.

Bunje, E. T. H., H. Penn, and F. J. Schmitz. 1937. "Russian California, 1805–1841." Reprint. In *Cultural Contributions of California: Bay Area Cities Series*, ed. R&E Research Associates (Berkeley: University of California, 1970).

Buss, G. 1987. *The Bear's Hug: Christian Belief and the Soviet State, 1917–1986*. Grand Rapids, MI: William B. Erdman's Publishing Company.

Buttimer, A. 1976. "Grasping the Dynamism of Lifeworld." *Annals of the Association of American Geographers* 66:277–92.

Buttimer, A., and T. Hagerstrand. 1980. *Invitation to Dialogue*. Lund, Sweden: Department of Geography, University of Lund.

California. Department of Finance. Demographic Research Unit. 1991. *Estimates of Refugees in California Counties and the State*. Sacramento: State of California.

Carlstein, T., D. Parkes, and N. Thrift. 1978. *Making Sense of Time*. London: Edward Arnold.

Chamisso, A. von. 1873. "A Visit to San Francisco in 1816." *Overland* 10 (March): 201–8.

Chernenko, A. M. 1989. *Rossiiskaia Revoliutsionnaia Emigratsiia v Amerike*. Kiev: Vyshcha Shkola.

Chernievsky, M. 1966. "Old Believers and the New Religion." *Slavic Review* 25:1–39.

Chevigny, H. 1965. *Russian America*. New York: Viking Press.

Chmykhalov, T. 1986. *The Last Christian: The Release of the Siberian Seven*. Grand Rapids, MI: Zondervan.

Chursenoff, C. 1969. "The Doukhobors." Sacramento. Photocopy.

Clark, A. 1960. "Old World Origins and Religious Adherence in Nova Scotia." *Geographical Review* 50:317–44.

Clark, S. M. 1990. "The Del Mar Ranch: From the German Rancho to the Sea Ranch, CA, 1845–1964." M.A. thesis, Sonoma State University.

Clarke, C. J. 1985. "Religion and Regional Culture: The Changing Pattern of Religious Affiliation in the Cajun Region of Southwest Louisiana." *Journal for the Scientific Study of Religion* 24:384–95.

Cole, D. B. 1976. "Russian Oregon: A History of the Russian Orthodox Church and Settlement in Oregon, 1882–1976." M.A. thesis, Portland State University.

Colfer, A. M. 1985. *Morality, Kindred, and Ethnic Boundary: A Study of the Oregon Old Believers.* New York: AMS Press.

Commager, H. S. 1973. *Documents of American History.* New York: Meredith Press.

Conovaloff, A. J. 1990. *The Molokan Directory.* Fresno, CA: author.

Conquest, R. 1968. *Religion in the USSR.* New York: Frederick A. Praeger.

Conybeare, F. 1962. *Russian Dissenters.* New York: Russell and Russell.

Cottingham, M. E. 1947. "A History of the West Kootenay District in British Columbia." M.A. thesis, University of British Columbia.

Couclelis, H., and R. G. Golledge. 1983. "Analytic Research, Positivism, and Behavioral Geography." *Annals of the Association of American Geographers* 73:331–39.

Crawford, R. G. 1989. *Making Sense out of the Study of Religion.* Oak Villa, UK: Lochee Publications.

Crowley, W. 1978. "Old Order Amish Settlement: Diffusion and Growth." *Annals of the Association of American Geographers* 68:249–64.

Crummey, R. O. 1970. *The Old Believers and the World of Anti-Christ.* Madison: University of Wisconsin Press.

Curtiss, J. S. 1965. *Church and State in Russia: The Last Years of the Empire, 1900–1917.* New York: Octagon Books.

Dabovich, S. 1898. *The Holy Orthodox Church: Ritual Services and Sacraments.* Reprint. Willits, CA: Eastern Orthodox Books, 1971.

Dafoe, J. W. 1931. *John Wesley Clifford in Relation to His Times.* Toronto: Macmillan.

Dana, R. H. 1846. *Two Years before the Mast.* New York: Harper and Brothers.

Davids, R. C. 1984. "The Aleuts: America's Oldest Civilization." *Exxon Magazine* 11:2–8.

Davis, J. D. 1922a. *The Russian Immigrant.* Reprint. New York: Arno Press, 1969.

———. 1922b. *The Russians and Ruthenians in America.* New York: G. H. Doran.

Davydov, G. I. 1977. *Two Voyages to Russian-America, 1802–1807.* Trans. C. Bearne. Kingston, Ont.: Limestone Press.

Dawson, C. A. 1936. "Group Settlement: Ethnic Communities in Western Canada." In *Canadian Frontiers of Settlement,* ed. W. I. G. Joerg. Toronto: Macmillan.

Day, G. 1934. *The Russians in Hollywood*. Los Angeles: University of Southern California Press.

De Blij, H. J., and P. O. Muller. 1992. *Geography: Regions and Concepts*. New York: John Wiley and Sons.

Degh, L. 1980. "Folk Religion as Ideology for Ethnic Survival: The Hungarians of Kipling, Saskatchewan." In *Ethnicity on the Great Plains*, ed. F. O. Luebke. Lincoln: University of Nebraska Press.

De Jong, G., J. Faulkner, and R. Warland. 1976. "Dimensions of Religiosity: Evidence from a Cross-cultural Study." *Social Forces* 54:866–89.

De Jong, G., and R. Gardner. 1981. *Migration Decision Making*. New York: Pergamon Press.

Desbarats, J. 1979. "Thai Migration to Los Angeles." *Geographical Review* 69:302–18.

Dinnerstein, L., and D. M. Reimers. 1975. *Ethnic Americans: A History of Immigration and Assimilation*. New York: Harper and Row.

Dmytryshyn, B., E. A. P. Crownhart-Vaughan, and T. Vaughan, trans. and eds. 1988. *Russian Penetration of the North Pacific Ocean, 1700–1799: A Documentary Record*. Portland: Oregon Historical Society Press.

———, trans. and eds. 1989. *The Russian American Colonies: A Documentary Record, 1798–1867*. Portland: Oregon Historical Society Press.

Doughty, R. W. 1981. "Environmental Theology: Trends and Prospects in Christian Thought." *Progress in Human Geography* 5:234–47.

Duflot de Mofras, E. 1937. *Duflot de Mofras' Travels on the Pacific Coast*. 2 vols. Trans. M. E. Wilbur. Santa Ana, CA: Fine Arts Press.

Duhaut-Cilly, A. B. 1929. "A Visit to the Russians in 1828." Trans. C. F. Carter. *California Historical Society Quarterly* 8:322–27.

Dunn, D. 1977. *Religion and Modernization in the Soviet Union*. Boulder, CO: Westview Press.

Dunn, E. 1966. "A Slavophile Looks at the Rasskil and the Sects." *Slavonic and East European Review* 44:167–79.

———. 1967. "Russian Sectarianism in New Marxist Scholarship." *Slavic Review* 26:128–40.

———. 1970. "Canadian and Soviet Doukhobors: An Examination of the Mechanisms of Social Change." *Canadian Slavic Studies* 4:300–326.

———. 1971. "The Importance of Religion in Rural Communities." In *The Soviet Rural Community*, ed. J. R. Millar. Urbana: University of Illinois Press.

———. 1976. "American Molokans and Canadian Doukhobors." In *Ethnicity in the Americas*, ed. F. Henry. Chicago: Aldine.

———. 1983–92. *The Molokan Heritage Collection*. Berkeley: Highgate Road Social Science Research Station.

Dunn, E., and S. P. Dunn. 1964. "Religion as an Instrument of Culture Change." *Slavic Review* 23:459–78.

———. 1977. "Religion and Ethnicity: The Case of the American Molokans." *Ethnicity* 4:370–79.

Dunn, S. P. 1969. "Sovietology, Old and New." *Canadian Slavic Studies* 3:565–74.

Dunn, S. P., and E. Dunn. 1967. *The Peasants of Central Russia.* New York: Holt, Rinehart, and Winston.

———. 1978. "Molokans in America." *Dialectical Anthropology* 3:349–60.

Durasoff, S. 1969. *The Russian Protestants.* Rutherford, NJ: Fairleigh Dickinson University Press.

———. 1972. *Pentecost behind the Iron Curtain.* Plainfield, NJ: Logos International.

Edinger, G. A. 1951. "Russia in California." *History Today,* Nov., 49–54.

Elder, M. L. 1966. "Agapius Honcharenko and Cyrillic Printing in San Francisco from 1867–1872." University of California, Berkeley. Photocopy.

Elkinton, J. 1903. *The Doukhobors.* Philadelphia: Ferris and Leach.

Elliot, M. 1988. "A Typology of Western-Soviet Christian Contacts." Institute for the Study of Christianity and Marxism, Wheaton College, Wheaton, IL. Photocopy.

Ellis, J. 1986. *The Russian Orthodox Church: A Contemporary History.* Bloomington: Indiana University Press.

England, R. 1936. *The Colonization of Western Canada, 1896–1934.* London: P. S. King.

Entrikin, J. N. 1976. "Contemporary Humanism in Geography." *Annals of the Association of American Geographers* 66:615–33.

Essig, E. O. 1933a. "The Russian Colonies in California." *Quarterly of the California Historical Society* 12:189–90.

———. 1933b. "The Russian Settlement at Ross." *Quarterly of the California Historical Society* 12:191–216.

Eubank, N. 1973. *The Russians in America.* Minneapolis: Lerner Publications.

Ex, J. 1966. *Adjustment after Migration: A Longitudinal Study of the Process of Adjustment by Refugees to a New Environment.* The Hague: Martinus Nijhoff.

Farafonteff, A. P., ed. 1937. *Fort Ross: 1812–1837.* San Francisco: Russian Orthodox Press.

Farris, G. 1990. "The Strange Tale of Saint Peter, the Aleut: A Russian Orthodox Martyr on the California Frontier." Sacramento: California Department of Parks and Recreation. Photocopy.

Fedorova, C. G., and B. A. Alexsandrov. 1985. *Novo-Arxangelsk.* Moscow: Nayka.

Federova, S. 1973. *The Russian Population in Alaska and California.* Trans. and ed. R. A. Pierce and A. S. Donnelly. Kingston, Ont.: Limestone Press.

Fedotov, G. P. 1946–66. *The Russian Religious Mind.* 2 vols. Cambridge, MA: Harvard University Press.

Ferguson, R. A. 1925. "The Historical Development of the Russian River Valley, 1579–1865." M.A. thesis, University of California, Berkeley.

Fickeler, P. 1962. "Fundamental Questions in the Geography of Religions." In *Readings in Cultural Geography,* ed. P. L. Wager and M. W. Mikesell. Chicago: University of Chicago Press.

Field, D. 1976. "Rebels in the Name of the Tsar." *Russian Review* 39:348–58.

Fletcher, W. C. 1971. *The Russian Orthodox Church Underground*. New York: Oxford University Press.

———. 1981. *Soviet Believers: The Religious Sector of the Population*. Lawrence: Regents Press of Kansas.

———. 1985. *Soviet Charismatics: The Pentecostals in the USSR*. New York: Peter Lang Publishers.

Fletcher, W. C., and A. J. Strover, eds. 1967. *Religion and the Search for New Ideals in the USSR*. New York: Frederick A. Praeger.

Forest, J. 1988. *Pilgrim to the Russian Church*. New York: Crossroads Publishers.

Fort Ross Citizens Advisory Committee. 1974. "Fort Ross: The Russian Settlement in California." Fort Ross, CA: author.

Foster, W. G. 1935. "Canadian Communists: The Doukhobor Experiment." *American Journal of Sociology* 41:327–40.

Fritz, E. 1980. "New Hope for the Siberian Seven." *Christian Century* 35:1064–66.

Fry, G. D. 1977. "The Doukhobors, 1801–1855: The Origins of a Successful Dissident Sect." Ph.D. diss., American University of Washington, DC.

Gale, D. T. 1973. "Belief and Landscape of Religion: The Case of the Doukhobors." M.A. thesis, Simon Fraser University.

Gale, D. T., and T. S. Koroscil. 1977. "Doukhobor Settlements: Experiments in Idealism." *Canadian Ethnic Studies* 9:53–71.

Gans, H. J. 1962. *The Urban Villagers: Group and Class in the Life of Italian-Americans*. New York: Free Press of Glencoe.

Garrett, P. D. 1979. *St. Innocent: Apostle to America*. Crestwood, NY: St. Vladimir's Seminary Press.

Gay, J. 1988. "Old Believers in a Time of Change." *Alaska Magazine* 54:22–27.

Gay, J. D. 1971. *The Geography of Religion in England*. London: Gerald Duckworth.

Geertz, C. 1973. *The Interpretation of Cultures*. New York: Basic Books.

Gerber, S. N. 1985. *Russkoya Celo: The Ethnography of a Russian-American Community*. New York: AMS Press.

Gerlach, R. 1976. *Immigrants in the Ozarks*. Columbia: University of Missouri Press.

Gibson, J. R. 1971. "A Russian Orthodox Priest in a Mexican Catholic Parish." *Pacific Historian* 15:57–66.

———. 1972. "Russian-America in 1833: The Survey of Kirill Khlebnikov." *Pacific Northwest Quarterly* 63:1–13.

———. 1976. *Imperial Russia in Frontier America*. New York: Oxford University Press.

———, ed. 1978. *European Settlement and Development in North America: Essays on Geographical Change in Honour and Memory of Andrew Hill Clark*. Toronto: University of Toronto Press.

———. 1980. "Russian Expansion in Siberia and America." *Geographical Review* 70:127–36.

―――. 1986. *Russian Expansion in Siberia and America: Critical Contrasts.* Washington, DC: Kennan Institute for Advanced Russian Studies.

Glazer, N., and D. P. Moynihan. 1963. *Beyond the Melting Pot: The Negroes, Puerto Ricans, Jews, Italians, and Irish of New York City.* Cambridge, MA: MIT Press.

―――. 1975. *Ethnicity: Theory and Experience.* Cambridge, MA: Harvard University Press.

Glazunova, A. 1972. "Bay Area Russian American Community: A Search for Its Identity." M.A. thesis, Dominican College.

Glock, C. Y. 1964. "The Role of Deprivation in the Origin and Evolution of Religious Groups." In *Religion and Social Conflict,* ed. R. Lee and M. E. Marty. New York: Oxford University Press.

Golder, B. F. 1968. *Father Herman: Alaska's Saint.* Platina, CA: Orthodox Christian Books and Icons.

―――. 1974. "Father Herman, Alaska's Saint." *Orthodox Alaska* 4:1–10.

Golder, F. A. 1914. *Russian Expansion on the Pacific, 1641–1850.* Cleveland: Arthur H. Clark Company.

Golledge, R. G. 1980. "A Behavioral View of Mobility and Migration Research." *Professional Geographer* 32:14–21.

Golovin, P. N. 1979. *The End of Russian America: Capt. P. N. Golovin's Last Report.* Trans. B. Dmytryshyn and E. A. P. Crownhart-Vaughan. Portland: Oregon Historical Society.

Gorbachev, M. 1988. *Perestroika: New Thinking for Our Country and the World.* New York: Harper and Row.

Gordon, M. N. 1964. *Assimilation in American Life.* New York: Oxford University Press.

Goricheva, T. 1987. *Talking about God Is Dangerous: The Diary of a Russian Dissident.* New York: Crossroads.

Gregory, B. 1972. *Orthodox America.* Kodiak, AK: St. Herman's Pastoral School.

―――. 1973. "The Beginnings of Orthodoxy on the West Coast." *Orthodox Church* 9:5.

―――. 1977. *A History of the Orthodox Church in Alaska.* Kodiak, AK: St. Herman's Theological Seminary.

―――. 1987. "Orthodoxy in Alaska." In *Russia in North America: Proceedings of the Second International Conference on Russian America,* ed. R. A. Pierce. Kingston, Ont.: Limestone Press.

Greinacher, N., and V. Elizondo. 1982. "Churches in Socialist Societies of Eastern Europe." In *Concilium: Religion in the Eighties,* ed. N. Greinacher and V. Elizondo. New York: Seabury Press.

Guelke, L. 1974. "An Idealist Alternative in Human Geography." *Annals of the Association of American Geographers* 64:193–202.

Hagerstrand, T. 1957. "Migration and Area." In *Migration in Sweden: A Symposium,* ed. D. Hannerberg, T. Hagerstrand, and B. Odeving. Lund, Sweden: Gleerup.

Hall, R. L. 1969. "The Russian Old Believers in Oregon." Woodburn, OR. Photocopy.

Handlin, O. 1951. *The Uprooted*. Boston: Little, Brown, and Company.

Hardwick, S. W. 1979. "A Geographic Interpretation of Ethnic Settlement in an Urban Landscape: Russians in Sacramento." *California Geographer* 19: 87–104.

————. 1986. "Ethnic Residential and Commercial Patterns in Sacramento with Special Reference to the Russian-American Experience." Ph.D. diss., University of California, Davis.

Hatch, F. F. 1971. *The Russian Advance into California*. San Francisco: R and E Research Associates.

Hawthorn, H. B., ed. 1952. *Report of the Doukhobor Research Committee*. Vancouver: University of British Columbia.

————, ed. 1955. *The Doukhobors of British Columbia*. Vancouver: University of British Columbia Press and J. M. Dent and Sons.

Hayward, M., and W. C. Fletcher. 1969. *Religion and the Soviet State: A Dilemma of Power*. New York: Frederick A. Praeger.

Heard, A. F. 1971. *The Russian Church and Russian Dissent Comprising Orthodoxy, Dissent, and Erratic Sects*. New York: AMS Press.

Heatwole, C. A. 1989. "Sectarian Ideology and Church Architecture." *Geographical Review* 79:63–78.

Heckrotte, W. N.d. "The Discovery of Humboldt Bay: A New Look at an Old Story." University of California, Berkeley. Photocopy.

Heitman, S. 1991a. "Analysis of Current Events." *Association for the Study of Nationalities* 2:1–8.

————. 1991b. *Soviet Emigration in 1990*. Cologne: Bundesinstitut für ostwissenschaftliche und internationale Studien.

Hill, K. R. 1989. *The Puzzle of the Soviet Church*. Portland, OR: Multnomah Press.

————. 1991. *The Soviet Union on the Brink*. Portland, OR: Multnomah Press.

Hirabayashi, G. K. 1951. "Russian Doukhobors of British Columbia: A Study in Social Adjustment and Conflict." Ph.D. diss., University of Washington.

Hoffer, E. 1951. *The True Believers: Thoughts on the Nature of Mass Movements*. New York: Harper.

Hollenwerger, W. 1972. *The Pentecostals*. Minneapolis: Augsburg Publishing House.

Holt, S. 1964. *Terror in the Name of God*. New York: Crown Publishers.

Hotchkiss, W. A. 1950. *A Real Pattern of Religious Institutions in Cincinnati*. Research Paper 13, University of Chicago, Department of Geography.

Huff, J. O., and W. A. V. Clark. 1978. "Cumulative Stress and Cumulative Inertia: A Behavioral Model of the Decision to Move." *Environment and Planning* 10:101–19.

Hugo, G. J. 1981. "Village-Community Ties, Village Norms, and Ethnic and Social Networks: A Review of Evidence from the Third World." In *Migration Decision Making*, ed. G. De Jong and R. Gardner. New York: Pergamon Press.

Hulley, C. C. 1970. *Alaska: Past and Present*. Portland, OR: Binfords and Mort.

Huntington, E. 1945. *Mainsprings of Civilization.* New York: John Wiley and Sons.

Hyatt, C. B. 1953. *Laws Applicable to Immigration and Nationality.* Washington, DC: U.S. Government Printing Office.

Innokentii. 1836. Journal. Bancroft Library Manuscript Collection, University of California, Berkeley.

Isaac, E. 1962. "The Act and the Covenant: The Impact of Religion on the Landscape." *Landscape* 2:12–17.

———. 1965. "Religious Geography and the Geography of Religion." In *Man and the Earth,* University of Colorado Studies, Series in Earth Sciences, no. 3. Boulder: University of Colorado.

Isaacs, H. R. 1975. *Idols of the Tribe.* Reprint. Cambridge, MA: Harvard University Press, 1989.

Iskra Magazine. 1991. Grand Forks, BC: Union of Spiritual Communities of Christ.

Ismail-Zade, D. 1976. "Russkie poseleniia v Zakavkaz'e." *Voprosy Istrorii* 30:18–31.

Iswolsky, H. 1962. *Christ in Russia.* Kingswood, UK: World's Work.

Iwanow, B. 1960. *Religion in the USSR.* Munich: Institute for the Study of the USSR.

Jackson, R. H. 1980. "The Use of Adobe in the Mormon Culture Region." *Journal of Cultural Geography* 1:82–95.

Jackson, R. H., and R. Henrie. 1983. "Perception of Sacred Space." *Journal of Cultural Geography* 3:94–107.

Jakle, J. A., and J. O. Wheeler. 1969. "The Changing Residential Structure of the Dutch Population in Kalamazoo, Michigan." *Annals of the Association of American Geographers* 59:441–60.

James, A. J. 1942. *The First Scientific Exploration of Russian America and the Purchase of Alaska.* Evanston, IL: Northwestern University Press.

James, W. 1902. *The Varieties of Religious Experience.* Reprint. Cambridge, MA: Harvard University Press, 1985.

Jamieson, S. 1955. "Economic and Social Life." In *The Doukhobors of British Columbia,* ed. H. B. Hawthorn. Vancouver: University of British Columbia and J. M. Dent and Sons.

Janzen, W. 1981. "Limits of Liberty in Canada: The Experience of the Mennonites, Hutterites, and Doukhobors." Ph.D. diss., Carlton University.

Jelezhov, M. 1929. *Moscow on the Hudson.* Reprint. New York: Harper and Row, 1969.

Jiobu, R. M. 1988. *Ethnicity and Assimilation.* Albany: State University of New York Press.

Joerg, W. I. G. 1932. *Pioneer Settlement.* New York: American Geographical Society.

Johnston, B. 1981. *Russian-American Social Mobility: An Analysis of the Achievement Syndrome.* Saratoga, CA: Century 21 Publishers.

Johnston, R. J. 1983. *Philosophy and Human Geography: An Introduction to Contemporary Approaches.* London: Edward Arnold.

Jordan, T. G. 1966. *German Seed in Texas Soil.* Austin: University of Texas Press.

———. 1980. "A Religious Geography of the Hill Country Germans of Texas." In *Ethnicity on the Great Plains,* ed. F. O. Luebke. Lincoln: University of Nebraska Press.

Kaups, M. 1966. "Finnish Place Names in Minnesota: A Study in Cultural Transfer." *Geographical Review* 56:377–97.

Khlebnikov, K. T. 1940. "Memoirs of California." Trans. A. G. Mazour. *Pacific Historical Review* 9:307–36.

———. 1835. *Baranov.* Trans. C. Bearne. Reprint. Kingston, Ont.: Limestone Press, 1973.

———. 1976. *Colonial Russian America: Kyrill T. Khlebnikov's Reports.* Trans. B. Dmytryshyn and E. A. P. Crownhart-Vaughan. Portland: Oregon Historical Society.

———. 1979. *Pycckaya Amerika.* Leningrad: Nayka.

Klibanov, A. I. 1973. "In the World of Religious Sectarianism: At a Meeting of Prygun Molokans." *Soviet Sociology* 13:80–93.

———. 1982. *History of Religious Sectarianism in Russia, 1860s–1917.* Trans. E. Dunn. Reprint. New York: Pergamon Press.

Kolarz, W. 1961. *Religion in the Soviet Union.* London: Macmillan.

Kollmorgan, W. M. 1949. "The Agricultural Stability of the Old Order Amish." *American Journal of Sociology* 49:233–41.

Kondratieff, G. 1976. "Fiftieth Anniversary of the Holy Myrrhbearer's American Orthodox Church in Bryte, California." Bryte, CA. Photocopy.

Kong, L. 1990. "Geography and Religions: Trends and Prospects." *Progress in Human Geography* 14:355–71.

Koslova, K. I. 1970. "Experiences Gained while Studying the Molokans of Armenia." *Soviet Sociology* 3:318–28.

Kotzebue, Otto von. 1830. *A New Voyage around the World, in the Years 1823, 24, 25, and 26.* London: Sir Richard Phillips and Company.

Krivoshein, G. V., and Cole, D. B. N.d. "The Beginnings of the Orthodox Church in Oregon." Portland, OR. Photocopy.

Kushner, H. I. 1979. *The United States, Russia, and Russian-America.* Washington, DC: Kennan Institute for Advanced Russian Studies.

Laatsch, W. G., and C. F. Calkins. 1986. "The Belgian Roadside Chapels of Wisconsin's Door Peninsula." *Journal of Cultural Geography* 7:117–28.

Lane, B. 1988. *Landscapes of the Sacred: Geography and Narrative in American Spirituality.* New York: Paulist Press.

Larkey, J. L., and S. Walters. 1987. *Yolo County: Land of Changing Patterns.* Northridge, CA: Windsor Publications.

Lee, C. S. 1983. *Revolutionary Struggle in China.* Berkeley: University of California Press.

Lee, E. S. 1966. "A Theory in Migration." *Demography* 3:47–57.

Legreid, A. M., and D. Ward. 1982. "Religious Schism and the Development of Rural Immigrant Communities: Norwegian Lutherans in Western Wisconsin, 1880–1905." *Upper Midwest History* 2:13–29.

Levine, G. J. 1986. "On the Geography of Religion." *Transactions of the Institute of British Geographers* 11:428–40.

Lewis, R. E., M. W. Fraser, and P. J. Pecora. 1988. "Religiosity among Indochinese Refugees in Utah." *Journal for the Scientific Study of Religion* 27:272–83.

Ley, D. 1980a. "Cultural/Humanistic Geography." *Progress in Human Geography* 5:249–57.

———. 1980b. *Geography without Man: A Humanistic Critique.* School of Geography Research Paper 24, Oxford University.

———. 1981. "Cultural/Humanistic Geography." *Progress in Human Geography* 5:249–57.

———. 1983. *A Social Geography of the City.* New York: Harper and Row.

Ley, D., and M. S. Samuels. 1978. *Humanistic Geography: Prospects and Problems.* Chicago: Maaroufa Press.

Lieberson, S. 1961. "The Impact of Racial Segregation on Ethnic Assimilation." *Social Forces* 40:52–57.

———. 1962. "Suburbs and Ethnic Residential Patterns." *American Journal of Sociology* 67:673–81.

———. 1963. *Ethnic Patterns in American Cities.* New York: Free Press.

Light, I. H. 1972. *Ethnic Enterprise in America.* Berkeley: University of California Press.

Litvintsev, K. 1887. "Amurskie Sektanty: Molokane i Dukhobory." *Khristianskoe Chenie*, Nov.–Dec.

Luebke, F. O., ed. 1980. *Ethnicity on the Great Plains.* Lincoln: University of Nebraska Press.

Lupinin, N. 1984. *Religious Revolt in the 17th Century: The Schism of the Russian Church.* Princeton, NJ: Kingston Press.

Lynch, K. 1980. "The Guests in the Basement." *National Review* 32:355–56.

McHugh, K. E. 1984. "Planning Migration Intentions and Destination Selection." *Professional Geographer* 36:315–25.

McQuillan, D. A. 1978. "Territory and Ethnic Identity: Some New Measures of an Old Theme in the Cultural Geography of the United States." In *European Settlement and Development in North America: Essays on Geographical Change in Honour and Memory of Andrew Hill Clark,* ed. J. R. Gibson. Toronto: University of Toronto Press.

Makarova, R. V. 1975. *Russians on the Pacific, 1743–1799.* Trans. and ed. by R. A. Pierce and A. S. Donnelly. Kingston, Ont.: Limestone Press.

Manning, C. A. 1953. *Russian Influence on Early America.* New York: Library Publishers.

Mannion, J. J. 1974. *Irish Settlements in Eastern Canada: A Study of Cultural Transfer and Adaptation.* Toronto: University of Toronto Press.

———. 1977. *The Peopling of Newfoundland: Essays in Historical Geography.* St. Johns: Memorial University of Newfoundland.

Manzo, J. T. 1983. "Italian Yard Shrines." *Journal of Cultural Geography* 4:119–25.

Markov, A. 1955. *The Russians on the Pacific Ocean.* Los Angeles: College Press.

Mattson, E. M. B. 1985. "Orthodoxy and the Aleuts: The Historical Significance of the Russian Orthodox Mission in Alaska." M.A. thesis, University of Idaho.

Mazour, A. G. 1941. "The Prelude to Russian Departure from America." *Pacific Historical Review* 10:311–19.

Mechling, J. 1979. "If They Can Build a Square Tomato: Notes toward a Holistic Approach to Regional Studies." *Prospects* 4:59–77.

Meinig, D. 1971. *Southwest: Three Peoples in Geographical Change, 1600–1970.* New York: Oxford University Press.

Meyendorf, J. 1962. *The Orthodox Church: Its Past and Its Role in the World Today.* New York: Random House.

Meyer, G. H. 1880. "The Legend of Fort Ross." *Californian* 2:191–93.

Meyer, J. W. 1975. "Ethnicity, Theology, and Immigrant Church Expansion." *Geographical Review* 65:180–97.

Miliukov, P. 1943. *Outlines of Russian Culture: Religion and the Church.* Philadelphia: University of Pennsylvania Press.

Moore, W. B. 1973. *Molokan Oral Tradition.* Berkeley: University of California Press.

Moorman, B. A. N.d. "A Short History of the Old Believer Community in Oregon." Woodburn City Library, Woodburn, OR. Photocopy.

Moquin, W. 1971. "Doukhobors." In *Makers of America,* ed. W. Moquin. Chicago: Encyclopedia Britannica Educational Corporation.

Morris, R. A. 1981. "Three Russian Groups in Oregon: A Comparison of Boundaries in a Pluralistic Environment." Ph.D. diss., University of Oregon.

Moser, L. J. 1985. *The Chinese Mosaic: The Peoples and Provinces of China.* Boulder, CO: Westview Press.

Mundy, W. B. 1964. "Sons of Freedom at Hope: A Study of the Interaction of a Settled Community and a Migrant Community." M.A. thesis, University of British Columbia.

Muranaka, T. A. 1988. "Spirit Jumpers: The Russian Molokans of Baja California." *Ethnic Technology Notes* 21:1–16.

Nesdoly, S. 1986. *Among the Soviet Evangelicals.* Carlisle, PA: Banner of Truth Trust.

Newell, C. M. 1971. "A Structural Analysis of Sobranija: Doukhobor and Russian Orthodox." M.A. thesis, University of British Columbia.

Newman, W. M., and P. L. Halvorson. 1984. "Religion and Regional Culture: Patterns of Change among American Religious Denominations, 1952–1980." *Journal for the Scientific Study of Religion* 23:304–15.

Nichol, J. T. 1966. *Pentecostalism.* New York: Harper and Row.

Nordyke, E. 1977. *The Peopling of Hawaii.* Honolulu: East-West Center.

Nostrand, R. L. 1970. "The Hispanic-American Borderland: Delimitation of an American Culture Region." *Annals of the Association of American Geographers* 60:638–61.

O'Brien-Rothe, L. 1989. *The Origins of Molokan Singing.* Molokan Heritage Collection, 4. Berkeley: Highgate Road Social Science Research Station.

Okun, S. B. 1979. *The Russian-American Company*. Trans. by C. Ginsburg. New York: Octagon Books.

Oleksa, M., ed. 1987. *Alaskan Missionary Spirituality*. New York: Paulist Press.

Oppolovnikov, A., and Y. Oppolovnikov. 1989. *The Wooden Architecture of Russia: Houses, Fortifications, Churches*. New York: Harry N. Abrams.

Oregon State Refugee Program: The Year in Review. 1990. Portland: Oregon Department of Human Resources.

Orthodox Church Directory. 1990. Syosset, NY: Orthodox Church of America.

Osborne, B. S., ed. 1976. *The Settlement of Canada: Origins and Transfer*. Kingston, Ont.: Queen's University.

Ostergren, R. C. 1979. "A Community Transplanted: The Formative Experience of a Swedish Immigrant Community in the Upper Midwest." *Journal of Historical Geography* 5:189–212.

———. 1981a. "The Immigrant Church as a Symbol of Community and Place on the Landscape of the American Upper Midwest." *Great Plains Quarterly* 1:224–38.

———. 1981b. "Land and Family in Rural Immigrant Communities." *Annals of the Association of American Geographers* 71:400–411.

———. 1988. *A Community Transplanted: The Trans-Atlantic Experience of a Swedish Immigrant Settlement in the Upper Midwest, 1835–1915*. Madison: University of Wisconsin Press.

Pallot, J., and D. J. B. Shaw. 1990. *Landscape and Settlement in Romanov Russia*. New York: Oxford University Press.

Palmer, F. H. E. 1901. *Russian Life in Town and Country*. New York: G. P. Putnam's Sons.

Paraskevas, J. E., and F. Reinstein. 1969. *The Eastern Orthodox Church: A Brief History*. Washington, DC: El Greco Press.

Parsons, H. L. 1987. *Christianity Today in the USSR*. New York: International Publishers.

Pascal, P. 1976. *The Religion of the Russian People*. Crestwood, NY: St. Vladimir's Seminary Press.

Petrov, V. 1988. *Pycckue b Uctopuu Amepuku*. Tenafly, NJ: Hermitage Press.

Pierce, R. A. 1965. *Russia's Hawaiian Adventure, 1815–1817*. Kingston, Ont.: Limestone Press.

———, ed. 1976. *Documents on the History of the Russian American Company*. Trans by M. Ramsay. Kingston, Ont.: Limestone Press.

———, ed. 1978. *The Russian Orthodox Religious Mission in America, 1794–1837*. Trans. C. Bearne. Kingston, Ont.: Limestone Press.

———. 1984. *Rossiisko Amerikanska's Kompaniia*. Kingston, Ont.: Limestone Press.

———. 1986. *The Russian Governors: Builders of Alaska, 1818–1867*. Kingston, Ont.: Limestone Press.

Pierce, R. A., and A. S. Donnelly. 1979. *A History of the Russian American Company*. Kingston, Ont.: Limestone Press.

Pollock, J. C. 1964. *The Faith of the Russian Evangelicals*. New York: McGraw-Hill Book Company.

———. 1979. *The Siberian Seven*. London: Hodder and Stoughton.

Poole, E. 1918. *The Village: Russian Impressions*. New York: Macmillan and Company.

Popoff, E. A. 1964. *An Historical Exposition on the Origin and Evolvement of the Basic Tenets of the Doukhobor Life-Conception*. Grand Forks, BC: Iskra Publishers.

Portes, A. 1969. "Dilemmas of a Golden Exile: Integration of Cuban Refugee Families in Milwaukee." *American Sociological Review* 34:508–18.

Portes, A., and R. G. Rumbaut. 1990. *Immigrant America: A Portrait*. Berkeley: University of California Press.

Pospielovsky, D. 1984. *The Russian Church under the Soviet Regime, 1917–1982*. Crestwood, NY: St. Vladimir's Seminary Press.

Priamur'e, F. 1909. *Fakty, Tsifry, Nabliudeniia*. Moscow: n.p.

Pronin, A., ed. 1975. *Russian Émigré Archives*. Fresno, CA: Faculty Press.

Pushkarev, S. 1989. *Christianity and Government in Russia and the Soviet Union*. Boulder, CO: Westview Press.

Raitz, K. B. 1979. "Themes in the Cultural Geography of European Ethnic Groups in the United States" *Geographical Review* 69:79–94.

Ravenstein, E. G. 1889. "The Laws of Migration." *Journal of the Royal Statistical Society* 52:241–305.

Rearden, J. 1972. "A Bit of Old Russia Takes Root in Alaska." *National Geographic* 142:401–25.

Reddaway, P. 1984. "Soviet Policies on Dissent and Emigration: The Radical Change of Course since 1979." Occasional Paper 192. Washington, DC: Kennan Institute for Advanced Russian Studies.

Relph, E. 1976. *Place and Placelessness*. London: Pion.

———. 1977. "Humanism, Phenomenology, and Geography." *Annals of the Association of American Geographers* 67:177–79.

Rezanov, N. P. 1972. *Rezanov Reconnoiters California*. Trans. R. A. Pierce. San Francisco: Book Club of California.

Riasanovsky, N. V. 1977. *A History of Russia*. New York: Oxford University Press.

Ricoeur, P. 1985. "The History of Religions and the Phenomenology of Time Consciousness." In *The History of Religions: Retrospect and Prospect*, ed. J. M. Kitagawa. New York: Macmillan.

Ridington, J. 1903. "The Doukhobor Pilgrimage of 1902." *Canadian Magazine* 20:211–22.

Ripp, V. 1984. *From Moscow to Main Street: Among the Russian Émigrés*. Boston: Little, Brown, and Company.

Ritchey, P. N. 1976. "Explanation of Migration." *Annual Review of Sociology* 2:363–404.

Robison, G. T. 1961. *Rural Russia under the Old Regime: A History of the Landlord-Peasant World and a Prologue to the Peasant Revolution of 1917*. New York: Macmillan.

Robison, M. 1948. "Russian Doukhobors in West Kootenay." M.A. thesis, Syracuse University.

Rochcau, V. 1973. "The Origins of the Orthodox Church in Alaska." *Orthodox Alaska* 2:1–5; 3:1–23.

Rodzianko, M. 1975. *The Truth about the Russian Church Abroad.* Trans. M. P. Hilko. Jordansville, NY: Holy Trinity Monastery.

Roseman, C. C. 1971. *Migration as a Spatial and Temporal Experience.* Washington, DC: Association of American Geographers.

———. 1977. *Changing Migration Patterns within the United States.* Resource Paper 77. Washington, DC: Association of American Geographers.

Rossi, J. 1970. "Evdokia Gregovna Zaharaoff." *Pacific Historian* 14:41–48.

Rossiisko-Amerikanskaiia Kompaniia, Opis' Delum. 1781–1825. Documents on the Russian American Company, Bancroft Library Manuscript Collection, University of California, Berkeley.

Rozhdestvenskii, T. S. 1910. "Pamiatniki Staroobriadcheskoi Poezii." *Zapiski Moskovskago Arkheologicheskago Instituta.* Moscow.

Rushbrooke, J. H. 1943. *Baptists in the USSR.* Nashville: Boardman Press.

Russell, T. C. 1926. *The Rezanov Voyage to Nueva California in 1806.* San Francisco: Private Press of Thomas C. Russell.

"Russians in America." 1988. *Insight* 4:10–19.

Russian Orthodox American Messenger. 1896–98. Bancroft Library Manuscript Collection, University of California, Berkeley.

"The Russian Orthodox Old Believer Community in Oregon." 1973. Woodburn, OR: Department of Human Services.

Sabey, R. H. 1969. "Starovery and School: A Case Study of the Education of Russian Immigrant Children in a Rural Oregon Community." Ph.D. diss., University of Oregon.

Samarin, P. I., ed. 1975. *Molokan Directory.* Los Angeles: Editor Press.

Saueressig-Schreuder, Y. 1985. "Dutch-Catholic Emigration in the Mid-nineteenth Century Noord." *Journal of Historical Geography* 11:48–69.

Sawatsky, W. 1981. *Soviet Evangelicals since World War II.* Scottdale, PA: Herald Press.

Scheffel, D. 1991. *In the Shadow of the Antichrist: The Old Believers of Alberta.* Peterborough, Ont.: Broadview Press.

Schmieder, O. 1929. *The Russian Colony of Guadalupe Valley.* University of California Publications in Geography, 2:409–34. Berkeley: University of California.

Schwartz, H. 1979. "Fort Ross, California." *Journal of the West* 18:35–48.

Schwind, P. J. 1971. "Spatial Preference of Migrants for Regions: The Example of Maine." *Proceedings of the Association of American Geographers* 3:150–56.

Seebarin, R. B. 1965. "Migration of the Sons of Freedom into the Lower Mainland of British Columbia." M.A. thesis, University of British Columbia.

Semple, E. C. 1903. *American History and Its Geographic Conditions.* Boston: Houghton Mifflin and Company.

Serafim, A. 1973. *The Quest for Orthodox Church Unity in North America in the Twentieth Century.* New York: Saints Boris and Gleb Press.

Shakhovskaya, Z. 1967. "The Significance of Religious Themes in Soviet Literature." In *Religion and the Search for New Ideals in the USSR*, ed. W. C. Fletcher and A. J. Strover. New York: Frederick A. Praeger.

Shenitz, H. A. 1959. "Father Veniaminov, the Enlightener of Alaska." *American Slavic and East European Review* 7:223–55.

Sherrill, J. L. 1985. *They Speak with Other Tongues*. Grand Rapids, MI: Zondervan.

Shortridge, J. R. 1976. "Patterns of Religion in the United States." *Geographical Review* 66:420–34.

Shur, L. 1990. *Russian Sources on American History*. Fairbanks: Alaska and Polar Regions Department, Elmer E. Rasmuson Library.

Siegel, M., and L. Canter. 1991. *United States Immigration Made Easy*. Tucson: Sheridan Chandler and Company.

Simerenko, A. 1964. *Pilgrims, Colonists, and Frontiersmen: An Ethnic Community in Transition*. London: Collier-Macmillan.

Smart, N. 1989. *The World's Religions*. Englewood Cliffs, NJ: Prentice Hall.

Smith, B. S. 1974. *Preliminary Survey of Documents in the Archive of the Russian Orthodox Church of Alaska*. Boulder, CO: Western Interstate Commission for Higher Education.

———. 1980a. *Orthodoxy and Native Americans: The Alaskan Mission*. Syosset, NY: Orthodox Church in America.

———. 1980b. *Russian Orthodoxy in Alaska*. Anchorage: Alaska Historical Commission.

Smith, B. S., and R. J. Barnett, eds. 1990. *The Forgotten Frontier*. Tacoma: Washington State Historical Society.

Smith, S. J. 1984. "Practicing Humanistic Geography." *Annals of the Association of American Geographers* 74:353–74.

Smithson, M. J. 1976. "Of Icons and Motorcycles: A Sociological Study of Acculturation among the Russian Old Believers in Central Oregon and Alaska." Ph.D. diss., University of Oregon.

Sologyb, A. A. 1968. *Russian Orthodox Church Abroad, 1918–1968*. New York: Rausen Language Division.

Solzhenitsyn, A. 1963. *One Day in the Life of Ivan Denisovich*. New York: Praeger.

Sopher, D. 1967. *The Geography of Religion*. Englewood Cliffs, NJ: Prentice Hall.

———. 1974. *Historical Atlas of the Religions of the World*. New York: Macmillan.

———. 1981. "Geography and Religion." *Progress in Human Geography* 5:510–24.

Sowell, T., ed. 1978. *Essays and Data on American Ethnic Groups*. New York: Urban Institute.

———. 1981. *Ethnic America: A History*. New York: Basic Books.

Spilka, B., T. Hood, and R. L. Gorsuch. 1985. *The Psychology of Religion: An Empirical Approach*. Englewood Cliffs, NJ: Prentice Hall.

Spinka, M. 1980. *The Church in Soviet Russia*. Westport, CT: Greenwood Press.

Spiro, M. E. 1955. "The Acculturation of American Ethnic Groups." *American Anthropologist* 57:1240–52.

Steeves, P. D. 1976. "Evangelistic Awakening in Russia." Ph.D. diss., University of Kansas.

———, ed. 1988. *The Modern Encyclopedia of Religions of Russia and the Soviet Union*. Gulf Breeze, FL: Academic International Press.

———. 1989. *Keeping the Faiths: Religion and Ideology in the Soviet Union*. New York: Holmes Meier.

Stewart, J. 1972. "The Largest Russian Colony in America and How It Grew." *San Francisco Magazine* 14:24–29, 44.

Stoochnoff, J. P. 1961. *Doukhobors as They Are*. Toronto: Ryerson Press.

Story, S. R. 1960. "Spiritual Christians in Mexico: A Profile of a Russian Village." Ph.D. diss., University of California, Los Angeles.

Straight, S. M. 1989. "Russian Orthodox Churches in Alaska." *Geographical Bulletin* 31:18–28.

Stromberg, P. G. 1986. *Symbols of Community: The Cultural System of a Swedish Church*. Tucson: University of Arizona Press.

Stump, R. 1984a. "Regional Divergence in Religious Affiliation in the United States." *Sociological Analysis* 45:283–99.

———. 1984b. "Regional Migration and Religious Commitment in the United States." *Journal for the Scientific Study of Religion* 23:292–303.

———. 1986. "The Geography of Religion: Introduction." *Journal of Cultural Geography* 7:1–3.

———. 1987. "Regional Variations in Denominational Switching among White Protestants." *Professional Geographer* 39:438–49.

Sturgis, W. 1799. "Extracts from Sturgis' Manuscript." Bancroft Library Manuscript Collection, University of California, Berkeley. Photocopy.

Sutcliffe, F. 1984. "Migrant Communities in an Industrializing Ethnically Homogeneous Society." *Geographical Review* 74:257–66.

Suttles, G. D. 1968. *The Social Order of the Slum*. Chicago: University of Chicago Press.

Svart, L. M. 1976. "Environmental Preference Migration: A Review." *Geographical Review* 66:314–30.

Swrerenga, R. P., ed. 1985. *The Dutch in America: Immigration, Settlement, and Cultural Change*. New Brunswick, NJ: Rutgers University Press.

Symanski, R. 1986. "Along the Salvadoran Pipeline." *Focus* 36:3–11.

Synan, Vinson. 1984. *In the Latter Days: The Outpouring of the Holy Spirit in the Twentieth Century*. Ann Arbor, MI: Servant Books.

Szczesnian, B. 1959. *The Russian Revolution and Religion*. Notre Dame, IN: University of Notre Dame Press.

Tarasar, C. J., ed. 1975. *Orthodox America, 1794–1976: Development of the Orthodox Church in America*. Syosset, NY: Orthodox Church of America.

Tarasoff, K. J. 1972. "Doukhobors: Their Migration Experience." *Canadian Ethnic Studies* 4:1–11.

———. 1982. *Plakun Trava: The Doukhobors*. Grand Forks, BC: Mir Publications.

———. 1990. *Spells, Splits, and Survival in a Russian Canadian Community.* New York: AMS Press.

Tarasov, K. J. 1963. "A Study of Russian Organizations in the Greater Vancouver Area." M.A. thesis, University of British Columbia.

Thompson, R. A. 1896. *The Russian Settlement in California Known as Fort Ross.* Santa Rosa, CA: Sonoma Democrat Publishing Company.

———. 1951. *The Russian Settlement in California.* Oakland: Biobooks.

Tikhmenev, P. A. 1940. *Historical Evolution of the Origins of the Russian American Company.* Trans. M. Dobrynin. Berkeley: Bancroft Manuscript Collection on Russian America.

Timasheff, N. S. 1942. *Religion in Soviet Russia, 1917–1942.* Reprint. Westport, CT: Greenwood Press, 1979.

Tolstoy Foundation. 1970. *Report on Duty Trip to Portland, Oregon, on Behalf of Settlement of Old Believers in the Woodburn and Gervais Areas.* New York: author.

Tompkins, S. R. 1953. *The Russian Mind.* Norman: University of Oklahoma Press.

Trepanier, C. 1986. "The Catholic Church in French Louisiana: An Ethnic Institution." *Journal of Cultural Geography* 7:59–75.

Tripp, M. W. 1980. "Russian Routes: Origins and Development of an Ethnic Community in San Francisco." M.A. thesis, San Francisco State University.

Trofimenko, H. 1989. "Long-Term Trends in the Asia-Pacific Region: A Soviet Evaluation." *Asian Survey* 29:237–51.

Troyanovsky, I., ed. 1990. *Religion in the USSR.* San Francisco: Harper.

Tuan, Yi-fu. 1976. "Humanistic Geography." *Annals of the Association of American Geographers* 66:266–76.

———. 1977. *Space and Place: The Perspective of Experience.* Minneapolis: University of Minnesota Press.

———. 1978. "Space, Time, and Place: A Humanistic Frame." In *Making Sense of Time,* ed. T. Carlstein, D. Parkes, and N. Thrift. London: Edward Arnold.

———. 1986. "Strangers and Strangeness." *Geographical Review* 76:10–19.

Tul'tseva, L. A. 1977. "The Evolution of Old Russian Sectarianism." *Soviet Sociology* 16:20–48.

Turyk, M. D. 1950. "Hillier's Doukhobors." *Canadian Welfare* 25:18–20.

Untiedt, J. A. 1977. "Impingement upon Old Believers in Oregon by Agents of Social Change." Ph.D. diss., United States International University.

Ushin, S. 1874–94. Diaries. Manuscripts in Library of Congress. Alaska Historical Document 3:1–117.

———. N.d. Records of Russian Orthodox Church in Alaska. Manuscripts in Library of Congress.

Van Cleef, E. 1933. "Finns on Cape Cod." *New England Quarterly* 6:597–601.

Van der Laan, L., and A. Piersma. 1982. "The Image of Man: Paradigmatic Cornerstone in Humanistic Geography." *Annals of the Association of American Geographers* 72:411–26.

Van Stone, J. W., ed. 1986. *Russian Exploration in Southwest Alaska: The*

Travel Journals of Petr Korsakovskiy (1818) and Ivan Ya. Vasilev (1829). Trans. D. H. Kraus. Fairbanks: University of Alaska Press.

Varnals, D. 1973. "The Doukhobors in the Kootenays: Signs of Stress." *British Columbia Perspectives* 1:15–20.

Veniaminov, I. 1836. "Diary of a Visit to California, 1836." Bancroft Library Manuscript Collection, University of California, Berkeley.

Verigin, J. J. 1963. *A Doukhobor History.* Grand Forks, BC: United Spiritual Community of Christ.

Walhouse, F. 1961. "Influence of Minority Ethnic Groups on the Cultural Geography of Vancouver." M.A. thesis, University of British Columbia.

Wallace, F. A. N.d. *The Tides of Change.* Chilliwack, BC: Synaxis Press.

Ware, T. 1964. *The Orthodox Church.* Baltimore: Penguin Books.

Waters, M. 1990. *Ethnic Options: Choosing Identities in America.* Berkeley: University of California Press.

Watkins, A. E. 1961. "A Historical Study of the Russian Orthodox Church in Alaska." M.A. thesis, University of Alaska.

Watrous, S. 1991a. "Early California through Russian Eyes: The Writers and the Artists." Sonoma State University, Rohnert Park, CA. Photocopy.

———. 1991b. "Fort Ross Brochure Notes." Sonoma State University, Rohnert Park, CA. Photocopy.

Weber, M. 1963. *The Sociology of Religion.* Boston: Beacon Press.

———. 1976. *The Protestant Ethnic and the Spirit of Capitalism.* London: Allen and Unwin.

Weightman, B. 1990. "Religious Symbolism in Landscape and Lifeworlds: A Humanistic Perspective." Paper presented to the Association of American Geographers, April, Toronto. Photocopy.

Wertsman, V. 1977. *The Russians in America.* Dobbs Ferry, NY: Oceana Publications.

West, E. N. 1989. *Outward Signs: The Language of Christian Symbolism.* New York: Walker and Company.

Whitney, N. J. 1966. *Experiments in Community Unity: Ephrata, the Amish, the Doukhobors, the Shakers, the Bruderhof, and Monteverde.* Wallingford, PA: Pendle Hill.

Willis, D. 1979. "Russian Christians: The Ambassador's Embarrassing Guests." *Christian Science Monitor,* 24 July, B4, B8.

Winsburg, M. D. 1986. "Ethnic Segregation and Concentration in Chicago Suburbs." *Urban Geography* 7:135–45.

Wittfogel, K. A. 1957. *Oriental Despotism.* New Haven: Yale University Press.

Wixman, R. 1980. "Language Aspects of Ethnic Patterns and Processes in the North Caucasus." Research Paper 191, Department of Geography, University of Chicago.

Wolpert, J. 1964. "The Decision Process in Spatial Context." *Annals of the Association of American Geographers* 54:537–58.

———. 1965. "Behavioral Aspects of the Decision to Migrate." *Papers and Proceedings of the Regional Science Association* 15:159–69.

Wood, A., and R. A. French, eds. 1990. *The Development of Siberia*. New York: Macmillan.

Wood, W. W. 1965. *Culture and Personality Aspects of the Pentecostal Holiness Religion*. The Hague: Mouton.

Woodcock, G., and I. Avakumovic. 1968. *The Doukhobors*. Toronto: Oxford University Press.

Wrangell, F. P. 1833. *Russian American Statistical and Ethnographic Information*. Trans. M. Sadouski. Reprint. Kingston, Ont.: Limestone Press, 1980.

Wright, D. M. 1941. "The Making of Cosmopolitan California: An Analysis of Immigration, 1848–1870." *California Historical Quarterly* 20:65–79.

Wright, J. F. C. 1940. *Slava Bohu: The Story of the Doukhobors*. New York: Farrar and Rinehart.

Young, P. V. 1929. "The Russian Molokan Community in Los Angeles." *American Journal of Sociology* 35:393–402.

———. 1930. "Assimilation Problems of the Russian Molokans in Los Angeles." Ph.D. diss., University of Southern California.

———. 1932. *The Pilgrims of Russian Town*. Chicago: University of Chicago Press.

Zelinsky, W. 1961. "An Approach to the Religious Geography of the United States: Patterns of Church Membership in 1952." *Annals of the Association of American Geographers* 51:139–67.

———. 1971. "The Hypothesis of the Mobility Transition." *Geographical Review* 61:219–49.

Zenkovsky, S. A. 1957. "The Russian Church Schism: Its Background and Repercussions." *Russian Review* 16:37–58.

———. 1970. *Russia's Old Believers: Spiritual Movements of the Seventeenth Century* (in Russian). Munich: Wilhelm Fink Verlag.

Zernov, N. 1961. *Eastern Christendom: A Study of the Origin and Development of the Eastern Orthodox Church*. New York: Putnam Publications.

———. 1963. *The Russian Religious Renaissance in the Twentieth Century*. New York: Harper and Row.

Newspaper Articles

"An American Melting Pot." *Eugene Register Guard*, 4 Aug. 1991, B1, B4–6.

"Del Mar Notes." *Point Arena Record*, 19 Dec. 1912, 6.

"Émigrés and Gorbachev: Survival and Celebration." *San Francisco Chronicle*, 31 May 1990, B3, B5.

"The Guests in the Basement." *National Review*, 21 March 1980, 355–56.

"Icons: Windows of Veneration." *Kenai Peninsula Clarion*, 8 April 1988, 12–14.

"New Age Pilgrims Find Their Freedom." *Sacramento Bee*, 5 July 1990, Neighbors Section, 1, 6–7, 12, 20.

"Old Believers Head Ranchers Off at the Pass." *Anchorage Daily News*, 19 July 1990, A1, A12.

"Old Way Is Hard to Keep." *Anchorage Daily News*, 15 April 1990, A1, A7.

"Pentecostals Find Refuge." *Los Angeles Times*, 16 Dec. 1991, A3, A30.

"Religious Refugees from Soviet Union Grow in Number in West Sacramento." *Daily Democrat,* 24 Aug. 1991, A3.

"Russian Evangelicals on the Move." *San Francisco Chronicle,* 9 April 1991, A1, A4.

"Russian Family to Worship Freely in West Sacramento." *Sacramento Bee,* 23 Nov. 1989, A1, A11.

"Russian Jews Seeking Asylum Face Uncertainties." *Honolulu Advertiser,* 17 Jan. 1992, D10.

"Russians in Carmichael?" *Suttertown News,* 7 March 1991, 1, 3, 8.

"Schools Get Influx of Soviet Students." *Sacramento Bee,* 4 Dec. 1989, B4, B5.

"Soviet Clans Escape Religious Persecution." *Seattle Times,* 11 July 1990, F1, F3.

"Soviet Immigrants Revitalize Churches in Area." *Sacramento Bee,* 29 June 1990, B1.

"Soviet Invasion." *Sacramento Bee,* 4 Sept. 1989, B1, B6.

"Soviet Now Free to Preach." *Sacramento Bee,* 27 Sept. 1990, A1, A20.

"Soviet Refugees Find Their Land of Promises." *San Francisco Chronicle,* 27 Aug. 1989, B1, B5.

"Steeped in Past, Faith in Future for a Soviet Sect." *New York Times,* 11 Sept. 1991, A10.

"Surge in Soviet Immigration to U.S." *San Francisco Chronicle,* 4 July 1990, A2.

"Trading Old Beliefs for a New Life." *Eugene Register Guard,* 10 Feb. 1991, A1, A4.

"Under One Roof." *Sacramento News and Review,* 18 June 1992, 14–16, 19.

INDEX